# THE LETTERS OF
# KATHERINE MANSFIELD

PUBLISHED BY

## CONSTABLE & CO LIMITED
10-12 ORANGE STREET
LONDON W.C. 2

*India . Central Europe*
*Scandinavia.*

OXFORD UNIVERSITY PRESS

| | |
|---|---|
| *Bombay* | *B. I. Building, Nicol Road* |
| *Calcutta* | *30, E. Chowringhee Road* |
| *Madras* | *Kardyl Building, Mount Road* |
| *Leipzig* | *Barthels Hof, Markt 8* |
| *Copenhagen* | *St. Kongensgade 40 H* |

*Canada*

THE MACMILLAN CO. OF CANADA LTD

*Toronto      St. Martin's House, Bond Street*

*Katherine Mansfield* 1913

# THE LETTERS

## *of*

# KATHERINE MANSFIELD

*Edited by*

## J. MIDDLETON MURRY

*Volume I*

**LONDON**
**CONSTABLE & CO LTD**

*First Published 1928*
*Reprinted 1930*
*Reprinted 1932*

543.

PRINTED IN GREAT BRITAIN BY ROBERT MACLEHOSE AND CO. LTD.
THE UNIVERSITY PRESS, GLASGOW

THESE VOLUMES ARE DEDICATED AFFECTIONATELY

TO

IDA CONSTANCE BAKER

# INTRODUCTORY NOTE

In arranging the letters of Katherine Mansfield for publication I have had two distinct aims in view : to present as fully as possible all those of her letters which seemed to me to possess an intrinsic interest, and secondly to retain such portions of other letters as would explain the various situations of her life. My hope is that, taken together with her *Journal*, the letters as now arranged will form an intimate and complete autobiography for the last ten years of her life.

It was our destiny that our life together should be broken by frequent and prolonged and most painful separations. During these times of separation she wrote to me every day, and these sequences of her letters have always seemed to me to convey her more truly as she was, with her alternations of joy and sorrow, than any of her writings save her finest stories. It is, naturally, impossible for me to have an unbiassed judgment upon this matter ; and it is possible that these letters may not be so remarkable and so beautiful as I believe them to be. But I have read them many times, and always with the feeling that she lived again in them.

Her letters of certain periods, notably in the three weeks (March 22-April 11, 1918) during which she was detained, seriously ill, in Paris during the bombardment, and again while she was isolated in Ospedaletti in January 1920, are too painful for publication.

A certain amount of criticism was directed

# Introductory Note

against the publication of her *Journal* on the
ground that the revelations were too intimate;
and no doubt the same criticism can be made with
equal justice of these volumes. But Katherine
Mansfield's one concern was to leave behind her
some small legacy of truth, and because I believe
that not a little of her 'truth' is contained in
these letters, I have tried to make the record as
complete as I could.

# Letters

THE first five letters were written from Cholesbury in Buckinghamshire where Katherine Mansfield and I rented a red-brick cottage during the summer of 1913. *The Blue Review*, mentioned in some of the letters, was a magazine which lasted for three months (May-July 1913). I believe it is now very rare. Wilfrid Wilson Gibson, the poet, assisted in editing it. K. M. contributed to it three sketches called *Epilogues* and a story, *Millie*. These have been re-published in *Something Childish, and other Stories*, pp. 90-127.

*To J. M. Murry*                                Cholesbury
                                                Summer 1913

Yes, Friday *will* be fun. I am beginning to ' pretend ' that you are a sailor—trading with all sorts of savages from Monday until Friday and that *The Blue Review* is your schooner and Secker the Fish Eyed Pilot. Could you not write a long—complicated—extremely—insulting—symbolical—serial round that idea with minute, obscene descriptions of the savage tribes . . . ? Thank you for Pa's letter. He was cheerful and poetic, but very loving. I feel towards my Pa-man like a little girl. I want to jump and stamp on his chest and cry " You've got to love me." When he says he does, I feel quite confident that God is on my side.

It is raining again to-day, and last night the wind howled and I gloomed and shivered, and heard locks being filed and ladders balanced against windows and footsteps padding upstairs . . . all the old properties jigged in the old way. I'm a lion all day, darling, but with the last point of daylight I begin to turn into a lamb and by

midnight—mon Dieu ! by midnight the whole world has
turned into a butcher !

Summer 1913

. . . The postman knocked into my dream with your
letter and the back door key.    I had locked myself in three
times three with Mrs. G.'s key, but I am glad you sent me
ours.

I have begun the story and meant to finish it this
evening : it feels pretty good to me.

Oh, dear ! I am afraid W. is having his birthday cake far
too soon—like all our young men (except you and me).
What a surprise for them when we sit down at the heads of
their tables—all among their cake crumbs and groaning
tummies—you, with a laurel wreath on your darling head,
and me trailing a perfectly becoming cloud of glory.

. . . Pride is a charming, sheltering tree : but don't
think I'm resting in it.    I'm only standing underneath
with my eyes turned up for a moment's grace.

Last night Mrs. G. and I had a glass of dandelion wine,
and over it I heard how Mrs. Brown's petticoat had
dropped off in the hurdle race " King Edward's Corona-
tion time."    Such goings on !

Good-bye for to-day.    " Not to-morrow, not the next
day, but the next."    Tell me what train you are coming
by.    I cannot quite believe that you are coming back here.
I feel . . . quite alone and as if I were writing to someone
in the air—so strange.

Summer 1913

I've nursed the Epilogue to no purpose.    Every time I
pick it up and hear " You'll keep it to six," I *can't* cut it.
To my knowledge there aren't any superfluous words :
I mean every line of it.    I don't " just ramble on " you
know, but this thing happened to just fit six and a half
pages.    You can't cut it without making an ugly mess
somewhere.    I'm a powerful stickler for form in this style
of work.    I hate the sort of licence that English people

give themselves . . . to spread over and flop and roll about. I feel as fastidious as though I wrote with acid. All of which will seem, I suppose unconvincing and exaggeration. I can only express my sincerest distress (which I do truly feel) and send you the Epilogue back. If you and Wilfrid feel more qualified for the job. . . . Oh, do by all means— But I'd rather it wasn't there at all than sitting in *The Blue Review* with a broken nose and one ear as though it had jumped into an editorial dog-fight. It's a queer day, with flickers of sun. The Epilogue has worried me no end : and I can still hear, tossing about, the aftermath of that thunder. " It's not fair. Swinnerton can do it . . . you've got to cut it " . . . etc., etc. Can't you cut a slice off the D. Brown ? I really am more interesting than he is—modest though I be. . . .

P.S.—Don't think of this letter. I'm frightfully depressed to-day . . . sad beyond words.

Summer 1913

No letter from you to-day. I am sending you the Banks drawings this evening. Enough string came with my parcel from Ida to make it possible. If you want any meat (and if—oh, well no—not necessarily) bring some down with you, please dear. *Meat* and *tea*. That is all we want. It is a very grey day again, here, half raining— and a loud roaring noise in the trees. This morning a robin flew into my room. I caught it. It did not seem at all frightened but lay still and very warm. I carried it to the window and I cannot tell you what a strange joyful feeling—when the little bird flew out of my hands. I am sorry you did not write to me. I count on your letters in the morning and always wake up early and listen for the postman. Without them the day is very silent.

Summer 1913

Thank you for the money : I'm going to start again keeping a strict account of every penny I spend and then we can see where the screw is loose or the shoe pinches—or whatever it is.

Last night as I got into bed the bed refused to have me and down I flew with my feet up in the air. I was terrified but I couldn't help laughing—and once started I kept on. It seemed no end of a joke to be all alone in what R. C. would call the " profound stillness of the June night " and to be served that age-old trick !

" Mrs. Walter " is here to-day and we're having clean pinnies from head to foot. Such relief that I've written my reviews again and started my Epilogue. I went in to see Baby G. this morning. He was sucking. Such a pretty sight as a rule. But Mrs. G.'s sharp wan face above him somehow filled me with horror.

Things have straightened out in my mind and I'm rather ashamed that I told you—what I did yesterday. It sings in my ears rather like the wail of the little girl left behind on the fence—more anger than anything else.

In November 1913, we went to live in Paris, in a flat at 31 rue de Tournon, not 32, as printed by mistake in the *Journal.*

*To J. M. Murry*          Paris : 31 rue de Tournon
                                     February 1914

Lesley writes me, the weather is beastly—and here it is so warm and sunny that I have sat with my window open yesterday and to-day. (Yes, dear, mentioned ' with intent.') I wish you would buy a pair of shoes as well as the pepper and salt trousers. Try to. You want them so badly and I've no faith in those cheap Boulevard beauties.

Everything, here, too ' is just the same.' The femme de ménage is singing in the kitchen—a most improbable song. It runs along, very blithe and nice—for about five notes and then it *drops*—any distance you like, but a little deeper each time. If the ' aspects ' were not good that song would 'frighten me no end ... *pro-vi-ded* that I was in a little house on the edge of the steppes with a mush-room shaped cloud over it and no smoke coming out of the chimney, etc., etc. But things being what they are, my romantic mind imagines it a kind of fifteenth century French Provincial Ride-a-Cock-Horse—you know the business . . . dashing off on someone's knee to get a pound of butter and being suddenly " tumbled into the gutter." Which, after all, is a very pleasant place to fall. I wonder if Queens played this Disturbing Game with their youngest pages.

My door has been mended. I am told that a workman came at nine, wrenched out the remains of the old panel, tapped the wood with an iron hammer, clapped in a new panel, clattered over the hall—but I did not hear a sound. I slept until a quarter to ten.

February 1914

You are good to me ! Two letters this morning and a telegram yesterday afternoon. I wished that I might have sent you one in return but I thought you would not expect it so I . . . guarded the money. It would be a great relief to talk over everything, but by the time you get this letter it will be Friday morning and unless your plans have changed you will have no time to reply to me except ' in person.' I talked over ' the business ' with you yesterday as much as I could by letter and without you. Depend upon us—we're quite strong enough now to find a way out of our difficulties and we *will* and be happy, too, and do our work. (By being happy I mean happy together in the ' odd times,' you know.) And if I can get a room in London that hasn't another opening out of it and isn't the logical end of a passage I can work there as well as anywhere—supposing we arrange to leave here at once.

After a miserable winter (1914-15) in a damp and draughty cottage near Great Missenden (*Journal*, pp. 15-23) during part of which K. M. was crippled by arthritis,

5

and was unable to write, she went to Paris in February, returning to Missenden at the end of the month, but only to escape again to Paris in March and again in May.

*To S. S. Koteliansky*                        Monday
                                      Rose Tree Cottage
                                   The Lee, Great Missenden
                                        March 1, 1915

I hope you are not waiting for me to-day—for I am unable to come to London. My rheumatism still makes walking an impossibility—and I suffer very much. However I am in hopes it will leave me suddenly and then I shall come. We are going to shut up this house and live in London until the Summer. Jack has seen some rooms (rather, they were my idea) in Fitzroy Street and as soon as I am able to move I am going to see them. So we shall be in London quite soon and more or less permanently. This cottage is too cold and too depressing.

When we are settled in London we must have some good times together. Make up a little basket of dreams—will you—and I will, too, and we shall be ready, then. I feel about 800, Koteliansky, for I can hardly walk at all—nor turn in my bed without crying out against my bones.

                                         Monday
                                      March 8, 1915

I have wanted to write to you ; you have been in my mind several days. I am in bed. I am not at all well. Some mysterious pains seem to like me so well that they will not leave me. . . . All the same I am grateful to your Ancestral Grandfathers—for, for some reason I can work. I am writing quite quickly—and it's good. Send me a little letter when you have the time. It is very cold here. It is winter and the sky from my window looks like ashes. I hear my little maid go thumping about in the kitchen and when she is quiet I listen to the wind. My God, what poverty ! So I write about hot weather and happy love
6

and broad bands of sunlight and cafés—all the things that make life to me. Yes, you are quite right. I *am* wicked. Would it be very rude if I asked you to send me a few cigarettes ? If it would—do not send them.

To-day I had a most lovely postcard sent me from my concierge in Paris—hand painted roses as big as cabbages— and so many of them they simply fall out of the vase !

Wednesday, late afternoon
March 11, 1915

Your parcel came at midday. You cannot think in what dramatic circumstances. I was 'up' for the first time and downstairs and because of my hideous wickedness I had begun to cry dreadfully—that is quite true—when in walked the cigarettes—the chocolates and the thrice blessed little bottle of whiskey. So I drank some whiskey and smoked a cigarette and dried my eyes and sent you a very superior form of blessing—which I hope you caught safely.

I am glad that you liked *The Little Governess* [1]—but wait. I've written such different things lately—much, much better—and I am going on writing them. Yes, I have a special disease. Pray your Ancestors for my heart.

March 17, 1915

I did not tell you all the truth last night. When you asked me if I was writing and I said 'Yes' it was not quite true. I *cannot* write my book living in these two rooms. It is impossible—and if I do not write this book I shall die. So I am going away to-morrow to finish it. Then I promise to come back shorn of all my wickedness. It is agony to go, but I must go. Write to me, will you ? I will write to you often—write to me *often often*, for I shall be very lonely, I know. Goodbye, just for now. I press your hands *tightly*—Goodbye.

[1] Published in *The Signature* (another short-lived magazine written by K. M., D. H. Lawrence and me) and republished in *Bliss*.

*To J. M. Murry*                    Paris : 13 Quai aux Fleurs
                                    March 19, 1915

I have just had déjeuner—a large bowl of hot milk and a
small rather inferior orange, but still not dressed or washed
or at all a nice girl, I want to write to you.   The sun is
very warm to-day and lazy—the kind of sun that loves to
make patterns out of shadows and puts freckles on sleeping
babies—a pleasant creature.

I had a vile and loathsome journey.   We trailed out of
London in a fog that thickened all the way.   A hideous
little frenchwoman in a mackintosh with a little girl in a
dirty face and a sailor suit filled and overflowed my
carriage.   The child combed its hair with a lump of brown
bread, spat apple in our faces, made the *ultimate* impossible
noises.   Ugh ! how vile.   Only one thing rather struck
me.   It pointed out of the window and piped its eternal
" Qu'est-ce ? "   " C'est de la *terre*, ma petite," said the
mother, indifferent as a cabbage.

Folkestone looked like a picture painted on a coffin-lid
and Boulogne looked like one painted on a sardine tin.
Between them rocked an oily sea.   I stayed on deck and
felt nothing when the destroyer signalled our ship.   We
were two hours late arriving and then the train to Paris
did not even trot once—sauntered, meandered.   Happily
an old scotchman, one time captain of *The California*, that
big ship that went down in the fog off Tory Island, sat
opposite to me and we ' got chatting.'   He was a scotchman with a pretty, soft accent ; when he laughed he put
his hand over his eyes and his face never changed—only
his belly shook.   But he was ' extremely nice '—quite as
good as 1/- worth of Conrad.   At Amiens he found a tea-
wagon and bought ham and fresh rolls and oranges and
wine and would not be paid : so I ate hearty.

Paris looked exactly like anywhere else ; it smelled
faintly of lavatories.   The trees appeared to have shed
their buds.   So I took a room (the same room) and piled
up coats and shawls on my bed to ' sleep and forget.'   It

8

was all merely dull beyond words and stupid and meaning-
less.

But to-day the sun is out. I must dress and follow
him. . . .

This is a silly old letter—like eating ashes with a fish
fork. But it is not meant to be. I rather wanted to tell
you the truth. . . .

March 19, 1915

I went to Chartier to lunch and had a maquereau grillé
and épinards à la crême. It was very strange to be there
alone. I felt that I was a tiny little girl and standing on a
chair looking into an aquarium. It was not a sad feeling,
only strange and a bit ' femmeseuleish.' As I came out it
began to snow. A wind like a carving knife cut through
the streets, and everybody began to run. So did I—into
a café, and there I sat and drank a cup of hot black coffee.
Then for the first time I felt in Paris.

It was a little café and hideous, with a black marble top
to the counter, *garni* with lozenges of white and orange.
Chauffeurs and their wives and fat men with immense
photographic apparatus sat in it. And a white fox-terrier
bitch, thin and eager, ran among the tables. Against the
window beat a dirty French flag, fraying out on the wind
and then flapping on the glass. Does black coffee make
you drunk, do you think ? I felt quite *enivrée* [*The
word is circled with a line and the following remark written
in :* " Oh, I won't do this : it's like George Moore.
Don't be cross."] and could have sat three years, smoking
and sipping and thinking and watching the flakes of snow.
And then you know the strange silence that falls upon your
heart—the same silence that comes one minute before the
curtain rises. I felt that and knew that I should write
here. I wish that you would write a poem about that
silence some time. It is so *peculiar*. It is a kind of dying
before the new breath is blown into you. As I write, I
can almost see the poem you will make—I see the Lord

9

alighting upon the breast of the man and He is very fierce.
(Are you laughing at me ?)

So after this intense emotion I dashed out of the café,
bought some oranges and a packet of rusks and went back
to the hotel. *Me voici !* The garçon has just polished
the handles of the door ; they are winking and smelling
somethink horrible. The sky is still full of snow, but
everything is clear to see—the trees against the tall houses,
so rich and so fine, and on the grey streets the shiny black
hats of the cabmen are like blobs of Lawrence's paint.
It's very quiet. A bird chirrups, a man in wooden shoes
goes by. Now I shall start working.

Sunday, early afternoon
March 21, 1915

Still no letter—perhaps I can be certain of one to-
morrow. I walked to the post this morning and then,
finding neither light nor murmur there, I went to the
Luxembourg gardens. About 3 of the biggest chestnut
trees are really in leaf to-day—you never saw anything
lovelier, with pigeons and babies adoring. I walked and
walked until at last I came to a green plot with the back
view of the head and shoulders of a pa-man rising out of an
enormous stone urn—*d'une forme de carotte.* Laughing
with my muff as my solitary habit is, I sped to see his face
and found that it was a statue of Verlaine. What extraordinary irony ! The head seemed to me to be very
lovely in its way, bashed in but dignified, as I always
imagine Verlaine. I stayed a long time looking at that,
then sunned myself off on a prowl. Every soul carried a
newspaper. *L'Information* came out on orange sails. *La
Patrie* lifted up its voice at the métro stations. Nothing
was talked of but the raid last night. (I'm dying to tell
you about this raid, but I'm sure I shan't be able to.)

Oh, Jack, it was really rather fine. I came home late.
I had been dining with B. at the Lilas. It was a lovely
night. I came in, made some tea, put out the lamp, and

opened the shutters for a while to watch the river. Then
I worked till about one. I had just got into bed and was
reading Kipling's *Simples Contes des Collines*, when there
was a sharp quick sound of running, then the trumpets
from all sides blaring *Garde à vous!* This went on,
accompanied by the heavy groaning noise of the shutters
opening and then a chirrup of voices. I jumped up and
did likewise. In a minute every light went out except one
point at the bridges. The night was bright with stars.
If you had seen the house stretching up and the people
leaning out! And then there came a loud noise like
*doo-da-doo-da* repeated hundreds of times. I never
thought of Zeppelins until I saw the rush of heads and
bodies turning upwards as the Ultimate Fish (see *The
Critic in Judgment*) passed by, flying high with fins of
silky grey. It is absurd to say that romance is dead when
things like this happen. And the noise it made, almost
soothing, you know,—steady and clear, *doo-da-doo-da*,
like a horn. I longed to go out and follow it, but instead
I waited, and still the trumpets blared—and finally when
it was over I made some more tea and felt that a great
danger was past and longed to throw my arms round some
one. It gave one a feeling of boundless physical relief,
like the aftermath of an earthquake.

B.'s flat is really very jolly. She only takes it by the
quarter at 900 francs a year—four rooms and a kitchen, a
big hall, a cabinet and a conservatory. Two rooms open
on to the garden. A big china stove in the salle à manger
heats the place. All her furniture is second-hand and
rather nice. The faithful J. conducts her shopping. Her
own rooms, with a grey self-colour carpet, lamps in bowls
with chinese shades, a piano, 2 divans 2 armchairs, books,
flowers, a bright fire, was very unlike Paris, really very
charming. But the house I think detestable ; one *creeps*
up and down stairs. She has dismissed D. and transferred
her virgin heart to P. Strange and really beautiful though
she is still, with the fairy air about her and her pretty
little head still so fine—she is ruined. There is no doubt

of it. I love her, but I take an intense, cold interest in noting the signs. She says, " It's no good my having a crowd of people. If there are more than you I go to the cupboard and nip cognacs until it's all over for me, my dear . . . " or, " Last Sunday I had a fearful crise. I got drunk on *rhum* by myself at the Rotonde and ran up and down this street crying and ringing the bells and saying, ' Save me from this man ! ' There wasn't anybody there at all." And then she says with a faint show of importance, " Of course the people here simply love me for it. There hasn't been a real woman of feeling here since the war. But now I am going to be careful."

Myself, I am dead off drink—I mean, the idea of being drunk revolts me horribly. Last time I was drunk was with B. here, and the memory stays and shames me even now. We were drunk with the wrong people. Not that I committed any *sottise*, but I hate to think of their faces and—ugh ! no, I shall not drink again like that—never, never.

As I write to you the concierge is doing the flat, and she will persist in talking. Do I like flowers ? Cold or heat ? Birds or beasts ? She is one of those women who can't lift or replace a thing without giving it its *ticket*. But she's a good soul and looks after me and fills the lamp without being told. Of course everybody she ever knew has died a grisly death in this war. The fact that C. is going to Turkey seems to delight her beyond measure. " Il ne reviendra jamais ! "

To-day everywhere they are crying " Voici les jolies violettes de parme," and the day is like that. Under the bridges floats a purple shadow.

I must start working. I believe now she is dusting simply to spite me and to keep me off my work. What a bore these women are !

*To S. S. Koteliansky*                    March 22, 1915

Write me a letter when you feel inclined to—will you ? I am staying here for a while instead of at the rooms in

London. I understood you that week-end at the Law-
rences' for I have been like that myself. It is a kind of
paralysis that comes of living alone and to oneself and it is
really painful. . . . I was silly and unsympathetic, for
Lawrence could not understand it because he has never
felt it and I should have been wiser. But come quite alive
again this Spring—will you ? I do not know how it is in
London just now but here the very fact of walking about
in the air makes one feel that flowers and leaves are dropping
from your hair and from your fingers. I could write you a
long letter but I am afraid you cannot read my hand-
writing. Tell me if you can and then I will. Yes, write
to me here.

The nights are full of stars and little moons and big
Zeppelins—very exciting. But England feels far far away
—just a little island with a cloud resting on it. Is it
still there ?

*To J. M. Murry*                     Monday night
                              March 22, 1915

I am sitting writing to you by the light of a candil, with
the whole house so quiet and closed and all the people in
the cellars. The trumpets sounded about an hour ago.
All the lights are out, except one on the bridge, very far,
and one by the police station at the corner. I have been
standing at the open window. Searchlights sweep the
sky ; they are very lovely, lighting up one by one the
white clouds. Now and then some one passes, or a cart all
dark gallops by. When the alarm sounded, the sirens and
fire-whistles and motors all answered. I was in the street
and in a moment or two it was almost pitch dark—just
here and there a flicker as someone lighted a cigarette.
When I arrived at the Quai aux Fleurs and saw all the
people grouped in the doorways, and when people
called out, " N'allez pas comme ça dans la rue ! " I was
really rather thrilled. The concierge, all the house, and
an obscure little old man who is always on the scene on

every occasion, asked me if I would ' descendre ' but I
hated the idea and I came up—of course all the gas was
turned off—and hung out of the window. It was
extremely terrifying suddenly ; in fact (prosaic !) I was
nearly sick !  But after that the wonderful things happening, and especially a conversation between a man at a fifth
floor window and a thin man on the Quai got me over my
mal d'estomac.  Those two men talking—their voices in
the dark and the things they said—are unforgettable.
Also a fool who came along the Quai whistling, his hands
in his pockets, and as big drops of rain fell shouted with a
laugh " Mais ils seront mouillés—ces canailles d'oiseaux ! "
The rain—the dark—the silence—the voices of the two
men—the beauty of the river and the houses that seemed
to be floating on the water . . . Ah, Jack !

As I wrote that more bugles sounded.  Again I ran into
the bedroom with the lamp and again opened the window.
A big motor passed, a man in front blowing a trumpet.
You heard from far and near the voices raised.  " C'est
fini ? "  " Fini, alors ? "  The few people in the street
ran blindly after the motor and then stopped.

I went on the landing with my big rusty key to put on
the gas again, because it's cold and I wanted a fire.  The
little man came up the stairs, and of course, I couldn't find
the letter or the number, and of course he knew all about
it.  " Attendez, attendez !  Voulez-vous aller voir si le
gaz prend ? "  He was a far greater fool than I.  But I
mercied him bien and managed it myself.

These raids after all are *not* funny.  They are extremely
terrifying, and one feels such a horror of the whole idea of
the thing.  It seems so cruel and senseless.  And then to
glide out into the sky like that and hurl a bomb n'importe
où is diabolic and doesn't bear thinking about.  (There
go the trumpets again and the sirens and the whistles.
Another scare !  All over, again.)  At B.'s this afternoon
there arrived " du monde " including a very lovely young
woman, married, and *curious*, blonde . . .(Oh God, it's all
off again !  I opened the shutters ; the motors flew by

14

sounding the alarm.) I can't talk about the tea-party
to-night. At any rate, it isn't worth it really. It ended
in a great row. I enjoyed it in a way, but B. was very
impossible ; she must have drunk nearly a bottle of brandy,
and when at 9 o'clock I left and refused either to stay any
longer or to spend the night here, she flared up in a *fury*
and we parted for life again. It seems such utter rubbish
in the face of all this—now. A very decent and pleasant
man saw me home, happily. Otherwise I think I might
have been sitting in a Y.M.C.A. until this moment ; it
was so very dark—but a lovely evening, very soft, with
rain falling. B. makes me sad to-night. I didn't touch
anything but soda-water, and so I really realised how the
other people played on her drunkenness, and she was so
. . . half-charming, and such an *utter fool*.

It is raining fast now, on the shutters, a sound I love to
hear. England feels so far away at this moment—oh,
very far. . . .

                                                            March 1915

I don't know what you think of yourself, but *I* think
you're a little pig of a sneak. Not a letter—not a sign—
not a copy of *The Saturday Westminster*—plainly nothing.
Why are you so horrid ? Or is it the post ? I'll put it
down to the post and forgive you. A baby in arms could
play with me to-day. The weather is so warm I'm sitting
with the windows wide open and nothing but a thin blouse
on (in a way of speaking). All the trees are popping and
the air smells of mignonette. Big open barges full of
stones are being towed by black and red beetles up the
river ; the steering men lean idly, legs crossed—you know
their way—and the water froths against the bows. The
carts passing make a merry jingle and the concierge has put
a pink hyacinth in her window. I'm a fool when I'm
alone. I turn into a little child again.

There is a woman on the opposite side of the river.
She sits with her back against a tree, her legs stretched out

in front of her, combing her long brown hair. To this side and to that she bends, and then with that charming, weary gesture she throws her head back and draws the comb all the length of it. If I were near enough, I am sure I would hear her singing. The idle time of the year is coming, Jack, when you can sit outside with a piece of bread and butter on your knee and watch it frisle. (How do you spell that?)

I felt very flat when I bought *La Patrie* at midday and found that no Zeppelins had arrived after all. Unfortunately I had already posted your letter, so you can laugh at me. This afternoon I am going to write about last night. I'll send it to you. Do what you will with it. Send it somewhere, will you please? . . .

I dreamed last night about G. I was at an opera with you, sitting on a converted railway carriage seat, and I heard G. talking of his wife to an American lady. Then he saw me and I went up and spoke to him. Just as I was saying I never had and never would love him, etc., Mrs. S. appeared and seeing us together she came up to me and said, " Oh Katherine, I always felt such love for you, and now I know why," and she pressed me to her and said " Frank is at home digging in the garden." This so touched me that I nearly sacrificed myself on the spot, but I knew you were waiting for me in a little house in South Kensington. The opera had disappeared, and I was sitting on the stump of a nut tree, and G. leant against it, toying with a top-hat. So I pressed his hand awfully kindly, picked up a very large rabbit that was watching us, with twitching ears, and walked away, saying over my shoulder to G., " There is always a beginning and an ending, G." But he burst into tears and called, " Ah, my dear, *don't—don't* be so wonderful." " If that is the case," thought I, " I'm wasting myself. I shall take some inexpensive but good dancing lessons." Then I woke up.

*Next day.* After all, I never wrote a thing. Yesterday I began reading and read on till past midnight. There are so many books of " the young men " here, and I glanced

through a number to get an impression. Heavens !
What a set of lollipops ! Really, I did not come across *one*
that counted. Upon the same stage with the same
scenery, the same properties, to the same feeble little
tune, one after another pipes his piece, and the audience,
being composed of a number of young men and females
exactly like himself, with precisely the same burning desire
to feel the limelight on their faces, applaud and flatter and
cherish. You can't believe they were not all littered at a
breath. Funny, if it weren't so damned ugly ; and the
trouble is that nobody will ever kick their little derrières
for them because they haven't got 'em to kick—seulement
" deux globes d'ivoire " ! Afterwards I began to read
Stendhal's " Le Rouge et le Noir." You can imagine
how severe and noble it seemed and does still by morning
seem to me. But what I feel most deeply is—how *tragic*
a great work of art appears. All these young ' nez-au-
venticistes ' have their place and their meaning in this
world ; but I seemed to see Stendhal, with his ugly face
and pot belly and his little pig's legs, confined within a
solitary tower, writing his book and gazing through the
window chink at a few lonely stars. (Don't whistle !)

I must go off to the post. I could write to you all day.
It is raining fast and my lung hates the weather.

Thursday morning
March 25, 1915

Yesterday I had your letters at last. . . . You seem to
have done perfect wonders with the rooms.[1] The car-
pentering job I saw and heard as plain as if I'd been there,
to the very sand-papering. All the things are floating in
my brain on a sea of blue Ripolin. I feel those rooms will
be lovely.

I had a great day yesterday. The Muses descended in
a ring like the angels on the Botticelli Nativity roof, or so it
seemed to " humble " little Tig, and I fell into the open

[1] Two top-rooms in Elgin Crescent which I was preparing.

arms of my first novel. I have finished a huge chunk, but
I shall have to copy it on thin paper for you. I expect you
will think I am a dotty when you read it ; but, tell me
what you think, won't you ? It's queer stuff. It's the
spring makes me write like this. Yesterday I had a fair
wallow in it, and then I shut up shop and went for a long
walk along the Quai—very far. It was dusk when I
started, but dark when I got home. The lights came out
as I walked, and the boats danced by. Leaning over the
bridge I suddenly discovered that one of those boats was
exactly what I want my novel to be. Not big, almost
grotesque in shape—I mean perhaps *heavy*—with people
rather dark and seen strangely as they move in the sharp
light and shadow ; and I want bright shivering lights in it,
and the sound of water. (This, my lad, by way of uplift.)
But I *think* the novel will be all right. Of course, it's
not what you could call serious—but then I can't be, just
at this time of year, and I've always felt that a spring novel
would be lovely to write.

To-day I went to Cook's with my last golden sovereign
in my hand to be changed. I am getting on all right as
regards money and being very careful. Cooked vegetables
for supper at 20 c. the demi-livre are a great find and I
drink trois sous de lait a day. This place is perfect for
working.

I read your letter yesterday in the Luxembourg Gardens.
An old gentleman, seeing my tender smiles, offered me
half his umbrella, and I found that it was raining ; but as
he had on a pair of tangerine coloured eyeglasses, I declined.
I thought he was a Conrad spy.

I have adopted Stendhal. Every night I read him now,
and first thing in the morning.

Saturday afternoon
March 27, 1915

I shall write you my letter to-day in this café Biard,
whither I've come for shelter out of a terrific storm—rain
and thunder. I'm soaked and my bones are in dismay

18

already. It is the most absurd *rot* to have to think like
an old pusson every time the rain falls. This is rheumatiz
for a dead spit for me. But I am not sad, I am only
surprised at God.

I am writing my book. *Ça marche, ça va, ça se dessine.*
It's good.

Last night I woke to hear torrential rain. I got up
with a candle and made the shutters firm, and that awful
line of Geo. Meredith's sang in my head : " And Welcome
Waterspouts that Bring Fresh Rain." Then I dreamed
that I went to stay with the sisters Brontë who kept a
boarding house called the Brontë Institut—*painfully* far
from the station, and all the way there through heather.
It was a sober place with linoleum on the stairs. Charlotte
met me at the door and said, " Emily is lying down." K.
I found was also there, taking supper. He broke an
orange into a bowl of bread and milk. " Russian fashion,"
said he. " Try it. It's very good." But I refrained.

Then the bell tinkled and the concierge gave me your
letter. . . . How can all these people afford cabs ? Even
girls in pinafores without hats are jumping into fiacres. I
cannot afford even the principle.

I found a photograph of Willy to-day. He looked like
Edward VII. in spirits of wine—an awful fathead. Of
course, he has got *something*, but he's terribly small beer,
I'm afraid. *And* a snob *and* heartless. So I feel. Frank
Harris is writing pro-Germanics in *The Continental Times.*
He is roaring down England and roaring up Germany. I
feel very disgusted. " And you ? " (as they are always
singing in Wagner's operas for a kick-off).

There goes Eve Balfour. Yes, it is. No, it isn't. Yes,
it is. No, it isn't. Alas, another case of mistaken
identity, like the darkey who was asked why he stole the
old lady's parrot and said, " A-aw Boss, Ah took it for a
lark."

" Tig, what a *fool* you are to-day."

" But it won't stop raining, and I'm stuck, and wondering if the waiter will flick me away next time he comes."

Saturday afternoon : Café Biard
March 27, 1915

A lovely woman sits in here with me. She's got a fool
of a man with her that she hates beyond words. So would
I. She wears a big rose under her chin—her eyes are
lovely, but very shadowed with a purple ring. She is not
only bored ; she is trying not to cry. Three fat jossers at
a table near by are vastly amused. Two dirty little
froggies, smoking pipes 'à l'anglaise' and ragging each
other, are next to me. They occasionally sing at me, or
snap their fingers. They are the most hideous little
touts.

Now—I ought to have known it—my lovely woman is
playing a game of cards with her cavalier. Mon dieu !
she does look lovely with the fan of cards in her hand, the
other hand hovering over, and her lip just pouting. I
must go. This is a fool of a letter. . . .

Pretty business this German-chasing ! And a pity they
have to photograph such decent honest-looking wretches
as the *belles proies*. It's a filthy trick ; there's no difference
between England and Germany when the mob gets a hand
in things. No difference between any nations on earth ;
they are all equally loathsome.

*To S. S. Koteliansky*                              March 29, 1915

I am extremely fond of you this afternoon. I wish you
would walk into this café now and sit opposite me and
say—" Do not look at these people ; they are extremely
foolish." But no, you will not ; you are dancing on the
downs with the fair Barbara and Kisienka is forgotten.
No, I won't come to any of your weddings. You will
marry some woman who will show me the door—because
I come and sing in the street you live in in my beautiful
Russian dress (given me by my anonymous friend) and you
dare to look out of the window. I have just finished Two
Frightful Hours trying to buy a corset—not really a corset

but a kind of belt—I have spent every penny that I haven't got upon an affair of violet silk which is so exquisite that I lament my lonely life. . . . Now Frieda would say that I was being *very* wicked, but you understand—don't you? All the while I write I am looking at you and laughing a little and you are saying to me, " Really, you are a *deplorable* creature ! "

Your letter was given to me and I read it while I was half awake—when in bed—and after I had read it I lay smoking and watching the sun dance on the ceiling—and I wondered why on earth I *had* fled away and could not find any answer. At any rate I can tell you frankly that the illness that I had in England and longed to be cured of —is quite gone for ever—I believe it was my ' heart ' after all, you know, but not the kind of heart that Dr. Eder punches. Shut your eyes a minute—do you feel frightfully happy—just now—just at this minute ? I do— I should like to lie on the grass beside a big river and look up at the sun until the sun went down—and then go slowly home to a little house hidden in a ring of poplar trees—carrying a large bunch of daisies. Do you see this house ? It is a new one—just built at this moment—it is in some place very far away and there are woods near, and this river. A tiny little balcony has a table on it with a red and white cloth and a jar of clovers—and we sit there in the evenings, smoke and drink tea. Now *you* can build a little of it.

To tell you the absolute truth, a friend of mine is coming to London at the end of this week. (Do not tell anybody.) Her name is Katherine Mansfield, and if she should ring up the Bureau on Friday—answer her. Will you.

Yes, Koteliansky, you are really one of my people—we can afford to be quite free with each other—I know.

. . . My dear, it is so hot in this café that if Mrs. E. were here she would have taken half a dozen sun baths !

*To J. M. Murry*                                          Jeudi
                                                     May 13, 1915

I cannot tell you how beautiful this place is by daylight.
The trees on the island are in full leaf . . . I had quite
forgotten the life that goes on *within* a tree—how it
flutters and almost plumes itself, and how the topmost
branches tremble and the lowest branches of all swing lazy.

It is very warm to-day.  All the windows are wide open.
From early morning people have passed along the Quai
carrying lilac . . . little stout men, the bunch upside down,
looped to a finger by a knotted string—young girls carrying
it along the arm—little children with their faces quite
buried—and old fat women clasping the branches, just a
frill of flower showing above their bosoms.

I ran out at seven to buy some oranges.  Already the
shops were open.  Already the sausages were looped
round a lilac jar—the tailoress bent over the machine had
a piece in her bodice.  (I shan't tell you any more because
you won't believe me.  It's everywhere.)  I'll tell you
where I saw it first yesterday.

" Oh, Tig, don't *harp* so."

Just this, and then I won't.  But we drew up alongside
a hospital train.  From my window I could see into the
saloon.  There were pallet beds round the walls.  The
men, covered to the chin, never moved an inch.  They
were just white faces with a streak of hair on top.  A doctor,
stout and ruddy, with a fine blond beard, stood at the
window drying his hands and whistling.  All round the
walls of the car kind female hands had placed big bunches
of purple and white lilac.  " What lovely lilac ! " said the
people in the train with me.  " Look ! how fine it is."
The wounded men did not matter a rap.

(Then came a cry from the étage above.  " Fermez vos
persiennes s'il vous plaît ! "  But I wasn't in time.
Whether the lady sheared a sheep outside her window or
merely shook her bedroom mat, I do not know.  A little
of both.  Damn her !)

22

And now there comes a little handcart with three babies
in it and a quantity of newspapers.  It is dragged by two
other infants—men of about eight or nine.  They stopped
outside here, let down a kind of false leg which steadied the
cart and strolled over to the lavatory, talking, unbuttoning
their breeches and shouting to the babies to keep tranquille.
But alas ! no sooner had they disappeared than the infants
with screams of rage began throwing the papers into the
wet gutter.  Back rushed their lords, and now they are
picking up the muddy papers and the culprits hang their
heads over the side of the wagon like people about to be
guillotined . . . terribly chastened.

Friday<br>
May 14, 1915

*Next morning.*  I went out to lunch yesterday at a very
good little brasserie, overlooking Place du Châtelet, *and*
cheap, quite as cheap as Chartier, and frequented only by
old men and a priest or two.  Afterwards, like a fool, I
took the métro to the Palais Royal and went to look for
Smith's to see if they had *The Golden Bowl*.  Oh, that
walk—it stretched for miles, and each moment I thought
it was going to end.  My leg finally trailed after me like a
tired child.  And they had not got *The Golden Bowl*.  So
I came home and worked and did not go out again.  We
had the thunder last night.  To-day it is silvery, and now
and then some rain falls. . . .

I don't want to complain, but I do think my leg is a bit
off, don't you ?  It hurts like billy-o to-day.

Saturday evening<br>
May 15, 1915

The lamplighter is just going his rounds, but I am sitting
in the dusk still.  I have just come in from a small walk.
I returned to the garden of Notre Dame.  It was dusky
already and the smell of the flowery trees a wonder to
enjoy.  Hardly anybody was there ; an old man on the

23

other end of my bench kept up a buzzing in his beard, and a
few extremely wicked babies without any hope of bed
played ball, just their heads and knees and flying hands to
be seen.   How black the tree stems were and how fine the
leaves !   They were like a tune given out in the bass with
a wonderful running treble,—and above the trees uprose
Notre Dame in all her venerable beauty.   Little birds
flew among the towers—you know the little birds that
always fly about ruins.   Looking at them I wanted to
write a sonnet, using as an image of old age and the thoughts
of old age flying out and returning, the tower and the
birds.   I shall write it one day.

I have been writing my book all the afternoon.   How
good the fatigue is that follows after !

Lovers are idling along the Quai.   They lean over the
parapet and look at the dancing water and then they turn
and kiss each other, and walk a few steps further arm in
arm and then stop again and again kiss.   It *is* rather the
night for it, I must say.

The rain stopped after I had posted your letter to-day,
but it is still *un temps très lourd*.   I bought a litre of white
wine to-day for 45 c. (very good) and it is lying in a basin
of water in the kitchen zinc.   The butter and the milk sit
on a brick outside the kitchen window.   " *Some* summer,"
as a fool at the music hall would say.

Write to me as often as you can.   Of course, no human
being could compete with my effugions and well I knows
it, but alone in furrin parts is not the same as being even as
alone as you are in England.

*Sunday morning.*   I have just had your summer letter.
London does sound good, and the idea of drinking cider
and then sitting in my special little garden was very
alluring.   I know that garden [1] better than any other in
the world.   I see it now as I write.   But for some strange
reason, I have always gone there to cry.   I well remember
one dreadful New Year's Eve when I went there and sat
on one of the benches crying into a little black velvet

[1] The little garden in Leicester Square.

muff with blue ribbons (L. had it after) and an awful old
woman with a jet bonnet watched a long time, and then
she sighed and said, " Well, that's 'ow it is, my dear."

If you lean over the Pont St. Louis you look down on to
a little court which is called Port de l'Hôtel de Ville.   It is
a pleasant cobbled square with poplars and lime trees
growing against the wall ; where it slopes down to the
river there are two upturned boats.   An old man in a
straw hat sat by one of them to-day tapping it with a
hammer, and over the other two little boys wriggled,
dabbling their hands in the water.   There were some
mattresses propped against the wall in the sun and a
wooden frame set up, covered with a square of red linen.
An old woman in a lilac print dress with a white band over
her head and under her chin was tossing grey flock and
feathers on the red linen square.   An immense heap of
them beside her was lifted and shaken and gathered up for
her by a younger woman in black, wearing a cotton bonnet.
It was very warm in the sun, and the flock and feathers
were so dusty that the two women coughed and sneezed
as they worked, but they seemed very happy.   I watched
until the mattress was filled and folded over like a pie-
crust.   Then the young woman took a little camp-stool
and sat down with a needle and thread, stitching, and the
old one replaced the ' buttons ' in the cover with a long,
long needle like a skewer.   Now and again the two little
boys ran up to have their noses blown, or the old man sang
out something and they sang back. . . .

Whose fault is it that we are so isolated—that we have
no real life—that everything apart from writing and
reading is ' felt ' to be a waste of time ?

I walked on to-day and came to a garden behind Notre
Dame.   The pink and white flowering trees were so
lovely that I sat down on a bench.   In the middle of the
garden there was a grass plot and a marble basin.   Sparrows taking their baths turned the basin into a fountain
and pigeons walked through the velvety grass, pluming
their feathers.   Every bench and every chair was occupied

by a mother or a nurse or a grandfather and little staggering babies with spades and buckets made mud pies or
filled their buckets with fallen chestnut flowers or threw
their grandfathers' caps on to the forbidden grass plot.
And then there came a chinese nurse trailing two babies.
Oh, she was a funny little thing in her green trousers and
black tunic, a small turban clamped to her head. She
sat down with her darning and kept up a long bird-like
chatter all the time, blinking at the children and running
the darning needle through her turban.

But after I had watched a long time I realised I was in
the middle of a dream. Why haven't I got a real ' home '
—a real life—why haven't I got a chinese nurse with green
trousers and two babies who rush at me and clasp my
knees ? I'm not a girl—I'm a woman. I *want* things.
Shall I ever have them ? To write all the morning and
then to get lunch over quickly and to write again in the
afternoon and have supper and *one* cigarette together and
then to be alone again till bedtime—and all this love and
joy that fights for outlet, and all this life drying up, like
milk, in an old breast. Oh, I want life ! I want friends
and people and a house. I want to give and to spend.

*To S. S. Koteliansky*                    Monday night
                                          May 17, 1915

. . . It is a rainy evening—not at all cold, rather warm,
but rainy, rainy. Everything is wet ; the river is sopping,
and if you stand still a moment you hear the myriad little
voices of the rain. As you walk, the air lifts just enough to
blow on your cheeks. Ah ! how delicious that is ! It is
not only leaves you smell when you stand under the trees
to-day ; you smell the black wet boughs and stems, the
' forest ' smell. This evening I went walking in a park.
Big drops splashed from the leaves and on the paths there
lay a drift of pink and white chestnut flowers. In the
fountain basin there was a great deal of mixed bathing
going on among some sparrows— A little boy stood just

outside the park.   He thrust one hand through the railing among the ivy leaves and pulled out some tiny snails, arranging them in a neat row on the stone wall.   " V'là mes escargots ! "   But I was rather frightened, that, being French, he'd take a pin out of his jacket and begin eating them !   And then they locked the park up.   An old caretaker in a black cape with a hood to it locked it up with a whole bunch of keys.

There is a wharf not far from here where the sand barges unload.   Do you know the smell of wet sand ? Does it make you think of going down to the beach in the evening light after a rainy day and gathering the damp drift wood (it will dry on top of the stove) and picking up for a moment the long branches of sea weed that the waves have tossed and listening to the gulls who stand reflected in the gleaming sand, and just fly a little way off as you come and then—settle again.

This evening a mist rose up from the river and everything looks far away.   Down below, two nuns went by, their ample skirts gathered in one hand, the other holding an umbrella over their white hoods.   And *just below*— there is a court where the barrow men take their barrows for the night—their palms and their rose trees and china blue hydrangea bushes.   You see the barrows with waving shining leaves float by like miraculous islands.   Very few people are out.   Two lovers came and hid behind a tree and put up an umbrella—then they walked away, pressed against each other.   It made me think of a poem that our German professor used to read us in class.

> Ja, das war zum letzenmal
> Das wir beide, Arm in Arme,
> Unter einem Schirm gebogen . . .
> . . . . Alles war zum letzenmal. . . .

And I heard again his ' sad ' voice (so beautiful it seemed, you know !) and I saw again his white hand with a ring on it, press open the page !

But *now* I know the perfect thing to do on a night like

this. It is to ride in a little closed cab. You may have the windows open but you cannot keep out the smell of leather and the smell of *upholstered buttons*. The horse makes an idle klippety-kloppeting. When we arrive at the house there is a big bush of lilac in flower growing over the gate and it is so dark that you do not stoop low enough and drops and petals fall on you. The light from the hall streams down the steps.

### Scene II.

*K. :* "Tell me frankly. Does it, does it *not* feel damp to you ?"

*Visionary Caretaker :* "I've had fires in all the rooms, m'm. Beautiful fires they were, too. It seemed a pity to let them out ; they burned that lovely."

' *M. or N.' :* "It feels as dry as a bone to me, I *must* say."

The Visionary Caretaker beams at 'M. or N.' Her little girl puts her head round the door. In her pinafore she has rather a wet kitten.

*Visionary C. :* "And if you *should* like a chicken at any time, m'm, or a few greens, I'm sure my husband and I would be only too pleased, etc., etc., etc., etc. . . . "

I'm laughing. Are you ? The queer thing is that, dreaming like that I can't help living it all, down to the smallest details—down to the very dampness of the salt at supper that night and the way it came out on your plate the exact shape of the salt spoon. . . .

Do you, too, feel an infinite delight and value in *detail*—not for the sake of detail but for the life *in* the life of it. I never can express myself (and you can laugh as much as you please.) But do you ever feel as though the Lord threw you into Eternity—into the very exact centre of eternity, and even as you plunge you felt every ripple floating out from your plunging—every single ripple floating away and touching and drawing into its circle every slightest thing that it touched.

No, I shan't write any more. I see you, my wise one,

putting down this letter and saying—" No.   I must go to
Barbara to explain this . . . "

I feel a little bit drunk.   It's the air, and the noise the
real waves make as the boats, with long fans of light, go
dancing by.

We shall see each other again soon.   But I can't deny
that I feel a little neglected.   I had *counted* on a reply to
my letter, after all.   Don't forget me—don't go far away.
As I write I hear your voice and I see you swing out into
the hall of the bureau as though you were going to beat
to death the person who had dared to come in.


*To J. M. Murry*                              Saturday
                                        May 22, 1915

I don't know how money goes.   I keep a strict account
(one of those amazing fourfold affairs in which we are so
expert) and every penny is reckoned, and yet, it seems to
fly.   A franc in Paris is really 8d. in England just now.
But don't think I am complaining, because I am not—
merely stating my case—and I know my money *will* come
next week.   I have asked them to send it through Cook's.
It is the simplest way, and really the post-offices are
merely a collection of stools and stamp-paper.   Yesterday, after I had nearly cried through a grating about my
lost letter, the man suggested brightly, cleaning his nails
on an old nib, " Perhaps the postman *threw it away ! . . .*"

I wanted to tell you about a nice time I had on Thursday night.   At about seven I left the house, buttoned up
in my black and white coat and went for a walk behind the
Hotel de Ville.   I found most curious places, and I found
at last a little market place where every third body was
either frying or eating Polish pancakes.   The air smelled
of them and of ' petits gris,' tiny snails which you bought
by the shovelful.   It began to rain.   Under an old stone
arch three hags wrapped in black shawls were standing,
their hands crossed over their bellies.   At their feet there
lay three little baskets of herbs, dry twigs, withered

29

bundles and tiny packets. Their heads were raised, watching the drizzle, and the green light from a lantern fell on their faces. All of them were talking, whether to each other or to themselves you could not tell, for their voices did not pause. It sounded like a song. It was one of the most ancient things I have ever seen or heard.

I had to go into one of those little 10 c. places. In the passage stood an immense fat and rosy old market woman, her skirts breast high, tucking her chemise into her flannel drawers, and talking to an equally fat old ouvrier, who began to help her to arrange her affairs, saying as he tugged and buttoned, " Mais tu sais, *ma petite*, tu ne peux pas sortir comme ça."

I went on much further—then down an alley on to a quai. There was a bird shop there. The window was flying with canaries and java sparrows and green love-birds and white doves and parrots. Outside the shop two little girls were standing, their arms round each other's necks. One had rings in her ears and the other wore a bangle. They were watching the birds and eating an orange between them, quarter by quarter. The bird-seller was a dark young man with long black moustaches and narrow eyes. . . . I don't know why, but I had a curious sensation that I was in a dream and that I had seen all this years and ages ago.

Finally, it poured so with rain that I hunted and I hollered and found a café—very poor—the people eating, chauffeurs and rag bags of people. But a woman came in, skinny, enceinte, but very alive, and a curious rough boy followed her. They were so wet that the woman said " faut danser." And they danced. As far as I could make out this is what they sang as they turned round and round. The people who ate banged with their bread on the table and the plates clattered.

> *S'il en reste un bout, ce sera pour la servante.*
> *S'il en reste pas du tout, elle se tapera sur l'ventre.*
> *Et zon zon zon Lisette, ma Lisette.*
> *Et zon zon zon Lisette, ma Lison.*

All the while my hat dripped over the table. I kept taking it off and shaking it on the floor. But when the boy was greeted by a very smart young friend who came to my table and said " Je veux manger une belle fricassée avec vous, ma fleur," I paid and ran away.

Sunday evening
May 23, 1915

Instead of having dinner to-day I ate some bread and drank some wine at home and went to a cinema. It was almost too good. A detective drama, so well acted and so sharp and cruel, with a horrible décor—the environs of Calais. Wickedness triumphed to everyone's great relief, for the hero, an apache called ' l'Fantôme,' was an admirable actor. And there was a girl there, mistress of ' Bébé ' and ' le faux curé,' two other apaches. I wish you could have seen that girl act. She was very still, and then her gestures *sprang* from her. Pale, you know. A little round head and a black dress. All the while the orchestra played a tango that we have heard before, a very ' troubling ' tune.

Before going in I walked up to the Luxembourg Gardens. But the Sunday crowd . . . the women mincing in their high boots like fowls in the wet, and the shopwalker men, and the " Ah, c'est beau ! " " Dis—c'est joli," " C'est *très, très* joli," " Tout à fait beau." I felt exactly as if I were dead.

It is very beautiful outside the window this afternoon. The wind shakes the trees so.

There was a great excitement a few minutes ago. I saw the policeman before the station below suddenly stiffen, and then at the bottom of the steps that lead on to the quai—you know where I mean, below here ?—there came a grey little frog squirming in the grip of two gendarmes. They were evidently hurting him, but my policeman flew to their aid. He got behind the man and suddenly thrust his hand between the man's legs. You

31

should have heard the yell he gave and you should have seen the jerk that sent him forward. Life is a funny business.

Now there are birds wheeling and flying in the air and the sky is pink. It is evening. I have not spoken to anyone since Wednesday except to say " Combien ça fait ? " or to say " Oui, c'est bien terrible," to the concierge. It is curious for one who has been much alone— this *sinking back* into silence.

Café Baird, Rue de Rivoli.   Midi<br>May 24, 1915

Here is the history of my lunch. I decided I could never go to the Brasserie again because there was a black cat that frightened me there, so to-day I sought pastures new. All were impudently full, so I fell back on Chartier. I wanted something cheap, so I ordered *pied de veau*. My strike ! ... I had that removed, but still hungry I ordered *risotto milanais* and got a lump of rice originally covered in tomato sauce, but the sauce had run on to some one else's *crème d'Isigny* in transit. Then I ordered *compôte de rhubarbe*. " C'est fini." And looking down at that moment I saw on my thumb an immense BUG in all possible comfort and half full already. That was the limit. I fled here—and this coffee is just like squeezed wet flannel.

I wonder if it is the war that has made the people here so hideous, or if I am out of joint. They appear to me a nation of concierges. And the women look such drabs in their ugly mourning. I wish I had some new shoes and a straw hat. My head and my feet are always hot—but these are minor things. It is a brilliant day fine. Everything shines.

How terrible it is that waiters must have flat feet ! These are shuffling about—sweaty—ugly. If they were turned out of their cafés what would they do ? Plainly nothing.

My book *marche bien*.   I feel I could write it anywhere, it goes so easily, and I know it so well.   It will be a funny book.

Now I've finished my coffee.   I am going.

> Tuesday morning
> May 25, 1915

Yesterday was simply hellish for me.   My work went very well, but all the same, I suffered abominably.   I felt so alien and so far away, and everybody cheated me, everybody was ugly and beyond words cruel.   I finally got to such a state that I could go nowhere to eat because of the people and I could hardly speak.   At half past ten I shut up shop and went to bed, but not to sleep.   The three apaches of the cinema, l'Fantôme, Bébé and le faux curé, tried the key of the door all night and tip-toed on the landing.   Finally through the shutters there came two chinks of day.   Do I sound foolish and cowardly ?   Oh, but yesterday was simply hell.   In the evening (I'd gone out to get a lamp glass.   The concierge, with relish, had smashed mine) I sat in a little garden by a laburnum tree, I felt the dark dropping over me and the shadows enfolding me, and I died and came to life " time and time again " as Mrs. C. used to say.   I went to buy bread at a funny shop.   The woman hadn't got a nose and her mouth had been sewn up and then opened again at the side of her face.   She had a wall eye.   When she came into the lamplight with the bread I nearly screamed ; but she clapped her poor hand to her head and smiled at me.   I cannot forget it.

This morning things are better.   It is such a fine day. But I could not stand a month of yesterdays.   I'd come home in a coffin.

K. M. returned to London from Paris at the end of May.   In November we left together for the South of France.   I came back to England in December, leaving

K. M. in Bandol.   At the end of the year I returned to
Bandol, and we lived for three months at the Villa Pauline.

*To S. S. Koteliansky*                    Grand Bar de la Samaritaine
                                                   Marseille
                                          le 19 Novembre, 1915

I am glad that I came.   Many times I have realised
that Acacia Road and all that it implied is over, for ever.

This is a confused and extraordinary place.   It is full of
troops,—French, African, Indian, English.   In fact there
are types from all over the world and all walking together
down narrow streets choked with tiny carriages painted
yellow, white mules with red fringes over their eyes—all
those kinds of things you know.   The port is extremely
beautiful.   But I've really nothing to say about the place
unless I write to you for weeks—for all my observation is
so *detailed* as it always is when I get to France.   On the
mantelpiece in my room stands my brother's photograph.
I never see anything that I like, or hear anything, without
the longing that he should see and hear, too—I had a letter
from his friend again.   He told me that after it happened
he said over and over " God forgive me for all I have done "
and just before he died he said, " Lift my head, Katy, I
can't breathe "—

To tell you the truth these things that I have heard
about him blind me to all that is happening here—All this
is like a long uneasy ripple—nothing else—and below—in
the still pool there is my little brother.

So I shall not write any more just now.   But I think of
you often and always with love—

*To Anne Estelle Rice*                      Hotel Beau Rivage
                                                 Bandol (Var)
                                          December 8, 1915

I've been wanting to write to you for days, but this
morning is really my first free time and the first time that
I have been anything like settled since leaving England.

M. went back to London yesterday. Perhaps that will tell you a little what kind of a time we have had. I could write books about it until I died and then not finish the telling. It has been so funny and so tragic and so utterly unlike what we expected or imagined.

Marseilles became colder and colder. I got really very ill there with fever,[1] and spent my time drinking hot milk with sugar and orange flower water in the cafés and then keeping up my strength (!) with little glasses of brandy. Both of us got poisoned, I think from eating mussels and pistachio ices at the same time. The red stone floors started my rheumatism again. And everybody cheated Murry *at sight*. Even before he bought anything they put up the price.

So we decided to go to Cassis-sur-mer for *at least* a couple of months. We found there a very comfortable-looking hotel kept by a fat woman called ' Tante ' and two nieces. We had a huge room with four windows to get the lovely sun and read with great satisfaction in every single guide-book that Cassis was the first " station d'hiver sur la côte d'azur."

The day we arrived the mistral was blowing. I put my head out of the train window and it blew the trimming off my hat. . . .

*To J. M. Murry*                    Wednesday morning
                                              December 8, 1915

Yesterday after you had gone I bought some biscuits and oranges and after putting them in my room and entering the fact of them in my Account Book (!) I went for a walk. It was hot and sunny with big reine claude[2] waves breaking on the rocks. When I came back I picked my geraniums— toujours in a state of lively terror. I wanted to tell (1) the proprietor (2) the gardener (3) the girls hanging out washing (4) anyone in and out of sight that I had per- mission. I even suspected that the white dog had been

---

[1] See p. 40.          [2] *i.e.* greengage.

taught to hurle when one of the pensionnaires touches the
flowers. But there they are in the lovely little jug you
gave me—*un joli petit bouquet*.

The crepuscule descended just as it did the day before.
At six I took Jules Laforgue's rather cynical arm and
descended to the salon and read until dinner time. A
New Lady appeared in tight purple velvet, low neck and
short sleeves, tiny waist, big fat shoulders, marabout
scarf, little round head with curls like escargots on the
forehead. I was *quite overwhelmed*. After a chaste
repast (your serviette was still there—I got awfully sentimental over it) the man that we said was English, made
me a leg and offered me two copies of the *Times*. I took
about two hours reading them—picked them absolutely
clean and decided that the English newspapers were the
finest, *etc*., and that no other nation, etc., could possibly,
etc. But they were packed with meat. . . . An attack
on L.'s father as a pro-German—attempted suicide of Miss
Annesley Kenealy—Sir John Simon's attack on the *Times*
—the King's first excursion in a Bath chair (Note the
capital *B*. Heavens ! What a dignity it gave !). After
I had returned them the Englishman's lady opened a
rapid fire. But I kept under cover and she changed her
tactics and told me a lot of interesting things. For
instance : November is the very bad month of the year
for the South of France. ' Parisians ' never come then.
December is early spring. The flowers begin—the jonquils and the oranges. The villas open and the Parisians
arrive. The mistral *never* blows here—*never*. This place
abounds in charming walks and one can buy a map of the
forest paths for 50 centimes. (But shall I ' enter those
enchanted woods,' do you think, Boge, even with a map
of the paths ? Courage ! I must !) They are expecting
25 people at this hotel for Christmas. This was told to
encourage me, I think—and so on until bed-time.

I woke early and for a long time forgot you were not
with me but felt you beside me and only when I wanted to
tell you my Extraordinary Dream, I remembered.

It is a lovely day again—very bright and warm. They are still digging up the garden and prising up little rock borders with disused railway lines and telegraph poles. The boats with red sails are sailing on the sea and your ship is quite close in. Yesterday they lowered a boat and the exhausted crew 'tumbled' (see *The Lancet*) into it and were rowed to shore.

Thursday morning : A little before ten
December 9, 1915

I expect you are in London. I have just washed and dressed and put on my white broderie anglaise jacket (I really *do* look rather a pretty girl) and now I'm sitting in the sun by the open window smoking the first cigarette. The air is like silk to-day and there is a sheen upon the world like the sheen on a bird's wing. It's very quiet except for the gardener and his spade and warm as fine wool. Yesterday I walked to Sanary—which is the next bay to this, on the road that follows past the palm avenue. Really it was very hot. You walked along with your eyes and nose screwed up and breathed Hail Maries that you wouldn't freckle or be accosted by a black soldier. But I wish you could have been there and seen that bay. There is a long beach there too and on the other side of the road fields of jonquils in flower. Two women one in grey and one in yellow with black straw hats were picking them. As I passed they stood up and held the big nodding bunches before their eyes to see who was passing. There is a tiny villa there, too—with a glass verandah and a small garden. It could not have more than two rooms. It looks right over the bay to the open sea. Behind it rears up an old rock covered with that pink heath and rosemary. A board on the gate said 'à louer.' I confess to hanging over the fence for a long time and dreaming. . . . Coming home in the evening with driftwood to burn—the lamp on the round table—the jar of wild flowers on the mantelpiece. . . Sitting on the verandah in canvas chairs after supper and smoking and listening to the idle sea. But don't be frightened, you were not there. It was my Brother who sat on the verandah step stroking a kitten that curled on his knee.

I think the Oxford Book of English Verse is very poor. I read it for hours this morning in bed—I turned over pages and pages and pages. But except for Shakespeare and Marvell and just a handful of others it seems to me to be a mass of falsity. Musically speaking, hardly anyone seems to *even understand* what the middle of the note is— what that sound is like. It's not perhaps that they are even ' sharp ' or ' flat '—it's something much more subtle —they are not playing on the very *note itself*. But when, in despair I took up the French Book I nearly sautéd from the fenêtre with rage. It's like an endless gallery of French salon furniture sicklied o'er with bed canopies, candelabra and porcelain cupids all bow and bottom. Of course there *are* exceptions. Victor Hugo, by the way, reminded me very much of our white bull taking a railway ticket—to Parnassus. And I wasn't a bit ' surprised.'

December 10, 1915

Yesterday I went for a long walk round by the sea towards St. Cyr (which is very beautiful and wild and like my N. Z.) and then I struck inland and came home by little lanes and crooked ways bordered with olive trees— past the flower farms. I thought I should never get home again. I got quite lost and thought I kept hearing voices. The walls were always in the way and when I peered through the gates there was never a soul to be seen except jonquils and daffodils and big blue violets and white roses. The sun went down—I passed a little villa called " Allons-y " and coo-ed but a Fearful White Dog, happily attached to a pump, answered me so effectually that I decided to strike into a wood and have done with it But at that moment a far too agile malignant-looking goat appeared—vaulted over a wall just ahead of me. I rushed in the opposite direction and got found at last.

My work is shaping for the first time to-day—I feel
nearer it—I can see the people walking on the shore and
the flowery clusters hanging on the tree. . . . if you know
what I mean. It has only been a dim coast and a glint
of foam before.[1]    The days go by quickly.

December 11, 1915

The weather has changed. Last night a wind sprang
up—one of the lesser winds—a forlorn, piping creature
that I don't remember having heard on land before—a
wind I always connect with the open sea and night in the
cabin—and a hollow dread that the land has gone for ever.
I dreamed that I had a baby (Virtue always rewards me
with this elfin child) and Grandmother was alive. I had
gone to sleep after it was born and when I woke it was night
and I saw all the people in the house lying on their backs
asleep too. And I was sure my baby was dead. For a
long time I was too frightened to call anyone—but finally
called to Grandmother and she came in and said, " Nonsense, child, he's getting on beautifully (as though ' he '
were a cake in the oven)." She brought him in to
reassure me—a charming little creature in a flannel gown
with a tuft of hair. So I got up and kissed Grandmother
who handed me the baby and I went downstairs and met
you in the street. The moon was shining—you looked
lovely ; it shone particularly on your grey felt hat which
you wore à l'espagnole. But we were very poor ; we
lived in a tenement and you had put a banana box across
two chairs for the baby. " The only *brick* is," you said
—" how the hell can we go to a music hall ? " Then I
woke up, switched on the light and began to read *Venus
and Adonis*. It's pretty stuff—rather like the Death of
Procris.

Yesterday I had *de la veine* and wrote in the afternoon
and then went for a short walk along that bar that encloses
the harbour. It was sunset. It's a good place to walk—

[1] The reference is to *Prelude* (see *Journal*, p. 42).

the sea on either side rushes up and the town—just showing a glimmer of light here and there—looked marvellous. I sat on a stone and began thinking "I believe it is perfectly necessary to one's *spiritual balance* to be somewhere where you can see the sun both rise and set, etc., etc." and such like nonsense—très sérieux—when I remarked a gazelle-like military form approaching—in blue with a braided cap. This ensemble, thought I, is exactly like the cover of a 95 centimes novel. Myself on a rock—a red sunset behind—this graceful form approaching. . . . It came near—and than a blithe, cheerful dead sure voice positively *hailed* me. "Vous vous promenez seule, Madame ? " I had a good look at the upstart. Olive skin, silky eyebrows and silky moustache. *Vain*—there is no word for it. I said, " Oui, Monsieur, seule." " Vous demeurez à l'hôtel Beau Rivage, n'est-ce pas ? " Silence. " Je vous ai déja remarqué plusieurs fois." (His French was right. Mine isn't.) Then I looked up at him like Frank Harris would look at Dan Rider quoting Shakespeare—and he drew himself up, saluted, said "Ah, pardon je suis très indiscret." I said *exactly* like Harris— " Très indiscret, Monsieur," and walked home.[1] Scarcely had I gained the road when a gentleman in a cape approached and ' Vous vous promenez seule, Madame ? ' But that was a bit too steep. I said, " Non, Monsieur, avec une canne— " What a race ! They're like German commercial travellers ! Send me a bulldog in your next letter, sweetheart.

The sea is very choppy to-day. Far as you can see the waves break—like a school of fishes.

A windy Sunday
December 12, 1915

For some unaccountable reason I've got our Marseilles fever again with all its symptoms, loss of appetite, shivering fits, dysentry. What on earth can it be ? I really think it is a noisome fever from some black man in a café near

[1] For this incident, see *Journal*, p. 39.

to the Vieux Port.  At any rate its horrid and I am a
ragged creature to-day.  If I hadn't got William Shakespeare I should be in the ultimate cart, but he reads well
to a touch of fever.  However, I expect I shall be a better
girl by the time you get this, so don't go and worry.  I
bought a most superior exercise book yesterday for 4 sous
*but* at about five o'clock the eternal silence was broken by a
rap at my door and a pretty creature with gold rings in her
ears, spanish boots like yours, and flashing eyes and teeth
brought in a basket—My laundry.  I only sent a *morsel*—
the veriest fragment, and Lord ! there was a bill for 3.15.
*How* the rings, the teeth, eyes and boots vanished—
counting the precious money into her hand.  I paid for
them, every one.  I shall have to cut myself a little pair
of football shorts out of *Le Radical*, I can see that.

How are you ?  Where are you ?  What are you doing
now ? . . .

The salon has become impossible ground while the wife
of that Englishman remains in this hotel.  Did you
remark her ?  She is a Belgian—I never met her like.
She out-Belgians anything imaginable.  However, I'll
be even with her and put her to paper and be done with
her.  I shall creep to the post and back but that's my
limit to-day.  Otherwise I'll keep my room and try to
write and read.  Send me a book, when you can.


Sunday night before dinner
December 12, 1915

I have just put on my *spencer*, an extra *pair* of *stockings*
and another shawlet and I'm still frozen.  I rang for
Mary Anne to make me a fire but she is evidently gone
a junketing for I can't find her.  The only minion I did
find said they could not mont any bois until demain.
Which seemed to me absurd.  Suppose I were in con-
vulsions and had to be wrapped in blankets and laid on an
hearth (would that I were !)?  Also I am as empty as the
little French boy's tirelire and there's nothing to eat here.

And the salon is full of travellers a-sitting round the fire a-toasting of their unworthy toes—Oh, what a wretched little swinging-on-a-bare-twig of a goblin you have got to-night—and her maladies have been such that she has been forcée to garder her chambre all day except for to post my letter. At about five I nearly swallowed the tea-spoon and had done with it. For I have added a sore throat to my fever and I am trying to gargle every 2 hours with three sous worth of borax and it's tasted awful. Just when I wrote in my diary " Adieu chère terre "—a nice little boy who belongs to the hotel brought me a letter from you—it was a gift from heaven. Never was a letter more welcome—It was indeed one of my great-aunt Charlotte's ' direct answers ' to prayers. I read it once and then twice and then I absorbed it, you know—If you are not careful and less sweet to me I shall say TOUJOURS, too, and then you'll be finally caught out. I do hope they give you a bed among the pottery.[1] Can you choose your jug and basin from the stock ? I saw that shop the day Munro flouted me and nearly entered in (Forgive me ; I am all sticky with eating so much and such continuous Shakespeare). You told me very little of Kot. Didn't he fall down dead when he saw I wasn't there ? And where did you sleep that first night, sirrah ?

After lunch to-day a kind gentleman lent me an Historical Roman. (Je vous remercie, maman. Bon soir, chèr Père.) But I also saw the last two numbers of *La Vie Parisienne* left in the salon by a bald-headed old party who brought his own oysters to luncheon.

*Monday morning.* Then the bell for dinner and I went down and afterwards sat in the salon and talked with the lender of the Roman. What a night I spent, Bogey ! My left leg rushed up to reinforce my other ills and it has won the battle—In fact I'm a complete prisoner to it to-day and shall have to give this letter to foreign hands to post for I can't walk at all—However, it's just my old

[1] They did. It was the Peasant Shop in Devonshire St., and my landlady was kindness itself.

rheumatism—you know what it's like.   Dressing took me nearly two hours and I nearly gave it up, wore only one stocking, one leg of my ' pantalons ' etc. to-day, but the old trick of looking at myself in the glass and saying ' Courage, Katherine ' won after all—and here I am complete even to Flowering Gorse.[1]

I got two papers from Kot to-day.   They will be a great feast and as always happens I am now so tied and bound, so *caged* that I know I'll *sing*.   I'm just on the point of writing something awfully good, if you know that feeling.   So there is compensation.

The sun shines to-day but the wind is still high and ' foam flies white over rocks of black,' opposite.

I feel cut off from all human kind—but I am not sad to-day.

Monday
December 13, 1915

After giving your letter to my ' bonne ' yesterday I gave up the fight and retired in good order to bed, where I am still.   The day seemed very long yesterday, but I must say my ' bonne ' was very good to me.   She gave me an extra pillow, kept me supplied with boiling bottles, brought me Vichy, and my meals on a little round table, actually produced a bottle of alcool camphré and frictioned me and gave me some lime flower tea before I went to sleep.   Not counting the number of times she put her fat face round the door and said nodding and *smiling* as only a French-woman can—with an air of delighted gaiety (!) " Vous souffrez toujours ? "   You see little Wig giving her smile for smile and nod for nod and saying " Ah, oui, un peu ! ' She's the only creature I've seen.   I am rather surprised that neither of the kind ladies who were so ready to welcome us to their haven should not at least have inquired. But no—And I must confess that notice that the repasts served in the rooms *se paient en supplément* rather rings in my ear.   But my money has come and as I am spending

---

[1] ' Genêt Fleuri.'   K. M.'s favourite perfume.

nothing else it will be *perfectly all right*. It is such a
heavenly day to-day. Oh, so lovely—There seems to be a
ring of light round everything. It is still and sunny, so
still you could hear a spider spin. I dreamed last night
that I sat by a fire with Grandmother and my brother and
when I woke up I still held my brother's hand. That is
true. For my hands were not together—they were
holding another hand. I felt the weight and the warmth
of it—for quite a long time.

December 14, 1915

Don't you worry about me. My femme de chambre,
when she goes off duty leaves me in her ' friend's ' charge
and her ' friend ' is a little spry creature with a pale blue
nose who is very gentille indeed to me. " Il ne faut pas
vous gêner." She keeps saying to me—" Je veux faire
tout ce que je peux pour vous." In fact, the servants here
seem to think I'm a *dear* little thing ! *And* after midday
that Englishman, terribly shy, knocked at my door. It
appears he has a most marvellous cure for just my kind of
rheumatism—Would I try it ? All this was explained in
the most preposterous rigmarole, in an attempt to appear
off hand and at his poor unfortunate ease. I never saw a
man so shy ! Finally he says that if the pharmacien can't
make it up here he will take the first train to Toulon this
afternoon and get it for me. It is a rubbing mixture which
he got off a German doctor one year when he was in
Switzerland for winter sports and had an attack of sciatic
rheumatism. It sounds to me very hopeful,—but I'd
catch any straw !

So I thanked him and bowing and humming and hawing
he went off. I can't think what frightened him so, I shall
have to put on a hat and a pair of gloves when he brings
me back the unguent. Oh, that postman is a tortoise, a
detestable tortoise—half a tortoise—for I am hot and he is
slow. (Bogey, I am an awful little cod, my bed is going
to my brain. Now I'll wait for your letter before I
go on.)

*Later.*  I did wait with a vengeance.  At half past three I rang the bell.  " Le courier, a-t-il déja passé ? "  " *Ah, oui,* Madame—une *bonne* demi-heure ! "  " Merci bien." But when she had gone I confess I turned to the wall and cried bitterly. . . .  I think mostly from rage.  Then I began to think how my Father always had time to write every single day to my Mother, etc., etc., etc.  Then in despair I climbed out of bed, found a piece of ribbon and sat up and made myself a hat.  Once before, I remember when I was ill at Rottingdean and alone and waiting for a letter that didn't come I made myself a hat out of pins and fury and it was the hat of my life.  So is this.  But I think it is awfully cruel.  Once I get better I'll forgive you if you don't write, but Oh—to lie in this silent room and know the postman has *been.*  You wouldn't like it, Bogey.

Now I've had dinner, an omelette, some cauliflower and a stewed apple.  I am getting thin.  There are two hollows in my cheeks but no little love kisses there.  My Englishman has arrived with his pot of ointment and refuses to take even a pin or a bead in payment.  How kind he is—It's easy to see *he* hasn't lived with me three years.

I should like to be at a large circus to-night : in a box— very luxurious, you know, very warm, very gay with a smell of sawdust and elephants.  A superb clown called Pistachio—white poneys, little blue monkeys drinking out of chinese cups.  I should like to be dressed beautifully, beautifully down to the last fragment of my chemise— and I should like Colette Willy to be dressed just exactly like me and to be in the same box.  And during the entr'actes while the orchestra blared Pot Pourri from *The Toreador* we would eat tiny little jujubes out of a much too big bag and tell each other all about our childhood.

December 16, 1915

I am better but still in bed, for there is a bitter east wind blowing to-day and I feel it is not safe for me to start my normal life in it.  I think my Englishman's stuff is going

to do me a great deal of good and he has made me so perfectly hopeful—and has been in so many ways such a
*comfort* to me. Should this stuff not quite cure me he has
given me the address of a place in Normandy where one
goes for a cure once a year. The cure only takes three
weeks; it is a small inexpensive place and he says it's
simply miraculous. Well, I am sure I can get my Father
to give me a little extra a year for this purpose. "You'll
be skipping like a two year old after a week there" says
my nice, funny man. I am being rubbed twice a day and
dieting carefully and only drinking Vichy. This man isn't
really a doctor. He's the Head of Guy's Dental Hospital
—but he is a queer, delightful, good-natured person and
he has certainly been a comfort to me.

I feel very sober to-day. I am afraid you will think my
last letters very silly. They won't happen again. I
understand you far better now, somehow—and I'll not
ask for the moon either.

*A knock at my door.* A letter in pencil from you and
funnily enough almost the second sentence is about crying
for the moon. Thank you darling for your letter; it's
an awfully sweet one. I do hope you get your studio at
Haverstock Hill, it sounds really delightful—et pas trop
cher. Your present room must be horrid. I am sorry
too—you do not know how sorry, that we have not talked
more about the things we have read and seen and felt.
Still, it was fate and can't be altered.

Tell you all that I am doing? Why, Bogey, I'm lying
down or sitting up in bed. All I'm feeling? Ah, I can't
—I've lost the key just for the minute—you know how
things do get lost in bed.

Since I have been alone here the loss of my little brother
has become quite real to me. I have entered into my loss
if you know what I mean . . . always before that I shrank
from the final moment—but now it is past.

As I write it is raining fast with a loud noise on the
windows. I have the bed covered with copies of the
*Times,* marked at certain places with large blue crosses

and a copy of *Le Temps* with arrows in the margin and
" this will interest you " written underneath.  All from
the same kind and only donor.

Vendredi<br>December 17, 1915

I am afraid the courier is past and my letters are drowned
for it is as wild a day as ever I have seen—a sky like lead, a
boiling sea, the coast hidden by thick mist, a low noise of
wind and such rain dashing on the windows.  It is very
cold, too, and (3.30) dark already.  My maid, however,
lit me a splendid fire this morning and after lunch when
the room was warm I got up and am sitting by it now in
the armchair.  I don't feel *very grand* and though the fire
isn't like that wretched affair at Cassis and burns merrily
and warm, it seems to light the shadows and to prick an ear
to the quiet—How quiet it is !  except for the storm
outside !  Much quieter than Day's Bay !

No, the courier has just come and there *is* a letter after
all.

I am sorry I made you sad about that little villa.  I
heard of another last night from my Englishman—four
rooms—good stoves—electric light, heating, a verandah, a
garden all furnished, and so sheltered that you can dine out
every day—80 francs a month.  The man who has just
taken it says he buys fish at 1d. a dozen, so I should live
off fish and rosebuds.—But no, I'll not speak of these
things, for it's useless and foolish.

December 18, 1915

I must write a little more for ' le temps ' is so exciting.
I had a very vivid dream last night that I and my brother
were in Berlin without passports.  We were having lunch
in the waiting room of a railway station at a long table, with
several German soldiers just back from the front with their
equipment, etc.  I see now the proud wives carrying the
men's coats for them, etc.  Suddenly in a dreadful pause

I began to speak in English. I said the woman reminded
me of a Miss Lindsay, bootmaker's assistant on Lambton
Quay. In a flash I knew we were done for. Brother said,
" Make for the telephone box," but as we got in a soldier
smashed his helmet through the glass door—Crash! I
woke to a violent clap of thunder. It was raining, hailing,
the shutters flashed pale yellow with the lightning. I
heard the bells ringing in the hotel—the servants in felt
slippers running along the corridors. Bang! went the
thunder, rolling and tossing among the hills. The air was
so electric that one's hands and feet sang. Finally I got
up, put on my mackintosh and opened the shutters. I
felt sure that I'd be struck, especially as my room, being
at the corner for the full force of the storm. It was a
wonderful sight. I shall never forget the dignity of the
sea. It drew back from the land a long way. There were
no waves, only a fold or two where it touched the shore—
and it looked as cold as a stone. Above the coast the sky
was bright silver and above that a bright fantastic green.
As I opened the window I smelled the sharp smell of the
wet blue-gum trees. Oh, it was exciting—it was lovely
and all the while the hail springing against the window
pane and the low thunder and the fluttering light. I
rang for my breakfast and that became a kind of thrilling
feast, too. I put the milk jug under the *édredon* when I
had poured out my first cup of coffee and it stayed there
warm as a pigeon and I had a second boiling cup. That
seemed a miracle of ingenuity and forethought! Then
the spry maid tripped in and lit the fire—I heard the little
twigs cracking : she sat back on her heels and told me
which rooms the water had flooded—when such a thing
had happened before, etc. I felt that I was going to jump
out of bed, wash and dress as quickly as possible, pack a
small bundle and catch the ark at about half past ten.
But it is half past ten now and the wind has dropped,
two roosters are crowing somewhere and the sky is
silver.

I am very much better—in fact to all intents and pur-

poses *cured* I believe by that unguent.    Here is a geranium
—I quite forgot they were there.    Here is your Xmas
box. . . .

Sunday morning
December 19, 1915

From sheer laziness I am sitting up in bed.    The ' l'eau
chaude ' is warming its enamel bosom before a fresh-
lighted fire, and I ought to be up—but it's so pleasant
here and the smell of burning wood is so delicious and the
sky and the sea outside are so pearly.    After I had written
to you yesterday down came the rain again, and this time
the courier really was drowned, so I got a letter of yours
about the landlady, etc., just this moment.

My rheumatism this morning—*n'existe pas.*    I've not
been so free for a year.    I can positively jump.    I'm to go
on using the unguent and my Englishman is going to give
me the prescription to-day for he leaves here on Monday.
He is also going to conduct me to the post and see I'm not
cheated with my mandat—so that is all to the good.    I
dined down stairs last night.    A good many people have
arrived—and the hotel is rather changed.    More flowers,
more fires and an ' atmosphere.'    I met the ' Madame ' on
the stairs.    *Elle me demandait si je souffre toujours.*    I said
no—said she " Heureusement le climat est très sec ! "
What a *fool*, with rain teeming on everything !    I paid a
bill here too which was a relief off my mind.

Dear, *do* send me summat to read when you can.    I am
still confined to Shakespeare and the *Times*.    I don't know
what to ask for.    I'd like a 1/- Dickens that I haven't
read—or one I don't remember—but which is it ?    Oh,
I'd like to read *Oliver Twist* again, for one.    And I'll send
you something for *The Signature* but don't flatter me—
I'm only the jam in the golden pill—and I know my place,
Betsy.

I have a presentiment that I shall never see Albion's
shores again (but then I always feel like that when
I'm away).    Still, Bogey, in case I should be taken

sudden preserve these words and show them to the landlady.

It is such a Sunday morning—so quiet and so tending towards la messe. The lovely air must be the result of the storm, I suppose, for breathing is a delight. It's what you might call very *choice*, this morning, too.

I should like to embrace my Father this morning. He would smell of fine cloth with a suspicion of cigar added, eau de cologne, just an atom of camphorated chalk, something of fresh linen and his own particular smell—his ' blood smell ' as p'raps Lorenzo would say.

Lundi **matin**
December 20, 1915

A lovely ' gold dust ' day. From early morning the fishermen have been passing and the little boats with red sails put out at dawn. I am dressed to go to the post-office with my two mandats.

When I woke this morning and opened the shutters and saw the dimpling sea I knew I was beginning to love this place—this South of France. Yesterday I went for a walk—the palm trees after the rain were magnificent, so firm and so green and standing up like stiff bouquets before the Lord. The shop people, too, are very kind. You are a regular customer, after a day or two, and my Englishman says they are very honest.

Last night in the salon I had a long talk with a woman who is here for her health. A woman about fifty. She has been nursing since the beginning of the war somewhere near Arles. She is of the Midi and has a very pronounced accent, which is *extremely* fascinating—and she knows and adores ' mon pays.' She told me all about the coast, about all sorts of little places " de toute beauté "—and as she talked I began to see this place—not romantically but truly. I like it and more than like it. This woman was reading the letters of Taine. . . . She told me such good stories of the black soldiers—I must not forget them. I hope I shall speak a great deal with her because she is very

50

good for my French too. She has a good vocabulary and
a way of *spacing* her words giving them a very nice, just
quantity. Oh, Bogey, it is the most Heavenly day.
Every little tree feels it and waves faintly from delight.
The femme de chambre called to the gardener just now as
she beat the next door mattress out of the window—" Fait
bon ? " and he said, " Ah, délicieux ! " which seemed to
me very funny for a gardener, especially this little chap.
Now I must button my boots with a tiger's tail and go
out.

> Mercredi
> December 22, 1915

I wish you could see the winds playing on the dark blue
sea to-day, and two big sailing vessels have come in and are
rocking like our white boat rocked when you were here.
The sea is what I call very high this morning and the
clouds are like swans. It is a lovely morning ; the air
tastes like fruit !

Yesterday I went for a long scrambling walk in the
woods, on the other side of the railway. There are no
roads there—just little tracks and old mule paths. Parts
are quite wild and overgrown, then in all sorts of unexpected faery places you find a little clearing—the ground
cultivated in tiny red terraces and sheltered by olive trees
(full of tiny black fruit). There grow the jonquils,
daffodils, new green peas and big abundant rose bushes.
A tiny (this word is yours really : it's haunting me to-day)
villa is close by with a painted front and a well or a petite
source at the bottom of the garden. They are dream
places. Every now and then I would hear a rustle in the
bushes and an old, old woman, her head tied up in a black
kerchief would come creeping through the thick tangle
with a bunch of that pink heath across her shoulders.
" B'jour ma petite dame " she would munch and nod—
and with a skinny finger point me my way. Once I found
myself right at the very top of a hill and below there lay
an immense valley—surrounded by mountains—very high

ones and it was so clear you could see every pointed pine, every little zig-zag track. The black stems of the olives showing sooty and soft among the silvery green. One could see for miles and miles. There was, far in the distance a tiny town planted on a little knoll, just like a far away city in a Dürer etching, and now and again you would see two cypresses and then if you looked carefully you found a little house, for two cypresses planted side by side *portent bonheur*. On the other side of me there was the sea and Bandol and the next bay, Sanary. Why weren't you with me ? Why didn't you lean over the fence and ask the old, old man what that plant was and hear him say it was the immortelle, and it flowers for eight years and then dies and its yellow flowers come out in June ?

The sun went down as I found the Saint-Cyr road back to Bandol. The people were coming home, and the children were running from school. As I came into Bandol I heard a loud chanting and down the Avenue des Palmiers there came four little boys in white, carrying a cross and incense braziers—an old priest with white hair, chanting—four men following each carrying a corner of a black and silver cloth—then a coffin carried on a table by six men and the whole village following—the last man of all being an old chap with a wooden leg. It was extremely fantastic and beautiful in the bright strange light.

December 23, 1915

The sailors in the sailing ships have been washing. They are all pegged out along the masts and spars. It's a very still primrose and cowslip day—I am going to drive in a kerridge to that little Dürer town I told you of. The Englishman did not go away on Monday. He stayed till the end of the week to show me the different walks he has discovered here and it is he who is taking me there this afternoon. How we get there Heaven only knows but he says there *is* a road. This man has certainly been awfully kind to me. . . . I can't persuade him that I am more than six years old and quite able to take my own ticket and manage my own affairs.

You know I really am a little tempted to take a minute villa later on here. Would it be more expensive than living here, do you think ? It's not that I don't like this hotel—I *do*, and (this is like my brother) I am awfully popular with all the people here—You would laugh. I know all their separate histories and married lives, etc. I sit and listen—they talk. I feel sometimes very much like Fergusson. But a little villa with a handkerchief of garden is a very attractive idea—Talk to me about it.

Your two letters to-day for some reason have made me rather stiff—rather dumb. I feel it as I write—I don't know why. I feel I am talking over a fence, and my voice is tiny like a grasshopper's. Write to me again at length and know that this little stuffiness *n'est rien*, and that really and truly there isn't a fence and we are sitting hand in hand under a rhubarb leaf and I am showing you what I have got in my pocket and you are showing me what you have got in yours.

*To S. S. Koteliansky*     Nearly the end of the year
                            December 24, 1915

My extremely wicked and neglectful and utterly faith-less friend !

At last you have sent me a letter and although it only arrived a few moments ago and you certainly do not deserve an answer I *will* just write two words to prove once and for all my complete superiority of nature over you. You need not bother to write me letters if it is a trouble to you ; it's enough if, *occasionally* you send me a little card and tell me that you have not forgotten. For I shall not forget you. I often think of you. I wish you would come into my room now and smoke a cigarette with me. It is very quiet here and outside the window the sea is trembling under the moon. My room smells faintly of wood from the fire—you would like it.

I am very happy here. The place is so beautiful and the sun shines—or it doesn't—There is the sea and a wild beautiful coast—and behind the village there are woods and mountains. Already I have so many 'secret' places— The people are awfully nice too. They are honest; one can be oneself with them. You know, you can lean over the fence and talk to the old man who is cutting flowers or you can sit on a rock and talk to the old, old woman who is cutting heather—and you are " at home." There are many fishermen, too; fishermen are always very true.

Oh, my God! I am very happy. When I shut my eyes I cannot help smiling—You know what joy it is to give your heart—freely—freely. Everything that happens is an adventure. When the wind blows I go to the windiest possible place and I feel the cold come flying under my arms—When the sea is high I go down among the rocks where the spray reaches and I have games with the sea like I used to years ago. And to see the sun rise and set seems miracle enough.

When I first came here I was really very ill and unhappy but that is over now—and London, you know seems remote—remote—as though it did not exist. Those last hateful and wasted months are blotted out. Next time we see each other really we will be happy. Don't always remember the 'wicked' me. But one day we shall see each other again and be frightfully happy—Let us promise each other. I want to tell you all about the people here (but that would fill books) and all about the place (and that would not interest you). So pretend I have told you. At any rate it is too dark to see anything or anybody now. My brother is here often, laughing, and calling " Do you remember, Katy ? "

It is a beautiful night—so beautiful that you are half afraid to take it into your breast when you breathe.

This is not a letter at all—only a message—Take care of yourself. I do not know why but just this moment I see awfully clearly the elephant on your big inkstand.

And I want a reply *immediately* but you won't send me
one.   You will be wise and severe with me as you always
are—Goodnight.


*To J. M. Murry*                  The Morning of Christmas Eve
                                      December 24, 1915

Yesterday after I had posted your letter I went to the
Market.   You know where it is—in front of that square,
curious little Church.   Yesterday the Market was full of
branches of roses—branches of mandarines and flowers of
all kinds.   There was also a little old man selling blue
spectacles and rings " contre la rhumatisme " and a funny,
fat old woman waddling about and pointing to everything
she wanted with a fat fowl that she held by the legs.   The
fowl was furious.

Then I went up to that funny untidy villa with the
oranges growing against the walls close to the cemetery—
you know the one I mean ?   It has a long ' sticky ' garden
in front and a large blue board advertising apartments.
White roosters peck among the gravel and all the paths are
spanned over with brown sprigs of vine.   The villa is
stone and carved with doves, cauliflowers, lions, monkey
trees and setting suns.   Very gay.

In the garden, mounted on a very nervous chair, a huge,
old man in a blue apron and horn specs, was snipping twigs,
and below him a tiny little boy in pink and white socks was
receiving them in his pinny.   I asked if Mademoiselle
Marthe lived there.   Certainly, said the man, while the
chair wobbled fearfully and then he stood up, raised his
snippers, and hailed, " Marthe, Marthe."   Open flew a
window, out popped a little round head.   " On demande,"
said the old man.   Then a glass door opened and a little
creature in a white cotton jacket with red wool shoes on
stood smiling by me.   I asked her if she would lift the
shoulders of my brown jacket for me—and she said she
would—but after the days of fête—*n'est-ce pas* ?   And
then, her head a little on one side, with a charming timid

smile and one hand with a silver ring on it keeping the sun from her eyes she came to open the gate for me, because she said it was a very difficult gate. I went away longing to write a little play with this setting—I could even hear the music to it. I especially saw the garden by moonlight and the shadows of the oranges and Marthe with a shawl over her head—and her telling *him* it was a difficult gate.

Two of the big sailing ships have come right into the port this morning and are anchored close to the quai. I think they are unloading something; I must go and ask the paper woman all about it. She is a fund of cheerful gossip and she's a nice soul. When the air is ' frais ' she produces a tiny charcoal bucket with a pierced lid—and says—" Warm your hands one good little moment."

My dear ! Ten *children* with their parents and two nurses arrived here last night ; they are all ' une belle famille ' as my maid says. I have not seen them yet, but my brain reels at the idea of their weekly bills.

It is Xmas morning
December 25, 1915

When I went out to put your letter in the Palais d'Azur yesterday I found out why the boats had come in—for there was a procession of dark young sailors, bare legged, their bright blue trousers rolled to the thigh, in big full blouses and with their hair cropped " en pudding " carrying on their shoulders little red kegs and filling them at the fountain. A great dispute went on because it was midday and the women had come to draw water too—and the sailors would not take the kegs away and only laughed. They had a tiny boat rocking at the steps of the quai. On deck three sailors hung over the rail plucking three ducks. The feathers floated on the water. The boat is called the *Felicina* and she comes from Verraggia. The other boat hasn't got a name. To-day they are dressed and flying five or six snippets of flags.

Yesterday afternoon I went off by myself into the woods

and spent all the afternoon exploring little tracks and
' chemins de chamois ' ! I picked such lovely daisies too,
with pink tips. It got very faery after the sun went down
—and when I got to the road to come home, still deep in
the woods, there came a tinkle and round the corner came
an old man with a herd of brindled goats. As I came into
the town all the babies were flocking in the streets looking
at Xmas toys. Heaven knows they are a sorry little show,
but you should have heard the screams of joy—" Ah ah,
le beau chemin de fer—Dis, dis ! Qu'il est mignon le
p'tit chien ! Ah, la grande—la belle ! " I began to look
too and I nearly bought an elephant or a dog with one ear
standing up—or a *lovely* tea-set with roses painted on it
and a sugar basin with a tiny strawberry for the handle on
the lid.

Then the Captain of the *Felicina* landed and came
marching up the street—very grand—all gold braid—little
clipped beard, stiff linen. He was followed by two sailors
and he disappeared behind the bead curtain of the butcher's
shop. Then another ship came sailing in—which makes
*five*. Can you feel how thrilling they are in this tiny
place ? And how one longs to go on board and walk up
and down little ladders ?

There is a crèche in the Church. It has been all made
by the children. It is simply beautiful. A landscape
with painted cardboard houses—even shutters to the
windows. A windmill—little bridges of twigs, fountains
made of falling silver paper cut in strips—and the roads all
of fresh sand, the hills and the valleys all of moss that they
gathered in the woods. Trees are planted in the moss
and hung with silver stars (far too big for them). There
are sheep under the trees, shepherds, holy men, the three
Kings, one with a black face and awful whites to his eyes.
Fat little angels perch in all sorts of places and in a neat
cardboard grotto is Mary, St. Joseph (a very old dotty) and
a naked ' p'tit *Ch*esau ' as they say, who can open and shut
his eyes. The priest was showing this Marvel to a baby
when I was there but she could say nothing except in a

very hushed voice—" Il est tout nu." The dove is also perched on a tree—a drunken fowl bigger than the ox and the ass—and out of one house there is the head of the inn-keeper in a night cap with a tassel on it telling Mary he hasn't got a room. . . .

*Plus tard.* I have opened my letter (I am always doing that—it's like popping just one's head in again) to say that when I ran to the Post it was shut for all to-day and I am afraid this letter will not go until to-morrow.

I have just had a Xmas dinner—very dreadful and indecent to be partaken of alone. The ' belle famille ' had an *enormous* feed. I left the little tiny ones leaning back in their chairs with their legs stretched out utterly helpless—and slightly the worse for wine. For even the baby who is not yet three drank until her glass rested on her nose, where she left it and blew into it and stared at me through the top. Now I am going for a walk with the Englishman who leaves definitely the day after to-morrow.

*Later.* It was a long walk through the woods and then we left the paths and he taught me how to climb as taught by the guides in Norway. It was boring beyond words but absolutely successful—we scaled dreadful precipices and got wonderful views. Then I had to learn *how* to descend, and how to balance if the stones roll when you put your foot on them—What a pa-man ! All this, of course, he takes really seriously—and I find myself doing so too and I don't get one bit tired. I wish you could see my room. Even the blue glass vases we put away have had to come out for the big bouquets of yellow and pink roses. To-night I have promised to dine with this pa-man. I don't doubt I shall get a lecture on touring in Spain. I already know more about how to travel in Italy than any living being, I should think.

I am going to try to send you a nut shell in this letter for a little hat. It's dark now and the waves are breaking right up the road among the palms.

Monday morning
December 26, 1915

Even if you never came I cannot but love you more for
the evening and the night and the morning I have spent
thinking that you *are* coming.   It was Sunday, so I could
not send you a telegram until to-day.   I somehow—Oh,
how did I ?—got through last evening by sitting in the
salon among unreal fantastic people and sewing and talking.
For I knew I would not sleep.   I knew I would not sleep.
What drowsy bliss slept in my breast !   I hardly dared to
breathe.

A woman here told me how to buy our stores and what
to pay and how to make soup with 2 sous worth of bones,
and what day the woman with good apples was at the
market and how to manage une femme de menage.   I
heard.   I dared not look at her.   I felt my smiles chasing
in my eyes.   I saw the villa—perhaps a cactus near the gate
—you writing at a little table, me arranging some flowers
and then sitting down to write too.   Both of us gathering
pine cones and driftwood and bruyère for our fire.   I
thought of what I would have ready for you, soup and
perhaps fish, coffee, toast, because charbon de bois, which
is *much* cheaper than coal, makes lovely toast, I hear,—
a pot of confitures, a vase of roses. . . .   And then I saw
us waking in the morning and putting on the big kettle
and letting in the femme de menage.   She hangs her
shawl behind the kitchen door.   " Vous savez, il fait
beau."

December 27, 1915

Finally I could bear it no longer.   I came up to my
room and took a hot bath and then curled up in bed and
smoked and tried to read a new Dickens.   No use.   The
sea was very loud.   I looked at the watch and saw it said
25 to 12 and then I went to sleep.   When I looked again
it was nearly four.   So I turned on the light and waited,
waited for day.   How the light changed, I never shall

forget. I put on my big purple coat and opened the
shutters and sat on the window sill. It was all primrosy
with black mountains. A sailing ship put out to sea. I
saw all the little men on board, and how the sail was put up
and how when it caught the breath of wind the ship went
fast. Two more of our big ships, with a rattle of chains,
hoisted anchor and put out to sea. I saw the bending,
straining bodies of the men. And then came the fishers
bringing in their pots. Then the first bird—At seven I
heard my little maid lighting the stove so I ran out and
asked for my déjeuner—washed in cold water—kissed my
roses—put on my goblin hat and flew into the garden.
The market was there—with two funny Spaniards beating
drums. Such flowers! Such violets! But I kept my
pennies for you and me. I thought I should have to have
a small fête so when I went to the post office I put *new
relief nibs* in all the awful old crusty pens. The sea, and
sky this morning are LITERALLY a DARK NAVY (see Aunt Li).
I sent your telegram, ran home to find the maids beating
the carpets and the white dog overslept and pretending he
had been awake for hours on the terrace. Now I am going
with a gent in corduroys to look at a furnished villa of his.

December 29, 1915

If you *should* come I have found a tiny villa for us—
which seems to me almost perfect in its way. It stands
alone in a small garden with terraces. It faces the ' midi '
and gets the sun all day long. It has a stone verandah
and a little round table where we can sit and eat or work.
A charming tiny kitchen with pots and pans and big coffee
pot, you know. Electric light, water downstairs and
upstairs too in the cabinet de toilette. A most refined
' water closet ' *with* water in the house. . . . The salle à
manger is small and square with the light low over the
table. It leads on to the verandah and overlooks the sea.
So does the chambre à coucher. It is very private and
stands high on the top of a hill. It is called the *Villa*

*Pauline.* The woman (wife of the mobilier) who showed it me would also find me a servant for three hours every day. Yesterday I *ran ran* all day long to find something and saw such funny places. Every little street I came to there seemed to be an old woman in woollen slippers with keys in her hands waiting to show me " votre affaire." Oh, such funny experiences ! But I have been very careful to go to each woman I left in a state of uncertainty and to say I regret that I cannot take their particular treasure so that I shall not have to spend the rest of my days in dodging streets, houses and people as I usually do on these occasions. And they are neither heart-broken nor do they call me a ' sausage '—to my *great* surprise. It is a sunny windy morning with a high sea and dancing light on all the trees. The *vent de l'est* is blowing as a matter of fact, but it has no terrors for me now that I have my legs again.

Mdlle. Marthe has just been although I am still in my peignoire. She is not a girl ; she is a *sparrow*. It is so awfully nice to have your jacket mended by a charming little sparrow instead of a monster with icy hands and pins in her mouth and all over her non-existent bosom. But Marthe hops about, smiling, with her head a little on one side. She is a sweet little thing ; I wish to goodness I could somehow adopt her for us.

My roses—my roses are too lovely. They melt in the air (I *thought* that in French where it sounds sense but in English it's nonsense). I have 23. I just counted them for you and if you turn these blue glass vases back to front so that you don't see the handpainted horrors on them they are very lovely, the dark red stems and a leaf or two showing through the water.

. . . *Make* me wash and dress. I've lighted another cigarette now and in spite of my absolutely cold, calculating mind, my heart keeps on *perpetually* like this. One large vase of white and yellow jonquils in the middle of the table. Roses in the bedroom, some little red anemones on the mantelpiece. " This is the place, Bogey." A ring

at the door. The man with your boxes from the station—
Now we are sitting down, hardly daring to look at each
other, but smiling. Now you have unpacked and put on
your corduroys and your boots. I am downstairs and you
are upstairs. I hear you walking. I call out " Bogey, do
you want coffee or tea ? " We arrange to work every
morning—have lunch—go out until it is dark, come home
have tea and talk and read and get our supper—and then
work. On our walks we will take that satchel you bought
—for pine cones and wood and oranges—Oh God, this
place is as fair as New Zealand to me—as apart, as secret,
as much a place where you and I are alone and untroubled
—But so I dream.

Now I am going to get up. I've got some *awful* tooth-
paste. It is called Isis and it has funny woodeny birds on
the tube. It has all come out the wrong end, too. And
it's *much too pink*.

Wednesday night<br>
December 29, 1915

I am like that disciple who said : " Lord I believe.
Help thou my unbelief." As I was dressing and your
letter was already sealed the heavy steps really came along
the corridor. The knock at the door—the old man with
the blue folded paper that I scarcely dared to take and
having taken—could not open. Oh, I sat by the side of
my bed—and opened it little by little. I read all those
directions for the sending of urgent telegrams in the
night—At last I said : " He is not coming " and opened
it and read your message. . . . Since then I have never
ceased for one moment to tremble. . . . I felt " Now he
is coming that villa is taken " and I ran, ran along the
quai. One day I shall tell you all this at length, but it was
not taken until I saw the woman and took it. I went
through it again. It is quite perfect in its way. It is
always what I felt there was somewhere in the world for
us, in Spain or Italy. And the people to whom it belongs
who live next door are such good, decent, honest people,

eager to have us, eager to make us comfortable and
happy. " Je suis toujours là. Vous avez seulement de
frapper si vous auriez besoin de quelque chose." The sun
shone in every room and on the little stone verandah
danced the shadow of a tree. Is this true ? Is it coming
true ? I have to sign the agreement and pay a month in
advance to-morrow. Then to order the coal and wood
and see my femme de menage who has already been found
" pour 3 heures le matin et pour faire mes petites courses,
n'est-ce pas ? " All the rest of the day . . . I do not
know how I have spent it—such a lovely wild day brimming over with colour and light. I have found the
shortest way to our home by a road you do not know,
through fields of jonquils and past the olive trees that blow
so silver and black to-day. There are high walls on the
road and nobody goes.

Yes, I have found a lovely way—And I have made out a
list of our modest provisions that I shall buy on Friday.
In fact I have made out more than one list. For I can't
even write or read. . . .

This morning I went to the little Church and prayed.
It is very nice there. I prayed for us three—for you and
me and Chummie. It was so gay and yet solemn there.


                                        December 30, 1915

Money doesn't frighten me a bit. We'll be two little
silkworms and live on mulberry leaves. If you come here
we shall both write poetry—a mutual book which we will
publish together. Also we shall both write a kind of
' paysages ' and we shall both write—well, I shouldn't be
surprised if we both wrote *anything*.

The little house is there, waiting for us. Its eyes are
shut until I open them. The sun touches the verandah
and warms the place where your hand will rest. Tout bas,
tout bas mon coeur chante : " Cinquante kilos de charbon
de pierre—cinquante kilos de charbon de coke et des poids
pour allumer pour cinq sous—c'est presqu'un sac." I

have such a lot to do to-day. I must go out soon. Again I am not dressed but idling here with your letter beside me. I hardly slept at all.

December 30, 1915

*Midi.* This morning I went to the woman who introduced me to the Villa. She is a Spaniard, from Barcelona, and we are *really sincerely* friends. She is a dear creature and at first I knew she didn't like me but now really we have jokes together and she laughs, showing her pretty teeth. She tried to find me a femme de menage but could not so her daughter Marie, a dark-eyed Spanish beauty—a really fascinating creature with a fringe, big eyes and bright colour, is coming instead. But do we mind cuisine espagnole ? " Pas du tout." Then I went to the Church for a minute—I feel I must keep in close touch with God. They were dressing the altar with white and yellow jonquils—a sweet savour must have mounted. I prayed that my prayer was heard at the same moment and that God was pleased. Then I went to the station to ask what trains arrived and then to our villa by the path that you are coming. The door was open. The woman was inside hanging up saucepans. So we went through the inventory together and she said she would give me teacups and a teapot . . . because we were English. Also she offered to take me to any shops where I wanted to buy anything. I then went over the villa again. There is the loveliest green water pot like you admired. We must find something to fill it with. Then I went back to her house and together with her husband made out a lease, signed, paid, and put the key in my pocket. A friend came in and we sat talking a little. They told me not to buy flowers for your arrival. They had enough in their garden—and she said she would come in when Marie arrived on Saturday and show her how to make the fire. I walked home with the key in my hands.

*Friday.* Noon. Now I am just waiting. I have ordered the little stores and the wine and the wood. All

the windows are open—all the doors—the linen is airing.
I went to the flower market and stood among the buyers
and bought, wholesale you know, at the auction in a state
of lively terrified joy three dozen rose buds and six bunches
of violets.

We lived, very happily, at the Villa Pauline for the next
three months.  The next two letters were written on a
journey to Marseilles where K. M. had gone to meet her
sister (Mrs. Cecil Pickthall) who was returning from India.

                                    Hotel Oasis, Marseilles
                                         March 1916

I got through to the 2nd and had a very comfortable
journey.  I nearly fell out of the train at the last moment
looking for and then at you.  But no, you walked away.
It was rather awful—wasn't it ?  The country on the way
here is so lovely.  Where there used to be pink heather
there is gorse now and white and red trees everywhere.
Cook's weren't much consolation, but they referred me to
the P. and O. people, rue Colbert (opposite the Post
Office) and I found out from them that the *Sardinia* is
*definitely* expected at 8.30 a.m. on Thursday morning.
Also I explained my situation and obtained from them a
card permitting me to go on board.  So I must stay.  It's
a good thing I came.  She ' moors,' says my card further
at MOLE C—Bassin National.  I shall find it.  Cook's
will tell me the way.  The P. and O. people were not
inclined to over amiability.  Then (very hungry as usual
when en voyage) I went and bought my bag for 13 francs.
It was expensive, but it is just what you would have bought
(Oh, how she flatters him !)  Darling, it's a lovely bag,
though, *mouse blue*, well finished and strong, and with or
without a handle, AND the shape you said, AND deep
enough to hold my passport.  But my things somehow
don't belong, don't quite belong to me until you have seen
them—and they've spiritually passed through the customs.
Until you've more or less put a little white chalk squiggle

on this bag it isn't quite mine, though I'm very pleased
with it.   Then I came here and was remembered—but it
was " Eh, comment va Monsieur ? " from Monsieur,
Madame and especially that nice rather slatternly maid,
who was very friendly and shook hands.   I have the same
room (I'm in it now) the same flowers on the wall paper
(that came out and bowed when I had fever).   Only the
couch has been ' re-covered ' in large yellow and black
three-eyed beetles.   The same little chap has gone for my
bag, because it is pouring with rain and has been ever
since I set foot.   A nuisance—for I don't feel I *can* buy a
3.75 umbrella.   However, the rain is warm, and smells of
Spring.   I don't really mind it, but my boots do—and
they wouldn't be protected with an umbrella anyway—
I had two mingy eggs cooked in margarine, a pot of tea,
and one lumpish little roll for lunch, 1.70.   Two eggs are
1 *franc* : tea 60 *c*.—bread 10 *c*.   It was at the place we
always went to.   I protested, but was told a long story.
Everything has augmented.   I was very angry—especially
as I couldn't eat the eggs for all my hunger.   Our cooking
spoils one for anything else.   I bought 2 penny packets of
note-paper, a pen, a bottle of ink, a *Daily Mail* and *Radical*
and tabac.   So here I am waiting for the baggage—as
usual.

Madame Ferrand was at Cassis station ; in the corridor
of the train we met, and she did *not* acknowledge my bow.
Why are people so horrid ?

March 1916

Even though I hope to be home soon after this letter I
will send you a ' Bon jour '—I'm smoking my after-
breakfast cigarette.   This morning I am going to find my
way to the Bassin National in preparation for to-morrow.
Cook's could not explain exactly ; they advised me,
however, to take a cab (!) ; it is about half an hour's drive.
Très, très bien.   But the man here says I can go by train
from the Vieux Port all the way.   This I'll find out by

trying to do it this morning. Bogey—I had a funny night. All my fever came back. I shivered and my blood buzzed as though bees swarmed in my heart—and the lilies came out and bowed. Also it was rather late before I went to bed AFTER locking the door, fastening the bolt, etc., and to my Horror just as I began to fall asleep I heard SOMEONE turning the handle. Then the door was gently rattled. Then came a KNOCK. This is all true. I called out ' Qui est là ? ' No reply. So I leapt out of bed, threw my kimono on and, arming myself with a pair of scissors, I opened the door. There stood a horrid creature in his night-shirt who, began mumbling something about the wrong door—but he *leered*. Oh, I *slammed* the door in his face, and walked up and down my room—furious—I was not at all frightened.

To-day it is very warm (so far) and sunny. The trams roll up and down, and clatters and squeaks fly up. Now I have had a scrumptious, cat-like bath and washed my ears beyond words. I feel we are about 15 to-day—just children : you and I don't live like grown up people, you know. I keep seeing in my mind's eye, your back view as you go down to the *cave* for wood—and then your front view as you come up with your arms full. . . .

In April we left Bandol for Zennor, near St. Ives, in Cornwall.

*To S. S. Koteliansky*                              Thursday
                                            Zennor, Cornwall
                                            May 11, 1916

I am quite alone for all the day so I shall write to you. I have not written before because everything has been so ' unsettled ' ; now it is much more definite. I wish I could come and see you instead of writing ; next month I shall come to London probably for a little time and then we shall be able to meet and to talk. . . .

I am very much alone here. It is not a really nice place.

It is so full of huge stones, but now that I am writing I do not care, for the time. It is so very temporary. It may all be over next month ; in fact, it will be. I don't belong to anybody here. In fact, I have no being, but I am making preparations for changing everything. Write to me when you can and scold me.

Goodbye for now. Don't forget me.

*To Beatrice Campbell*                          Thursday
                                            May 1916

I have been wanting to write to you but felt that Ireland wouldn't permit. I can imagine what you and G. must have felt. This morning there is news that three leaders are shot and it's horrible reading. It's difficult to get any coherent account of anything down here but Garvin in *The Observer* last Sunday very nearly brought one off. There is no accounting for Ireland—The fact that while one street was under hot fire and people falling in all directions the milkmen with their rattling little cans went on delivering milk seemed, as Lawrence would say, " pretty nearly an absolute symbol."

If I had a box I'd send you flowers ; but I've nothing but a Vinolia Soap box and the violets would arrive in a lather. As soon as I have a box you shall have some. This country is very lovely just now with every kind of little growing thing—and the gorse among the grey rocks is, as Mrs. P. H. would agree, ' very satisfactory.' There are a great many adders here too. How does one cure oneself of their bite ? You either bathe the afflicted part with a saucer of milk *or* you give the saucer of milk to the adder.

There is a creek close by our house that rushes down a narrow valley and then falls down a steep cliff into the sea. The banks are covered with primroses and violets and bluebells. I paddle in it and feel like a faint, far-off reflection of the George Meredith Penny Whistle Overture, but awfully faint. Murry spends all his time hunting for his horn-rimmed spectacles for whenever he leaps over a stile or upon a mossy stone they fly from him, incredible distances, and undergo a strange and secret change into caterpillars, dragon flies or bracken uncurling.

To-day I can't see a yard, thick mist and rain and a tearing wind with it. Everything is faintly damp. The floor of the tower is studded with Cornish pitchers catching the drops. Except for my little maid (whose *ankles* I can hear stumping about the kitchen) I am alone, for Murry and Lawrence have plunged off to St. Ives with rucksacks on their backs and Frieda is in her cottage. It's very quiet in the house except for the wind and the rain and the fire that roars very hoarse and fierce. I feel as though I and the Cornish Pasty [1] had drifted out to sea— and would never be seen again. But I love such days— rare lonely days. I love above all things, my dear, to be alone. Then I lie down and smoke and look at the fire and begin to think out an EXTRAORDINARILY good story about Marseilles. I've re-read my novel to-day, too and now I can't believe I wrote it. . .

Sunday night
May 1916

It is still awfully difficult to credit what has happened and what is happening in Ireland. One can't get round it. This shooting, Beatrice, this incredible shooting of people ! I keep wondering if Ireland really minds. I mean really won't be pacified and cajoled and content with a few fresh martyrs and heroes. I can understand how it must fill your thoughts, for if Ireland were New Zealand and such a thing had happened there . . . it would mean the same for me. It would really (as *un*fortunately George-out-of-Wells would say) Matter Tremendously. . . . Dear woman, I am a little afraid of jarring you by writing about the whole affair, for I know so little (except what you've told me) and I've heard no discussion or talk.

[1] The name for the maid.

It is Sunday evening. Sometimes I feel I'd like to
write a whole book of short stories and call each one
Sunday. Women are far more 'sensitive' to Sundays
than to the moon. Does Sunday mean to you something
vivid and strange and remembered with longing ? . . .
Sunday is what these talking people call a rare state of
consciousness, and what I would call—the feeling that
sweeps me away when I *hear* an *unseen* piano. Yes, that's
just it, and now I come to think of it, isn't it extraordinary
how many pianos seem to come into being only on Sunday.
Lord ! someone, heaven knows where—starts playing
something like Mendelssohn's Mélodie in F.—or, miles
away, some other one plays a funny little gavotte by
Beethoven that you—simply can't bear. I feel about an
unknown piano, my dear, what certain men feel about
unknown women—no question of love—but simply " an
uncontrollable desire to stalk them " (as the Crown Prince
on Big Game Shooting says). Not that there is even the
ghost of a pianner here. Nothing but the clock and the
fire and sometimes a gust of wind breaking over the house.
This house is very like a house left high and dry. It has
the same 'hollow' feeling. The same big beams and
narrow doors and passages that only a fish could swim
through without touching. And the little round windows
at the back are just like portholes. Which reminds me—
there has been a calf lying under the dining room window
all day. Has anyone taken it in ? It has been another
misty Highland-Cattle-Crossing-the-Stream-by-Leader
day and the little calf has lain shivering and wondering
what to do with its far too big head all the day long.
What time its Mother has guzzled and chewed away and
looked into the distance and wondered if she were too fat
to wear a tussore coat like any Christian woman. Oh,
Lord, why didst Thou not provide a tucking away place
for the heads of Thy Beasts as Thou didst for Thy Birds ?
If the calf were only something smaller I could send my
soul out wrapped in a non-existent shawl and carrying a
non-existent basket lined with non-existent flannel and

bring it in to the dead out kitchen fire to get warm and
dry. . . .

I must stop this letter.    Write to me again very soon. . .


*To Lady Ottoline Morrell*
A Tuesday night.   No, it's Wednesday
May 1916

. . . We are going to leave here as soon as we can.    We
are at present, looking for a little cottage where we can put
our pieces of furniture, for we must have a tiny home and
a garden and we must be alive again. . . .    When we have
found our cottage we both shall love to come to you for
a little while.    We read your last letter sitting with our
feet in a little stream, all among primroses and wild
flowers—and dreadfully like the Overture to the Penny
Whistle chapter in Richard Feverel.    But your letter
saved us from piping . . . and at any rate, I'm never Lucy
and M. is never Dick.


*To Beatrice Campbell*                           Saturday
May 1916

. . . I am going to Cornwall on Monday to
Sunnyside Cottage,
Mylor, near Penryn,
and I will write you from there.    Do write to me, too,
darling, and tell me the news.

I arrived at Paddington to find the station crowded with
Sinn Feiners who had just arrived from Wormwood
Scrubbs and were being taken, on the points of innumer-
able bayonets to some other prison.

Heavens !   What a sight it was—but they all looked very
happy and they all wore bunches of green ribbon or green
badges.    I very nearly joined them, and I rather wish I
had.

*To Lady Ottoline Morrell*                    Thursday
                              Sunnyside Cottage, Mylor, near Penryn
                                             June 1916

I loved hearing from you this morning, and I had intended to write to you to-day and tell you that Lawrence has gone home again.  We walked with him as far as the ferry and away he sailed in a little open boat pulled by an old, old man.  Lawrence wore a broad white linen hat and he carried a rucksack on his back.  He looked rather as though the people of Falmouth had cried to him as the Macedonians did to Paul and he was on his way over to help them.

That journey with F.  I built myself a bower of newspapers and sat in it until the train reached Paddington but F. talked over and round it and kept pointing to little financial paragraphs . . . leaping upon them, you know, with a shout of excitement, with the ardour of a young man discovering mountains and torrents.  Fancy *thrilling* to the fact that Pig Iron is nominal and Zinc Sheets are unchanged. . . .


*To J. M. Murry*                        Very late Friday night
                                             September 1916

I shall not be able to post this letter until I have heard from you where you are going to sleep after to-night. Nevertheless I must write and tell you. . . .

That it only dawned on me this evening that perhaps you will not be here again for a long time . . . that you won't see the dahlias of this year again reflected in your mirror . . . and that the lemon verbena in a jar on my table will be all withered and dry.  As I thought that, sitting, smoking in the dusky room, Peter Wilkins [a black kitten] came in with a fallen-all-too-fallen leaf in his mouth, and I remembered that the Michaelmas daisies were out and, lo ! it was autumn.

Is it just my fancy—the beauty of this house to-night ? This round lamp on the round table, the rich flowers, the

tick of the clock dropping into the quiet—and the dark
outside and the apples swelling and a swimming sense of
deep water.   May brought me this evening some of this
year's apples. . .   " Good to eat."   They are small and
coloured like pale strawberries.   I wish that you were
with me.   It is not because you are absent that I feel so
free of distraction, so poised and so still.   I feel that I am
free even of sun and wind, like a tree whose every leaf
has ' turned.'

Saturday night
September 1916

Your girl has been so ' down ' to-day, so appallingly
' low.'   I knew I could not expect a letter—and cannot
until Monday.   Monday is 11,500 miles away. . . .   How
I loathed being here alone !   It gives me nothing really.
This place is only tolerable because of you, and even then
it never inspires. . . .

Mrs. H. called and asked me to come to a Sale of Work
on behalf of the Seamen's Mission.   Her thread glove
squeezed my hand. . . .   Her father was vicar here forty
years . . . she is a Widow. . . .   A girl called and asked
if I felt inclined to subscribe to the Red Cross. . . .
Little Keverns and parties from Kevern . . . " Please,
Mrs. Murry, can I go through ? " . . .   And then a
Mr. Watson with a boat for sale . . . £9 with a centre
keel, etc., etc. . . .   And that grocer and the oil boy . . .
and Mary has broken the Primus. . . .   And Mr. Mustard
says we use more than our fair share of water from the
pump.   That from *him* !

Then came your telegram which meant evidently that
we'll be in a state of suspense until Thursday at earliest
and dear only knows when I shall be in London.   Do you
want me ?   Would you love to have me ?   I want to
reach out my hand and take yours and say, " Oh I *should*
have come.   What is £2 10s. to us ? "

Oh, I could cry, I could cry, to-night.   I'll write no
more.

73

*To Lady Ottoline Morrell*                          September 1916

M. is away in London.   He left last Tuesday morning
and since then I have had no news from him.   I am very
anxious.   He went because of a letter from the Military
Intelligence Department who asked him to call with
reference to interpreterships.   I hope very much that he is
successful.

Being here alone in rather an ugly little house with no
news of what has happened is damnable.   I sit up at night
with all the doors and windows locked and wait for daylight with a hammer on the table by my side to bear me
companie.   What the hammer would do in an hour of
need I really don't know, but I feel that to come upon a
woman armed with a hammer *might* be damping to the
spirits of the most Hardened Fiend. . . .   The frightening
thing about this little house is its smugness—an eternal, a
kind of Jesus-Christ-yesterday-to-day-and-for-ever quality
of smugness which is most sinister.   It is a perfect setting
for a De Quincey murder.

I do not know in the least when M. will be home but if I
am not done to death before I'll gladly write something
for the *Garsington Chronicle.*

In the autumn of 1916 I received an appointment in the
War Office.   We went to London and at the beginning of
1917 K. M. took a studio at 141a Church Street, Chelsea,
where she lived until the end of the year.   I had rooms at
47 Redcliffe Road, to which K. M. came on her return
from France in April 1918.

*To the Hon. Dorothy Brett*                          Wednesday
                                        141a Church St., Chelsea
                                              August 1, 1917

. . . If this weather goes on, my girl, I'm afraid you'll
have to make a canvas boat of your picture and I will have
to turn my writing table upside down and float out of the
window.   But perhaps God in His goodness will allow us

to bob near each other for a moment. I have been informed by my great-aunt Charlotte (of Bangalore, Worple Avenue) that all those who are saved have expected a recurrence of the flood ever since the Kaiser was recognized to be Anti-Christ. And are Fully Prepared for it. Can't you see them " done up in impervious cases, like preserved meats "—like the Micawber family starting off for Australia ? . . .

I spent a mournful half morning yesterday being thumped and banged and held up by the heels by my doctor, who gave me no comfort at all, but half hinted, in fact, that given another hearty English winter or two the chances were that I'd bend and bow under my rheumatism until I become a sort of permanent croquet hoop. . . .

So, if in a year or two (I don't think the rain will stop before then) you *should* come through my gate and find me in the garden as a sort of decorative arch with a scarlet runner growing over me you will know then that the *worst* has happened.

Goodbye for now, mia bella. Salute my friends, frown on my enemies.

*To Mrs. Virginia Woolf*                                   August 1917

. . . I should love to come to Asheham on the 17th. Do have me. My story [1] I have sent to the typist who lets me have it back on Thursday. I couldn't cope with the copying : I've been so ' ill.' Rheumatics plus ghastly depression *plus* fury. I simply long to see you. I want to talk too about your *Mark on the Wall*. Now shall I write about it or talk about it ? Tell me, may I come and see you on Sunday at the tea time or after supper time or whenever it suits you ? Or when may I come ? I thought you had finally despatched me to cruel callous Coventry, without a wave of your lily-white hand.

[1] *Prelude.*

*To Lady Ottoline Morrell*                    Friday
                                          August 1917

. . . I am thankful to know that you are better and that
we shall soon be able to see each other again. What a
dreadful time you have had, I had no idea that the
measles were so formidable and overwhelming. I envy
you going to the sea—even for a few days. Oh, I have
such a longing for the sea as I write, at this moment. To
stand on the shore long enough to feel the land behind one
withdrawn into silence and the loud tumbling of the
waves rise and break over one's whole being. . . .

But the English summer sea is not what I mean. I
mean that wild untamed water that beats about my own
forlorn island. Why on earth do I call it ' forlorn.'
My bank Manager assures me that it's a perfect little gold
mine and whenever I go down to the Bank of New Zealand
I turn over a heap of illustrated papers full of pictures of
electric trains and American buildings and fashionable
ladies and gentlemen who might have walked out of the
Piccadilly Grill. . . . But all that sham and vulgarity is
hard to believe in : I don't believe in it all. There is
another side that you would believe in too. Ah, my dear, I
know the most heavenly places that cannot be spoiled—
and that I shall go back to as surely as if they were ' Dixie.'
And I shall think of you, and wish to God I expect that I
were sitting opposite you at the Maison Lyons ! Life is a
queer, a damn queer business !

It's a golden day. The blinds are down. I have some
big yellow lilies in the studio. The garden door is open
and the fig tree throws a wavy pattern on the floor and
walls among big soft spots of sunlight. Four o'clock in
the afternoon. I've been sitting at this table since
morning, writing and smoking. And somewhere quite
near someone is playing very old-fashioned dance tunes on
a cheap piano, things like the Lancers, you know. Some
minute part of me not only dances to them but goes
faithfully through, Ladies in the Centre, Visiting, Set to

Corners, and I can even feel the sensation of clasping
young warm hands in white silk gloves, and shrinking from
Maggie Owen's hand in Ladies Chain because she wore no
gloves at all—

Talking about dancing reminds me of last Saturday
night, when I really ' saw ' ――― for the first time.   It
was at a show at Margaret Morris's theatre.   He was there
with two very worn and *chipped* looking ladies—the
saddest looking remnants of ladies—in fact they reminded
me of those cups without saucers that you sometimes see
outside a china shop—all-on-this-tray-one-penny.   But
――― was really impressive looking.   I seemed to see his
mind, his haggard mind, like a strange forbidding country,
full of lean sharp peaks and pools lit with a gloomy glow,
and trees bent with the wind and vagrant muffled creatures
tramping their vagrant way.   Everything exhausted and
finished—great black rings where the fires had been, and
not a single fire even left to smoulder.   And then he
reminded me of that man in *Crime and Punishment* who
finds a little girl in his bed in that awful hotel the night
before he shoots himself, in that appalling hotel.   But I
expect this is all rubbish, and he's really a happy man and
fond of his bottle and a goo-goo eye.   But I don't think so.

Saturday night
August 11, 1917

There are three unfinished letters to you in my writing
case—one is even five pages long.   I could not re-read them
but I know why they were not sent.   They seemed to me
(and they were) as I wrote them hopelessly superficial and
fatiguing—fatiguing like a conversation by telephone can
be.   I heard my own little mocking, mechanical voice,
*loathed* it, and chose silence.   Quite suddenly, just after you
had been so near,—for no reason that I can explain away—
it was as if the light changed, and you vanished from me.
I wandered about in the wood among the wild smelling
bushes and sometimes I thought I saw the dark plume of

your hat, or your lips or your hands but when I went towards you—you *were* not. The strange part was that my memory of the days we had just spent together was as perfect as ever—as bright, as untroubled. I still saw the blue spears of lavender—the trays of fading, scented leaves, you in your room, and your bed with the big white pillow and you coming down in the garden swinging the gay lantern. But between these lovely memories and me there opened a deep dark chasm—it *trembled* open as if by an earthquake—and now it is shut again and no trace of it remains.

There—now I have told you ' all.'

Ever since I came back except for two *hellish* days, I have been ' at home ' and working. It is the only life I care about—to write, to go out occasionally and ' lose myself ' looking and hearing and then to come back and write again. At any rate that's the life I've chosen. But as soon as this bloody war is over I shall flee the country.

To-day has been so strange, very sunny, with a loud wind blowing and the sky a bright dazzle. One simply wanted to run about and be blown about and, if I dare quote Meredith, to cry like Diana : ' I am like a leaf.'

I am dying for something to read, but there is nothing. Every time my longing eye searches my shelves it sees *Horace for English Readers* or *Petit Larousse.* . . . *Where* are the books ?

Wednesday
August 15, 1917

Your glimpse of the garden, all flying green and gold, made me wonder again *who* is going to write about that flower garden. It might be so wonderful, do you know *how* I mean ? There would be people walking in the garden—several *pairs* of people—their conversation—their slow pacing—their glances as they pass one another—the pauses as the flowers ' come in ' as it were—as a bright dazzle, an exquisite haunting scent, a shape so formal and fine, so much a ' flower of the mind ' that he who looks at it really is tempted for one bewildering moment to stoop and touch and make *sure*. The ' pairs ' of people must be very different and there must be a slight touch of enchantment—some of them seeming so extraordinarily ' odd ' and separate from the flowers, but others quite related and at ease. A kind of, musically speaking, conversation *set* to flowers. Do you like the idea ? I see the Pig of the Party—rooting in her little dark mind. And I see B——, who hasn't the remotest idea of getting them into harmony. Perhaps that's not fair. But it's full of possibilities. I must have a fling at it as soon as I have time.[1]

I am sitting writing to you in the kitchen. I cannot *bear* at present my studio with its great Thou-God-seest-Me window. It is far more tolerable to sit up here with the saucepans and the nutmeg grater and the big swinging tree so close against the pane. Confound my poverty ! How I long to buy an exquisite room, absolute privacy, a devoted black woman, and some ravishing perfume. And I've been groaning for half an hour at having to pay the window cleaner four and sixpence ! And all the ugly makeshift furniture in the studio seems to be scrawled over with 1/11¾.

At that moment, appropriately enough, the window cleaner caught at my feet which weren't by any means flying and asked if it would be convenient to have 'em done again now. And since then a whole day has gone by—and I have read a long letter from Lawrence—He has begun to write to me again and quite in the old way—all about the leaves of the melon plant ' speckled like a newt,' and all about ' the social egg which must collapse into nothingness, into *non-being*.' I am so fond of him for many things. I cannot shut my heart against him and I never shall.

Don't you think one really must run away as soon as possible and as far as possible—

[1] See " Night-Scented Stock " in *Poems*, by Katherine Mansfield.

*To Mrs. Virginia Woolf*          August 1917

I had a last glimpse of you just before it all disappeared and I waved ; I hope you saw.

Thank you for letting me see Asheham. It *is* very wonderful and I feel that it will flash upon one corner of my inward eye for ever.

It was good to have time to talk to you ; we have got the same job, Virginia, and it is really very curious and thrilling that we should both, quite apart from each other, be after so very nearly the same thing. We are, you know ; there's no denying it.

Don't let THEM ever persuade you that I spend any of my precious time swopping hats or committing adultery. I'm far too arrogant and proud. However, let them think what they like. . . . There's a most wonderful greengage light on the tree outside and little white clouds bobbing over the sky like rabbits. And I wish you could see some superb gladioli standing up in my studio very proud and defiant like Indian braves.

Yes, your Flower Bed is *very* good.[1] There's a still, quivering, changing light over it all and a sense of those couples dissolving in the bright air which fascinates me—

Old Mother Gooseberry, my char from Ludgate Hill, has hung up her beetle bonnet : " Please m'm, if you would let me have the place to myself." So I am chased off, to sit among those marble pillars of brawn at the Library and read, *not* Henry James.

*To Lady Ottoline Morrell*          Sunday night
                                  September 1917

I feel as though I have returned from the seaside with one hot cheek and a feeling of sand between my toes, as I sit down to write to you. Your wonderful letter which seemed with its spray of verbena to come flying through the gold and green September air dropped in my lap and

[1] Mrs. Woolf's story, *Kew Gardens*.

I read it and sniffed and sniffed the sweet spray and put it at the bottom of a blue jar.

M. has had a holiday this last week and we've been so immensely occupied that I have had no time " to myself " at all. I haven't been able to shut a gate or a window or a door—and now at the end of these exquisite days I feel that it is High Time to lie down and be covered with these fresh fallen yellow leaves. But—to discover that it still is possible to laugh so much, to linger, to gaze in at shop windows and long so ardently for that lovely mirror, to walk under these bright trembling trees and high tumbling clouds, to watch children, and to lean over bridges.

*Ottoline :* " But dear Katherine. This is like Walt Whitman *too dreadfully* in the home ! "

Yes, I feel it is. But what am I to do ? I am hung about with memories like these and cannot move for them —Next week I must be abominably sober but *this* week is still here, and no, I cannot be calm.

(A dreadful, cold thought : can this be all hypophosphites ?) Ah well ! I must think that over carefully, " profoundly question it " (as B. R. might say) and if I feel it is true do not be surprised upon opening *The Daily Mirror* to find a picture of me with my hair parted down the middle and a black velvet band round my neck : Portrait of Katherine Mansfield, 141a Church Street. . . . You may make what use you like of this letter. . . .

But I had rather think that it was something quite, quite different—

None of *those people* ought to be " considered " ; it is only consideration which makes them swell so huge and loom so large. They cannot spoil September—Ah, Ottoline, will there really be winter again after all this rich beauty ? Cold and rain again, dark little days, dingy little days gripping one with frigid fingers like those hateful little dressmakers of my childhood. Must one really stand passive to them and be draped and pleated and folded into a kind of awful mackintosh parcel again ? . . .

London has a lap so full of pears and plums that every mean child hath a bellyful—

But B. and H. says in the *Evening News* : Now is the time to think of those cosy bloomers. . . . What Can One Do ?

*To the Hon. Dorothy Brett*                    Thursday
                                           October 11, 1917

It is a cold, sharp day.   I can see the sun flying in the sky like a faint far-away flag.   My Japanese doll has gone into boots for the winter and the studio smells of quinces. I have to write all day with my feet in the fringe of the fire—and oh alas ! it is sad to think that I shall be warm in front and cold behind from now until next June.

It seems to me so extraordinarily right that you should be painting Still Lives just now.   What can one do, faced with this wonderful tumble of round bright fruits ;  but gather them and play with them—and *become them*, as it were.   When I pass an apple stall I cannot help stopping and staring until I feel that I, myself, am changing into an apple, too, and that at any moment I can produce an apple, miraculously, out of my own being, like the conjuror produces the egg. . . .   When you paint apples do you feel that your breasts and your knees become apples, too ? Or do you think this the greatest nonsense.   I don't.   I am sure it is not.   When I write about ducks I swear that I am a white duck with a round eye, floating on a pond fringed with yellow-blobs and taking an occasional dart at the other duck with the round eye, which floats upside down beneath me. . . . [1]   In fact the whole process of becoming the duck (what Lawrence would perhaps call this consummation with the duck or the apple !) is so thrilling that I can hardly breathe, only to think about it. For although that is as far as most people can get, it is really only the ' prelude.'   There follows the moment when you are *more* duck, *more* apple, or *more* Natasha than

[1] See *Prelude*, p. 49.

any of these objects could ever possibly be, and so you
*create* them anew.

*Brett* (switching off the instrument) : " Katherine I
*beg* of you to stop. You must tell us all about it at the
Brotherhood Church one Sunday evening."

*K. :* " Forgive me, but that is why I believe in tech-
nique, too. (You asked me if I did.) I do just because I
don't see how art is going to make that divine *spring* into
the bounding outline of things if it hasn't passed through
the process of trying to *become* these things before re-
creating them."

I have left your letter unanswered for more days than I
could have wished. But don't think it was just because
I am so careless and faithless. No, really not. I enjoyed
keeping silent with the letter just as one enjoys walking
about in silence with another until the moment comes
when one turns and puts out a hand and speaks.

I threw my darling to the Wolves [1] and they ate it and
served me up so much praise in such a golden bowl that I
couldn't help feeling gratified. I did not think they
would like it at all and I am still astounded that they do.

" What form is it? " you ask. Ah, Brett, it's so difficult
to say. As far as I know, it's more or less my own inven-
tion. And " How have I shaped it ? " This is about as
much as I can say about it. You know, if the truth were
known I have a perfect passion for the island where I was
born. Well, in the early morning there I always remember feeling that this little island has dipped back into
the dark blue sea during the night only to rise again at
gleam of day, all hung with bright spangles and glittering
drops.[2] (When you ran over the dewy grass you positively
felt that your feet tasted salt.) I tried to catch that
moment—with something of its sparkle and its flavour.
And just as on those mornings white milky mists rise and
uncover some beauty, then smother it again and then

[1] *Prelude* was one of the first publications of Mr. and Mrs. Woolf
at the Hogarth Press.

[2] See *At the Bay.*

again disclose it, I tried to lift that mist from my people and let them be seen and then to hide them again. . . . It's so difficult to describe all this and it sounds perhaps over-ambitious and vain. But I don't feel anything but intensely a longing to serve my subject as well as I can.

But the unpardonable unspeakable thrill of this art business. What is there to compare ! And what more can we desire ? It's not a case of keeping the home fire burning for me. It's a case of keeping the home fire down to a respectable blaze, and little enough. If you don't come and see me soon there'll be nothing but a little heap of ashes and two crossed pens upon it.

Are you coming to London soon ? Let me know—let us meet. I shall see you float across my window upon a chariot of bright umbrellas ? . . . Venus laughing from the Skies. . . .

Isn't it a beautiful title, when all is said and done. . . . Goodbye, goodbye, goodbye.

It's all *too* wonderful.


*To Mrs. Virginia Woolf*                    November 1917

I have not been able to get to a telephone even. For I am alone here, and nobody has visited me. Murry is at Garsington and my rheumatism has ramped and raged. When it really descends on me I become a crawling thing without the power of doing anything except cursing my fate. The attack ought to be over in a day or two when I will come and make my apologies in person if I may—but Lord ! what a curse the flesh can be—or the bones rather. I am so down in the depths that I cannot imagine anything ever fishing me up again.


*To J. M. Murry*                    Sunday
                    November 5, 1917

. . . By the way, isn't *Furnished Rooms* a good title for a story which plays in the Redcliffe Road ? I can't resist it.

Come and look over my shoulder. The meeting on the
dark stairs, you know,—someone is coming down and someone is coming up. *Is* someone there? The fright, the
pause—the unknown in each other glaring through the
dark and then passing (which is almost too terrifying to be
borne). Then the whole street. And for backcloth—
the whole line of the street—and the dressmakers calling
to the cat, the Chinamen, the dark gentlemen, the babies
playing, the coal cart, the line of the sky above the houses,
the little stone figure in one of the gardens who carries a
stone tray on his head, which in summer is filled with
flowers and in winter is heaped with snow, the lamenting
piano, and all those faces hiding behind the windows, and
the *one* who is always on the watch. I see the heroine
very small, like a child, with high-heeled boots and a tiny
muff of *false* astrachan, and then the restless despairing
hero for whom all is over. She cannot understand what
is the matter with him. Does she ever know? And what
happens?

It is the extreme coldness of my room and the brown
paper wagging over the sooty fireplace which gives me such
a *veine*. Nothing will go up the chimney while this
tempest lasts. And I begin to feel ' The blighted Mongol '
stir and clamour in me.

On a journey to Garsington K. M. caught a severe chill,
which ultimately developed into tuberculosis.

Friday<br>December 14, 1917

. . . It's not so cold to-day, and I feel a great deal better.
I will tell you what the medicine man says to-morrow. I
am sure he will be surprised. I feel quite different—
rather quiet still—rather like a doll that has been mended
but put on a high shelf to dry before it can be played with
again. . . .

It's a nice day here—very quiet and warm. Even the
milkman crying milk sounds to me like a bird trying its

note—a funny sort of bird, you know—a bird penguinian. The clock ticks on tip-toe and the yellow curtains wave gently. I love such a day. It's such a rest—not having been outside for three days. I love to be out of the streets and buses, out of the nudging crowds. Oh, I must work. The very shadows are my friends. Don't forget to weigh yourself again when the week is up, and if you are not heavier you must melt a horse-shoe in your next glass of milk so as not to disappoint me. . . .

*To Anne Estelle Rice*                    Saturday
                                   December 22, 1917

The reason why I have not replied before to your letter and book has been that I have been strictly in bed for days, nearly weeks, with my left water-wing (alias my lung) entirely out of action for the time and strapped up in plaster which gives off waves of smell like new varnish on an inside cabin wall. *Dry Pleurisy*, ma chère, an old complaint of mine ! It has been most hellishly annoying, as you know my views on the subject of ill health. Picture me, lying very close to the wall, with my darling Japanese doll for an innocent bed companion, dressed in a pair of pyjamas which look as though they ought to take off and on with a spoon, they are so like a glace napolitaine, with one immense faux nichon, *i.e.*, the one that the strapping goes over and that is therefore mounted in cotton wool, and upon which the eyes of my visitors are immediately rivetted.

However, the worst is over and I am up to-day, feeling as light and airy as what dear Bates used to call a *gash* balloon, and still quite unable to grasp the fact that life really has given me such a cuff and a kiss as this old attack. *For* the doctor says I must never stay in England for another winter but must leave in September and not come back until April, and at present as soon as I am well enough he has given me a medical certificate for the South of France, and I hope to be able to leave in January.

This must sound like an absolute plant to you.    It did to
me.    When I heard the medicine man say : " You ought
to go to some place like Teneriffe or Madeira, but as you
can't go there, Spain or the South of France *will do*," I
would not have swopped my lung with any man alive.    If
I stay in England he says I may become consumptive.
Alors, je m'en vais !    But I can't really believe that this
will happen and I won't, until I see a pink house with two
cedars in front of it.    It is too good luck.    But talk about
the knock-out blow—I've had it !    Why can't you come
too ?    I mean to find a little house somewhere down there
with a good garden and really make it a pied à terre so that
my *rare* darling friends can camp in it too and always
feel that it is there if they want to come.    I shall beat
along the coast slowly this spring *if if if* I ever do get
there. . . .

London has been just lately like a big brimming bowl of
the very best pea soup.    One looks up at the studio window
at a kind of green, thick mixture with the tree outside
swimming in it like a bunch of dry herbs.    There has not
been a breath of wind, but if you put your head out of bed
a cold whistling draught from nowhere blows it back again.
Through it the rag and bone man has cried up and down
the road with quite peculiar relish, and just when the fog
was at its brightest and best some carol singers started :

" Christians !  Awake !  Salute the Happy Morn . . . "
Quel pays !  when you are living " as you might say three
hundred and sixty-four days under an umberellar like any
dratted mushroom."    Since the raid the gas supply is
almost cut off, and the gasman informed me yesterday
that if these raids go on there will be no knowing whether
London will have any gas at all.    So nice, plus the coal
shortage.

Looe sounds a real find.    I am thankful you are there
and out of this.

A thousand thanks for *Nounette*.    My God, after a visit
from *well-meaning* relatives and friends who assailed me
with :

" Don't you think Lloyd George is *too splendid* ? "

" I do think the King has behaved *splendidly* during the war. Don't you ? It must be *too splendid* to be a man at a time like this, don't you think ? "—

I have simply lain in bed gasping and fanned myself with ce livre charmant. It breathes of France. I shall be here until about the second week in January. I'd simply love a poulet and it's very sweet of you to think of sending me one. I wanted to send you some candies but they are not to be had so I shall send dates instead. Quelquechose de bien sucré.

Forgive a dull dog of a letter. My mind feels so bald and my faithful L. M. who has all the intentions of an angel has almost made me an imbecile with this sort of thing :

*She :* Which would you rather have, hot milk or Oxo ?
*Me :* Oxo, please.
*She :* Oh, don't you think you'd rather have hot milk ?
*Me :* No, thanks, Oxo please.
*She :* But don't you think hot milk is more nourishing ?
*Me :* Oxo, please.
*She :* I wish you would have hot milk, just to please me.
*Me :* Oxo, please.
*She :* Very well, dear. But what about having Oxo in the hot milk ? Isn't that a good idea ?
*Me :* Plain Oxo, please.
*She* (from the kitchen) *:* Oh Katya, dear, I find there isn't any Oxo left. Will you have milk ?
*Me :* ! ! ! ! ! ! ! ! !


*To J. M. Murry* December 24, 1917

. . . Here is the certificate which the doctor has just given me. Is it all right ? He says that left lung of mine that had the *loud deafening* creak in it is " no end better," but there is a SPOT in my right lung which " confirms him in his opinion that it is absolutely imperative that I go out of this country and keep out of it all through the

future winters." It is *evidemment* rather a bad 'un of its
kind. At any rate it would become so if I did not fly. . . .
The programme seems to be (if I don't want to do this
mysterious crocking up) to sit tight, pack and make for the
sun. See ? What do you think ?

Although I am still snapping up fishes like a sea-lion,
steaks like a land-lion, milk like a snake (or is that only a
' tale ' ?) and eggs, honey, cream*b*, butter and nourishing
trimmings galore, they seem to go to a sort of Dead Letter
Office. However, he has given me a tonic to-day which
will put that right. Of course, I feel now that I've only
to get into the sun and I'll simply burst into leaf and
flower again. It is this old place that does it to me.

I know quite well, I appreciate absolutely that you must
be faithful to England. Hell it would be to know you
were away and felt its call, but all the same you will have
to have two houses and we shall have to have all our babies
in pairs so that we possess a complete set in either place.


December 1917

. . . Mrs. N. brought me her son for tea yesterday. She
left him with me. I think it is the first time I have spent
an hour alone with a thoroughly modern enlightened
child. I found out that the method practised on him had
been to treat him exactly like a grown-up on a small scale.
You can imagine the result. I sat and gaped at him. He
had brought with him a dairy-farm from Heal's—exactly
like a real dairy-farm *on a small scale*. And of course he
did not play with it, because he can't play. He ran it as a
little going concern, and I bet he made it pay. God
forbid that any child of mine should fall into modern
ways. . . .


December 1917

. . . I am spending an idle day in bed. Ribni [1] sits by
me, and I have made myself a sort of a Pirate cap which I

[1] K. M.'s Japanese doll.

think, hope, nay, am sure, will startle the doctor's young eye. It's all sunny outside and I am bored. After he is gone I've a mind to throw away my wings and go off for a frisk. But I won't. I am almost terrifically well again.

Mrs. N. came in last night and wanted to whisk me off to her house for a few days. Oh, what a dread prospeck! The amount of whisking that people want to do with me and a-wrapping of me up in bundils is quite terrifying. I said I was being superbly looked after by old Mrs. Harris, who was a very good cook. Oh! What fun! Do you know who I meant? Sairey Gamp's friend. I laughed so much inside that I thought she would hear the laughs running up and down in me. Even to write it makes me laugh again, and Ribni stuffed the ends of his necktie in his mouth, stood on his head and waved his feet when I told him.

*Later.* Really, I'm very nearly in love with this old doctor. He *is* such a find. No, that's not my feeling. What I do feel is that he's the sort of man we might all be talking to in a café in the good Paris days. I don't have to alter my vocabulary or pretend a bit and ah, you know how rare *that* is. He is coming again on Monday. So you can see how careful he is. He says I am much better and look much better and I've no temperature at all—but I must still go a bit slow and not go out. I think he thought I was a pirate. Yoho! Yoho! So don't you worry a bit. I am almost 2 lively and gay.

*To Lady Ottoline Morrell*                    Friday
                                        January 4, 1918.

I was so *more* than glad to hear from you yesterday. . . . Yes, indeed I appreciate what Xmas cares are yours and I didn't really expect a letter (though I longed for one).

M. and the Mountain have just gone off to the Foreign Office, armed with medical certificates enough to ensure one a State Burial. The Mountain has to come, too, and knock down the English and French policemen on the way.[1] She has a month's leave from her factory for the purpose—and by the end of that time I really shall be well enough to run about the farmyard and pick up grain for myself again. It's an absurd situation—

I *shall* miss you. I shall be awfully lonely at times—wanting a talk with you and wanting to have you there in the sunlight away from this hideous, evil England.

If it would not be too much trouble may I come down to Garsington on Tuesday for a few days ? The doctor wants me to go away before I ' make the journey ' and my flat has to be dismantled and done with next week. I should *hate* to go anywhere except to you—if you will have me—and then I thought my passport will be ready in a few days time and I could come up to London just for one night with M. before I go away. I am not an invalid really—I am up and ' bobbish.' Would I worry you too much ?

It is extraordinary how *changed* life feels to me now that I know that this life in England will not be mine, even as little as it has been. I simply don't feel that I shall ever come back if only they let me go. But perhaps that is partly because it is winter and because I have sat so long in this studio listening to the rag-and-bone man and the man crying coals. . . .

This is not a letter—I am still gasping rather after trying to move the Mountain *in time*.


*To J. M. Murry*                          Paris : 5.30 p.m.
                                               January 9, 1918

. . . I shall not be able to write you a proper letter until I arrive in Bandol. It is so difficult to get calm and I have spent an immense day rushing after my luggage and to Cook's (who wouldn't ' arrange ' my affair for me) and to the P.L.M. However, it is all done now and I am in a café near the station with my *grande malle enregistrée* and

[1] Most unfortunately, **she was** not allowed to accompany K. M. who had to travel alone.

my little 'uns at the consigne, writing to you before I go to that Duval where we went, to get some dinner before the train goes.

Everything on the whole has gone wonderfully. It's not a nice journey nowadays, and it was immensely complicated this time by the blizzard. We left Southampton at about 9 o'clock and did not arrive at Havre until after 10 next morning. We anchored for hours outside Havre in a snow-storm and lay tossing and pitching and rolling. . . . You won't believe me when I say that I enjoyed it. I did. For one thing I had a splendid supper when I got on board—a *whack* of cold, lean beef and pighells, bread, butter *ad lib.*, tea, and plenty of good bread. Then I took a nip of brandy and went right to bed, in a little cabin, very clean and warm, with an excellent stewardess in attendance. The upper berth was a general's widow (more of her later) and except for her imitations of a cat with a fish-bone in its throat I was divinely comfortable and slept and woke, slept and woke, but did not move until we reached Havre. Then I tumbled up on deck to find everything white with snow. I shall tell you nothing in detail now, for I mean to write it all. It was too wonderful to miss.

We had to spend the day in Havre. So I took a bedroom at a hotel, had breakfast and washed and went to sleep until late lunch. The food in France is simply wonderful. *Bread* that makes one hungry to look at it, butter, sugar, meat, 7 kinds of cheese for lunch and 7 hors d'oeuvres. Then we started for Paris at 5 to arrive at 9.20. The carriage was packed, *un*heated, with a broken window and the snow drifting in. This was very vile. But a Red Cross old party took me in charge and rubbed me and cosseted me and finally made me eat a dinner which cost 6 francs ! but saved me, as we did not arrive until 2 a.m. Then a plunge into the pitch dark and snow, as all the entrances to the *Terminus* were shut, except the one in the street. God ! how thankful I was that I had reserved a room. Crowds were turned away.

But I staggered up a palatial staircase, through ball-rooms, reception-rooms, *hollows* glittering with chandeliers, to a yellow and blue brocade bedroom which seemed to be worth £50 to me. I slept like a top and got up early and—*L'Heure! Liberté! La Presse!*—saw about all my affairs. It is snowing hard. The streets are all ice and water and so slippery *qu'on marche comme un poulet malade.*

All the same, I am unreasonably deeply happy. I thought I would be disenchanted with France this time. But for the first time I seem to recognise my love for it and to understand *why*. It is because, whatever happens, I never feel *indifferent*. I feel that indifference is really foreign to my nature and that to live in a state of it is to live in the only Hell I really appreciate. There is, too, dispassionately speaking, a wonderful spirit here—so much humour, life, gaiety, sorrow. One cannot see it all and not think with amazement of the strange cement-like state of England. Yes, they do feel the war, but with a difference. But this, too, I must write about seriously....

> Hôtel Beau Rivage
> Bandol (Var)
> Friday
> January 11, 1918

... My enthusiastic letter from Paris has been in my mind ever since. *And* mocked me. I took it to post ; it was dark by then, piercing cold and so wet underfoot that one's feet felt like two walking toads. After a great deal of bother I got established in the train (No pillows to be had nowadays) and then the fun began. I liked my fellow-passengers, but God! how stiff one got, and my feet hurt and the flat-iron [1] became hot enough to burn the buttoned back against which I leaned. There was no refreshment car on the train—no chance of getting anything hot—a blinding snowstorm until we reached Valence.

[1] K. M.'s name for the burning sensation in her lung.

I must confess the country was exquisite at sunrise—exquisite—but we did not arrive at Marseilles till *one* o'clock. Good ! As I got out a pimp getting in to hold a seat for some super-pimp gave me such a blow in the chest that it is blue to-day. I thought : " This is Marseilles, *sans doute*." Feeling very tired and hungry I carried my baggage three miles to the consigne, and finding that the train left for Bandol at 3.30 decided to have a snack at the buffet just outside—that place under a glass verandah. It was rather full, so I sat down opposite an elderly lady who eyed me so strangely that I asked if " cette place est prise ? " " Non, Madame," said she, insolent beyond everything, " mais il y a d'autre tables, n'est-ce pas ? Je préfère beaucoup que vous ne venez pas ici. D'abord, j'ai déjà fini mon déjeuner, et c'est très dégôutant de vous voir commencer car j'ai l'estomac délicat, et puis . . . " And then she raised her eyebrows and left it at that. You can judge what I ate after that and what I thought.

At 1.30 I went to get my baggage registered, waited for one hour in a queue for my ticket and then was told I could not have one until my passport was viséd. I had that done, waited again, carried my luggage to the platform finally at 3 o'clock *juste*, and waited there in a crowd until four. Then a train came in at another platform, and the people swarmed in just like apes climbing into bushes, and I had just thrown my rugs into it when it was stated that it was only for *permissionaires* and did not stop before Toulon. Good again ! I staggered out and got into *another* train on *another* platform, asked three people if it was the right one, who did not know, sat down in the corner, completely dished.

There were 8 Serbian officers in the compartment with me and their 2 dogs. Never shall I say another word against Serbians. They looked like Maiden's Dreams, excessively handsome and well cared for, graceful, young, dashing, with fine teeth and eyes. But that did not matter. What *did* was that after shunting for 2 hours, five yards forward and five back, there was a free fight at the station between a mob of soldiers and the civilians. The soldiers demanded the train and that *les civils* should exacuate it. Not with good temper, but furious—very ugly—and *vile*. They banged on the windows, wrenched open the doors and threw out the people and their luggage after them. They came to our carriage, swarmed in, told the officers they too must go, and one caught hold of me as though I were a sort of packet of rugs. I never said a word, for I was far too tired and vague to care about anything, except I was determined not to *cry*. But one of the officers then let out, threw out the soldiers, said I was his wife and had been travelling with him five days, and when the *chef militaire de la gare* came, said the same, threw *him* out, banged the door, took off their dogs' leads and held the door shut. The others then pressed against the connecting door between the carriages, and there we remained in a state of siege until seven o'clock when the train started. You should have heard the squalling and banging. They pinned the curtains together and I hid behind them until we were under way.

By this time it was pitch dark, and I knew I should never find the station, as a terrific *mistral* was blowing and you could not hear the stations cried. But as we came to each stop, they pulled the window down and shouted in their curious clipped French to know which it was. Ah, but they were very nice chaps, splendid chaps—I'll not forget them. We reached Bandol at 9. I felt that my *grande malle* was gone for ever, but I seized the other 2 and dashed across the line. I could not have walked here, but happily the boy from the Hôtel des Bains was at the station and though he said *qu'il n'était pas bon avec le patron* he brought me.

When I arrived the hall was rather cold and smoky. A strange woman came out, wiping her mouth with a serviette. I realised in a flash that the hotel had changed hands. She said she had received *no* letter, but there were plenty of rooms, and proceeded to lead me to them. My own was taken. I chose finally the one next door which

95

had 2 beds on condition she removed one. Also it was the cheapest, 12 francs a day. The others have had *de l'eau courante* put into them and cost 13. The big stoves were not lighted in the passages. . . . I asked for hot water and a hot water bottle, had some soup, wrapped up to the eyes, and simply fell into bed after finishing the brandy in my flask. For I felt that the whole affair wanted thoroughly sleeping over and not thinking about. . . .

In the morning when I opened the *persiennes* it was so lovely outside, I stayed in bed till lunch. *Ma grande malle* really did turn up. Then I got up, and after lunch went into the town. The Meynets are gone for the present. The *tabac* woman did not know me and had no tobacco. Nobody remembered me at all. I bought writing things and a few bull's-eyes—about a penny for two, they were—and suddenly I met Ma'am Gamel. She, too, did not recognise me until I had explained who I was. Then she was very kind. " Ah ! Ah ! Ah ! Vous êtes beaucoup changé. Vous avez été *ben* malade, n'est-ce pas ? Vous n'avez plus votre air de p'tite gosse, vous sa-avez ! " I went with her to the shop which is just the same and saw the old mother who was most tender about you. I bought a tiny pot of cherry jam and came home— to find my room not yet done. You can see, I am depressed. I feel faible still after ce voyage, but I shall get better and I shall arrange things here as soon as I have la force nécessaire. The place is, even to my blind eyes, as lovely as ever, glittering with light, with the deep hyacinth blue sea, the wonderful flashing palms and the mountains, violet in the shadow and jade-green in the sun. The mimosa outside my window is in bud. Don't worry about me. Having got over that journey and that Paris thaw, I shall never fall by the way ; and when my room is ready, I shall *work*. That I do feel, and that is what matters. I am not even very sad. It has been a bit of a bang, though, hasn't it ? I feel like a fly who has been dropped into the milk-jug and fished out again, but is still too milky and drowned to start cleaning up yet.

Letters will take a long while—perhaps 6 or 8 days—so do not worry if you do not hear.

Saturday
January 12, 1918

You are to write as often as you can at first—see ? Because letters take so long, so long, *et je suis malade*. I have just got up and am sitting wrapped up in all my clothes and my woolly coat and your geranium jacket and the Kashmir shawl over that and Ottoline's pink one round my legs and the rug folded on the floor. The fire is alight, but it won't burn unless I keep the iron shade right down ! ! The old, old story. It is bitterly cold, and a deep strange fiery light over the sea and sky. I have got up because I *must* work and I can't in bed. If I am going to languish in Foreign Parts alone, I must have a great deal of work done, or it will be no use. Please write me warm letters—*tellement il fait froid.* . . .

Sunday
January 13, 1918

I got so cold yesterday that I decided, willy-nilly, to take a small walk and try to ' warm up ' before the evening. So I made myself into a bundle, and started off. First I went to the Mairie to be registered. The old secretary was there at one desk in his braided cap ; the drum stood in a corner. He was very solemnly engaged in cutting a Spanish beauty's picture off a card and gumming the same on to the back of a pocket-book, breathing like a grampus. The Mayor did not (as usual) want to have anything to do with my passport. However, I persuaded him that it really *was* necessary, and when he did make up his mind, he went very thoroughly into the affair. Result. I am written in the book as *Kadreen, fille d'Arnold Beaucamp et Anne Dysa de Nouvelle Zélande*, etc. I could not make him get anything more accurate, so I just let him go on. Then I saw that the Meynets' blind was up and went

in. M. only was there. He sat on a stool stitching a
long red leather boot, more X-eyed than ever. Didn't
remember me. Madame is away but he expects her back.
" Marie est allée à Marseille il y a deux ans, et puis—elle
n'est pas revenue ! Voilà ! " Did I want a villa ? And
he began to press villas *de quatre pièces* on me, but I felt
a bit sick and went off. I then decided to go and see
Ma'am Allègre. The afternoon was very cold and grey
and just growing dusky. The sea was high and made a
loud noise. When I passed the vineyard where the two
little boys used to work I realised suddenly that I was
suffering—terribly, terribly, and was quite faint with this
emotion. Then came at last the road with GRAVIER 2K
written on the post. And then came our little home in
sight. I went on, though I don't know how, pushed open
the Allègres' singing gate, walked over those crunching
round stones. . . . The outer door of our villa was open.
When I reached the stone verandah and looked again upon
the almond tree, the little garden, the round stone table,
the seat scooped out of stone, the steps leading down to
the *cave*, and then looked up at our pink house, with the
swags of shells painted over the windows and the strange
blue-grey shutters, I thought I had never, in my happiest
memories, realised all its beauty. I could not get any
answer from the Allègres, but I felt certain I heard someone moving in our villa, so finally I knocked on our door.
You remember how hard it was to open. It tugged open
and there stood Ma'am Allègre, in the same little black
shawl, lean and grey as ever.

" Vous désirez, Madame ? " said she. I just managed
to say, " Bon jour, Madame. Vous m'avez oubliée ? "
And then she cried, " Ah ! Ah ! I know your voice.
Come in, come in ! I am just airing the villa. Come into
the little salon. Comment ça va ? Et votre mari ?
etc., etc."

I crossed the hall ; she opened one half of the persiennes
and we sat on either side of the table, she in your place, I
with my back to the fire in mine, and had a long talk. She

remembers us well.  Many times her husband and she have talked of us and wished to have us back again.  Her husband always wondered what had happened to us.  We were like " deux enfants," said she, and it was a happiness to them to know that we were there.  Her son is wounded and is now on the Swiss frontier in a post office.  They went all the way to Paris to see him.  I asked her what had happened to the flowers ; for there is not a single flower— not a jonquil, not a geranium, not a rose, not an orange— and she promised they would all be here " plus tar', plus tar'.  C'est la faute du mauvais temps, vous sa-avez ! "

But oh, as we sat there talking and I felt myself answer and smile and stroke my muff and discuss the meat shortage and the horrid bread and the high prices and *cette guerre*, I felt that somewhere, upstairs, you and I lay like the little Babes in the Tower, smothered under pillows, and she and I were keeping watch like any two old gnomes.  I could hardly look at the room.  When I saw my photograph, that you had left on the wall, I nearly broke down, and finally I came away and leaned a long time on the wall at the bottom of our little road, looking at the violet sea that beat up high and loud against those strange dark clots of sea-weed.  As I came down your beautiful narrow steps, it began to rain.  Big soft reluctant drops fell on my hands and face.  The light was flashing through the dusk from the lighthouse, and a swarm of black soldiers was kicking something about on the sand among the palm-trees—a dead dog perhaps, or a little tied-up kitten.

It is so quiet to-day.  I remember Sundays like this here.  Not a hint of sun.  A leaden sky.  A sea like oil. . . .  I had a very bad night, coughing and sweating so that I had to keep sponging my face and kept thinking, " It *must* be five o'clock," and finding it was only a quarter past one.  Oh, these long, long, lonely nights when one is ill !  They are unforgettable !  But after breakfast this morning I slept till eleven o'clock.  I heard all the noises in the corridor, but still I *was* fast asleep . . .

Monday
January 14, 1918

The Lord took Pity on me to-day and sent me a letter
from you.   As it was only written on Wednesday I thought
that very good.   I had been told that letters took 8 days
at least !   I read it from beginning to end and then from
end to beginning—upside down and then diagonally.   I
ate it, breathed it, and finally fell out of bed, opened the
shutters and saw that the day was blue and the sun shining.
So Wig put on her clothes and went for a walk round by
the Golf Hotel.   It was very exquisite, cold in the
shadows, but warm in the light.   I still have an appalling
cold, cough and flat-iron, but your letter was the best
medicine, poultice, plaster, elixir, draught I could have
had. . . .

A word more about this place.   There is a destroyer
anchored here close to the Quai, and sheds, etc., erected
for the sailors, who spend their time ½ in the urinals, ½
flirting with the girls.   Quantities of black soldiers everywhere.   I saw that woman whose husband was in
Salonique yesterday.   She is quite changed, very made up,
but pale, and impudent and horrid.   I realised yesterday
she is a type for negroes.   You remember the lovely
geraniums in this garden.   They are little scrubby bushes
now, with broken bottles and bits of lead piping chucked
among them.   These hotel people are no good.   A
widowed mother and two Bragian daughters.   And now
there are only 2 people here beside me.   However, I can't
leave. *Je n'ai ni la force ni l'assurance.*   It may improve.
Certainly the weather has.   I shall be back now, when you
get this, in 14 weeks. . . .

Wednesday
January 16, 1918

It is a very grey misty day.   After that one fine one it
has relapsed into winter again.   A plaintive wind howls
in the corridors.   I shall light my fire this afternoon and

sit tight.   Oh dear ! a panier of wood only lasts me two
days, try as I may to economise.

I still feel far from as well as I did when we went to
Harvey Nichols' together.   I lie in bed all the morning
until 12 and go to bed again as soon as dinner is over.
The *interval* I spend in going for a very small walk and in
working :  I have begun, thank God, to work a bit.   But
my back hurts horribly and I cough an awful lot.   However, I did not compose a single farewell telegram last
night in bed, so that is *one up.*

Our butcheress isn't there any more.   The pig-faced
woman is, and an old man.   The pâtisserie where the girl
was always eating is closed, sadly, with big official notices
plastered on the windows.   The shop with the funny
smell where we bought our *charbon de bois* is now the
Municipal Food Depot.   I went round by the Golf
Hotel yesterday, and just as I got to the place where it
says you are responsible for your own *dégâts* and *frais,* the
sheep with their little lambs passed by.   God ! what a
woeful company.   The sheep with just a saddle of dirty
wool on their backs, their bellies shaven, many of them with
swollen feet, limping pitifully, the lambs tottering past—
but *they* were pretty, there was one ginger one that
managed to give a hop or two.   Between them went a
shepherd who was half a dog, I think.   But he whistled
to them in a way I had forgotten.

There are 2 submarines in the bay and a black steamer
with a big white cross on her bows.   The officers take
their meals here.   Their talk and grouping, etc., is pure
Maupassant—*not* Tchehov at all, not deep enough or
*good* enough.   No, Maupassant is for France.

I read Wordsworth's sonnet beginning :

"Great Men have been among us :  hands that
        penned. . . ."

Look it up and read it.   I agree with every word.   There
is a change of front, if you like !   Whenever I am here, I
seem to turn to William Wordsworth. . . .

This old sort of pen-woman with a croak and a sad eye is not really me. Still not a cigarette to be had in all the land. It is sad. Please try and send me a book, a Dickens would do. I have read *Barnaby Rudge* twice. What about *Our Mutual Friend*? Is that good? I've never read it.

This letter goes like one of those sheep I saw. . . .

*To Lady Ottoline Morrell*                    January 18, 1918

My note from Paris has mocked me ever since I threw it so gaily into the letter box by the Gare de Lyon. That action was indeed the end of the movement, the end of the allegro, the end of anything inclining ever so faintly towards the major.

No, no, never come to France while this bloody war is on. It is tolerable as far as Paris but after that it is the most infernal weariness and discomfort and exasperation. Unendurable! The trains are not heated, they are hours upon hours late, one can obtain nothing to eat or what is much more, nothing hot to drink—they are packed to overflowing; the very lavatories refuse to work.

In such a case I crawled to Marseilles, and caught the most plaguey chill, stiff neck, sore throat, streaming cold that I ever had. Staggering out of the train, carrying my luggage, a pimp in white canvas shoes, eager to reserve a place for a super pimp, swung up the steps and dealt me such a blow on the chest that I am still blue with it. This, thought I, is joliment Marseilles. And it was indeed very typical, in a *mild* way, of the hours I spent there. Finally, when I had *thrown* myself into the 2 hours late Bandol train there was a fight between the soldiers and the civilians. The soldiers rushed the train, commandeered it and threw the civilians out, bag and baggage on to the platform—not in any high-tiddly-i-ty take me back to Blighty spirit but in a very nasty temper indeed—in fact, as ugly a crowd as I ever wish to see. They crawled into and over the carriages like apes, banged on the windows,

wrenched open the doors—This seemed to me the *comble*.
But I had happily got into a carriage with 8 Serbian
officers *and* their two dogs and *they* put up a fight against
the soldiers. They took off their dogs' leather leads and
tied up the doors, barricaded the entrance to the next
carriage and generally behaved as though their eight
mothers had born and bred them in the most expensive,
rare and exclusive cinema de luxe. Finally after com-
plications innumerable, in the midst of which I became for
the railway officials a Serbian, too, and the wife of one of
them, they gained the day. It only needed that I should
arrive here to find I was *not* expected, that the hotel
had changed hands, was far more expensive and was *not*
heated.

No, I lay down my weapons after that.

Since then I have been getting into bed and out of bed
and doing very little else, in no gay fashion. As soon as I
have recovered from this cursed chill I'll write again.
But at present my jaundiced eye would as lief gaze on the
Fulham Road as on this lilac sea and budding mimosa.
As the night wears on I grow more and more despondent
and my thoughts walk by with long black plumes on their
heads while I sit up in bed with your pink quilt round my
shoulders and think it must be at least 4 o'clock and find it
is just a quarter to 2 !

My lovely gay shawl lies upon a chair and I gaze at it
feeling rather like David Copperfield's Dora, and wondering when I shall wear it again.

But I suppose all this will pass. It's just another little
hell that must be gone through. . . .

*To J. M. Murry*                                      Monday
                                              January 21, 1918

I am only going to write you a note to-day just to say
that I still feel better. The weather is 1000 times rougher.
Never, not even on shipboard, or in my own little country,
or anywhere, have I heard such wind. And in the night

when one lay quiet in bed and listened, God knows how
many Ancient Mariners cried in it or how many lost souls
whirled past.   I thought then what agony it must be to
be wife to a fisherman.   How could a poor soul comfort
herself and to whom could she pray when such a wind and
such a sea fought against her ? . . .   I thought, too, it
must have been just such a storm when Shelley died.
This morning at red dawn a destroyer and a submarine
tried to put out to sea, but they were obliged to return.   I
despised them for that and thought no English sailors
would not have mastered it.   But you know, for all my
big talk, I never believe the Frenchies can sail a boat, or
throw a ball, or do anything at all which is a patch upon
the English. . . .   If you could see this sea to-day rearing
and smoking like a herd of monsters run mad !

Last night my little maid brought me a present, of
rosebuds.   Two green jars full of them and some yellow
*soleils d'or* besides.   She had been for a walk in the
country, she said, and a friend had made her a present.
She came to the door with them—so pretty—wearing a
black woollen cap, and her cheeks were red.   Shortly
after, the Madame came to ask if I would like some hot
wine at night for my cough.   " Je ne savais pas que vous
avez été si fatiguée."   Well, though it's a bit *tard* for
remedy as I'm such a much better girl, I said Yes to
the wine—and it was a rare fine posset.   3rd, the submarine captain, having heard me try to get tobacco,
presented me with a whole packet of Maryland—not
cigarettes but tobacco—so I feel people have been
unusually kind. . . .

As I write the sun pushes his head through a positive
monk's hood of a cloud and blesses you and me upon this
page.   I thought this morning : In February I shall be
able to say I come back the month after next.   And
February is a very tiny little month, too, so that after it is
gone and March has blown in, there will only be a few
weeks before April.   Does this comfort you as it does
me ?

Friday
January 22, 1918

I will just tell you, so that you may know how I am taking care of myself. I stay in bed every day until lunch. Then I dress by a fire. If it is fine I go for a small walk in the afternoon, then I come back to my fire. After dinner, at about 8.30 I go to bed. The food here has got much better since the submarines have taken to lunching and dining here. It is now very good and they have begun giving me portions so big that I think they suspect me of at least twins *sous le cœur*. I set sail across tureens of nourishing soup, stagger over soft mountains of *pommes purées* and melt in *marmelades*. So you see how well I am looking after *my*self. . . .

The wind still blows a hurricane here. In the night the rain joined in, but now the sun beats in the air like a kite. It is like living on a ship. The hotel is all bolted and barred up, the big doors closed and a strange twilight in the hall. People go about in shawls and coats. If a window is opened the seas of the air rush in and fill it. The great palm trees have snapped like corks, and many a glittering plume trails in the dust. They say it never has been known before. I have begun to like it. . . .

Wednesday
January 23, 1918

Last night, when I had finished capturing all I could of this wind and rain and cold, it ceased, and this morning the sun came out. There is still a stiff breeze, but it's warm in the sun and indescribably lovely. Every mortal thing looks sheathed in a glittering beauty.

I got up at about eleven and went out to buy myself une canne *avec une frique*. The disagreeable shop has become amiable. I bought a small stout one for 1.25 and then walked up the road behind the front, past Ma'am Gamel's, to the top of the hill and a little way further. The sky over the sea was like an immense Canterbury bell, darkly, transparently blue. Towards me came walking an old woman in a pleated black dress with a broad straw hat tied under her chin with a linen band, and she carried a pack of jonquils. Then there came a butterfly, my little sister, weak in the wing and staggering a little, but *basking*. The cats lay on the window sills. In a field against the sea a man and a woman were digging ; the olive trees blew silver, and the sea, very wild still, embraced the shore as though it loved it. As I came back I saw an old man sitting in the corner of a field, some wine and bread in a basket by him. He had a pair of breeches over his knees that he was carefully darning. They looked awfully forlorn, as though he had just given them a beating.

But how can all this have happened in a night ? Yesterday—midwinter—. I walked to the post wearing your wadded coat, my woollen one, my great blue one over all, and was perished. I staggered home, and decided that I must ask you to send me an anchor, a small one, shaped like a crab perhaps, with whiskers, that I would draw behind me on a string, to keep me from blowing (*a*) into the sea or (*b*) over *le grand cerveau*—and here's to-day come to mock me. *On a vraiment chaud.* . . .

Oh, the washer-girl came to-day while I was in bed. You remember her ? How fine she was, always so *gauffrée*, with frills over her hands and gold rings in her ears, and very expensive sparkling eyes. Now, poor wench, she's so changed. There can't have been a soul in Bandol with *pyjame de laine* at 2.50 the washing since you left. She has shed all her brightness, *jusqu'à ses pieds*, which were covered in lovely red kid slippers. I hope it will *monte* again. She charged me 3.30, but it was not a swin really.

I must tell you, my little maid is becoming more and more friendly. She looks like the girl you read of who spreads the linen to dry in the orchard while the young boy up the ladder fills her apron with pears. She was saying yesterday she did not like the hotel to be so empty.

We sit together, said she, there's nothing to do. " Alors, nous nous regardons—nous causons—mais, c'est triste, vous savez, ce n'est pas si gai que la service ! " What do they talk about and where do they sit ? I began to wonder.

I am doing all I can to live without spending, to wear my old clothes and shoes. We shall feast and array ourselves when we are together, " and fleet the time carelessly as they did in the golden world."

Now that you know I am so much better, you will tell me all about yourself, and you will take care of yourself.

> And this is not a boon.
> 'Tis as I should entreat you wear your gloves
> Or feed on nourishing dishes, or keep you warm,
> Or sue to you to do a peculiar profit
> To your own person. . . .

Thursday
January 24, 1918

Yesterday I took your letter with me and we walked our old familiar way—along by the coast and then inland. . . . Well, I suppose we looked as though we were walking, but, good God, my spirit never kept worse time with my toes . . . . A sea like quilted silk, the lavender bushes growing among the rocks all in new leaf. Such air as you and I have drunk together, and a whole flock of little winds to shake every perfumed bud and flower. The almond trees, if one stands close and looks up, are thick with white and red buds ; the lanes have a thick border of white and yellow—wild candytuft and small marigolds. The mimosa is coming out over the gate of our house, which is still sealed up—still as remote, more beautiful, more desirable than ever. This place is so full of ourselves that every little walk I take is a passionate pilgrimage. There is the villa—*allons-y*. Here is the field where we saw all the anemones, here the wall where the lizard lay basking. One could hear everywhere the voices of people in the fields, one could see, through the blue, fresh-painted gates, women bending to the earth and rising up again, with the old leisurely grace. They passed me, the dark people we know so well, with their loads of little olive branches *or* a squeaking barrow of manure—and as I came home I went by the Villa Pauline and saw over the wall the geraniums in leaf and bud. (Ah, I did of course go in, and while you put the kettle on, I took out the flowery cups, put our honey-biscuits in a dish, and we sat down, faint and warm and smiling we knew not why.) . . . These incredible people who *avant-hier* were wrapped in every inch of fur or wool they could find were yesterday dabbling their legs in the water down on the shore. . . .

I had a lie-down when I came home, and then I worked. When it grew dusky I opened the window to close the shutters. The moon was up ; the sky over the sea faint rose, and there was a strange bright glitter on the palm trees. After dinner in the hotel library I found a copy of *Martin Eden* (which O. always thought a famous good book) and a large shabby tome—*Tissot : Littérature Française*. But I couldn't stomach the former. No, a little Shakespeare makes one's nose too fine for such a rank smeller as Jack London. The other is *rare* meat. It is examples of French literature from the 9th century to the end of the 18th, and it is followed by a *Revue* of the state of the whole world at that time, each country taken separately—very excellent amusement. And, too, there are hundreds of the little engravings and fantastical letters that we love. I shall guard this in my room and bury Jack London again.

I heard from Madame G. yesterday *and* she included *une* poème. I send you both. By my passport I shall not be permitted to stay at Carpentras, you know. But I'll tell her that later. It would kill me. After the war, with you to fly to, I will : but alone to sustain that *parfaitement*, *Madame—justement—mais bien sur*—for more than half an hour would turn me into a parrot for life.

When we have a house here I think I'll try to get this

maid to come. She's just our style, but I wish she wouldn't give me a fresh bouquet more than once a day. The last is feathery mimosa. I write to you thus and tell you all because you *must* share it. For the present you are the King in the Counting-House counting out his money, and I am the Queen in the parlour eating bread and honey. . . . Oh, I could weep like a child because there are so many flowers and my lap is so small and all must be carried home. . . .

Thursday
January 24, 1918

I *must* add this to to-day's letter. I have chuckled over it for hours. As I went out this afternoon I met the widow hurrying up from the town, *très pandaresque,* and all a-flower with smiles. *Justement* she had come to look for me. One demanded me at the Mairie, and the Mayor waited. I said that I had better get my passport first, and she agreed. I told her that I was already registered, but she said they were very strict now. She had *no* idea (mark that !) what I was wanted for, but *enfin—voilà* ! Off I went. In that office of theirs the Mayor, his deputy, and old Drum waited for me. The Mayor wore white shoes with blue-strings and his cap back to front and a *bout* of cigarette in his mouth, *mais il était très sérieux.*

" You are, Madame, the lady to whom these papers refer ? " (The papers I had filled for the hotel.)

" Yes, Monsieur."

" Bien ! Will you follow me, Madame, to the Salon du Conseil ? "

" Très volontiers, Monsieur."

My spirits mounted with every step of the stairs. *He* is lame and had to get up them like a pigeon—you know, both feet on one step before he could reach to the next. Came a black door, heavily gilded, hugely labelled SALON DU CONSEIL. This was unlocked, and I had a glimpse of a chambre sich as my irreverent British eye has never twinkled on before. A black paper with gold stamping—

a huge table covered with a heavy black cloth fringed with gold. A few trunks of dead men, coloured, on brackets round the wall, and one of those portraits with a striped glass over, so that if you looked at it from your side, it was La Liberté, but if you looked at it from his, it was—*je ne sais pas*. There were also an immense number of bundles covered in black cloth—dead Mayors, I think. We sat down on a couple of velvet chairs with gold fleurs de lys so heavily stamped on their seats that if you had any chance *vous pouvez montrer à votre ami une derrière—mais vraiment chic*—and he produced a perfect mass of papers.

" Connaissez-vous, Madame, un certain *M. Parquerre* ?"

" Non, Monsieur."

" You are not expecting a gentleman to follow you to France ? "

" Non, Monsieur."

Then, of course, " I saw it all." It was *Baker*. He had heard from the British Consulate at Marseilles that a lady had tombéd gravement malade at Bandol. Was there such a lady ? Her friend M. *Parquerre* prayed for permission, etc. This was, I think, the first official document he had ever received from the B.C. He could not get over it—its importance—the whole affair. So I explained. We had a lot of chat. Then said he, " But do you want the lady ? I can arrange it. *C'est vite fait*." That is so like the Midi. And I said *No* without hesitating—just like that. Are you surprised ? I did right, didn't I ? I hope she will understand. . . . I left the Mayor, his deputy, and old Drum preparing the answer to this document—trying pens, stamping the rubber stamp on the backs of their hands to see if it would work, etc.

BUT : There was one unpleasant fly. He says *le crise des chemins de fer* will last—will grow worse with the spring, and at times the railway will be, as now, absolutely closed to civilian traffic. So he warned me, if I want to get home, to choose a moment well in advance. How awful it would be if I got stuck here, wouldn't it ?

No, it is much better that I remain alone now. I am

really (except for one local funny ' spot ' of pain about
which I wrote Dr. A. yesterday) such a well girl. I
hardly cough. They go on giving me wine at night and
with my café au lait a jug of milk that must be a *whole
goat*, and two fishes in place of anybody else's *one*—and the
weather is if possible lovelier than ever. I sat on a warm
stone this morning until my neck got burnt. The two
windows of my room are wide open. It is much warmer,
incomparably more exquisite than I have ever known it
here. The sea is so clear (and every shade, blue and green
and violet) that you can see, like a map outspread beneath
you, a whole new uncharted country with little lakes and
forests and bays. The coast is pink like the flesh of a
peach, and everybody is out fishing—you know, hanging
over the end of the boat and spearing the fish. . . . They
are mending and tarring the boats outside my window—
you can hear the little hammers, and a whiff or two of tar
breaks across the mimosa. *La Ciotat—Marie Réjane* :
the boats we know.

Another month has nearly gone. Six more days and it
is gone. Then comes little February (can't you see little
February, waiting and pleased : ' I can't stay very *long* ' ?)
and then March—but I shall be making my preparations
in March—and then. . . .

Saturday<br>January 26, 1918

Of *course* I did see and read what was inside the envelope.
Do you imagine I don't always turn the envelope upside
down and breathe into them and shut one eye and stare
up at them, always thinking one of your eyelashes or
perhaps a tiny twinkle out of your eye may still be there ?
Oh, I like the Wordsworth story : it makes my heart warm
to him.[1]

---

[1] The story is contained in the following extract from my letter :
" He [my brother] told me a story about Wordsworth—where he
can have got it from I don't know. It's stupid, but characteristic, and
it makes me love the old fellow rather. One day Wordsworth was

It is a different kind of day to-day, *il y a un peu de vent*. But with the bright sun it makes the sea an incredible, almost violet colour. I went for a walk yesterday and got lost—you know how one can. I couldn't find either the path to the shore, or the main road inland. And it kept getting on for sunset and the shadows great appeared before I was found. You should see the *swerves* I take past the dogs. They really are Bragian upstarts and their bold eyes and lifted lips terrify me. I thought : What if *I* had a bull-dog of my own ? Would that help ? But then I should always be frightened it would wait until we got to a lonely bit and then turn on me. No, the only thing would be a very awful imitation dog—one that I could make smoke come out of its eyes and fire out of its mouth when it passed one of these mongrels. Look out for one for me. . . .

Sunday
January 27, 1918

I am just up. It's ten past eleven. It has been a dead quiet golden morning and I lay in bed feeling as quiet as the day, thinking. I decided to tell you as far as I could—*how* and of *what*. . . . Something like this.

Why don't I get up now and sit at the table and write before lunch ? No, I can't. I am too tired. I have overdone it these last perfect days and walked too far and been out too long. For when I come back at 4 o'clock in the afternoon with three absolutely undisturbed hours

dining with a friend. Some rather aged, yellowish peas were served. The friend, in order to turn it off said to W., " Forgive me, but I forgot to send these peas to Kensington.' ' To Kensington ? ' says W. 'Why, pray ? ' 'Because that is the way to Turnham Green.' W. thought this an extremely good joke, resolved to remember it, and to let it fly on the first opportunity. It came very soon. He dined with a friend whose peas were also rather passé. He turned to the lady of the house. ' Madam, I am afraid you forgot to send these peas to Kensington.' 'To Kensington, Mr. Wordsworth ? Why, pray ? ' ' Because that is the way to make 'em green.' And he roared with laughter."

before me, I get into my room—lie on the bed—' collapse '
—and then get up, light my fire, sit down at the table,
leaning on anything I can find, leaning on my *pen* most of
all, and though I do write—it is only a matter of ' will ' to
break through—it's all a sham and a pretence so far. I am
so tired I can only just brush my fringe and get down to
dinner and up here again to bed. Ah, how devilish it is !
I am so tired I can't think of *anything*, and really can barely
read. Still, my lass, this won't last. Don't walk so far or
so fast. It's months since you really have walked, and
your legs are bound to turn backwards. But if only I
had the stickle-back [1] to lie on ! These little chairs are
for mean French behinds and they make me ache. However, none of this is serious. 'Twill pass. I'll go on
grinding until suddenly I throw away the stone and begin
to create something. It's no use being peevish. Are you
sure this is not hypochondria ? You are not getting ill
here ? Supposing you had a string kit and 10 little
children ? Oh, I'd sit in public houses and on steps. No,
it's a feeling of confounded physical weakness—preparatory to great physical strength, I'm sure. It's the change :
and then I get so fearfully excited, and that exhausts me.
Keep your head. You'll be all right in a week. . . .

After this consoling homily, I put my legs out of bed and
dropped after them and got into the basin for a bath. But
it is true. I have written two *Patrias* (they are the pink
cahiers) full here, and whenever I re-read the stuff, I can't
believe it's mine. Tame, diffuse, " missed it." Don't
blame me. I shall perk up. And I shall go slower till my
legs get more *wiry* ! I know what I want to do as soon as
I can do it. I have no doubts or false alarms at all. . . .

You know what I feel just at this moment ? Rather
dashed because I have been such an *enfant gâté* and now
the old post has nothing for me. It's these trains again.
Even if I had the money, I would not travel about here,
you know. Yesterday I saw a train come in here all
boarded up, all the carriages locked, full of soldiers, and

[1] K M.'s private name for a small sofa she possessed.

those who wished to get out to go " to the base," as Marie calls it, had to fling themselves through the windows and back again. A few poor civilians who were at the station were well jeered at by these braves.

I left off there and went down to lunch. I stood on the terrace a moment in the sun, wondering why French dogs and cats are so very unsympathetic, and suddenly there at the end of the palm avenue sparkled the brightest jewel—the postman. Yes, a letter from you and a paper. . . .

This country, *quâ* country, is really ideally beautiful. It is the most exquisite entrancing place. Yet I am very sincere when I say I hate the French. They have no heart—no heart at all.

Sunday night
January 27, 1918

I have been indoors all day (except for posting your letter) and I feel greatly rested. Juliette has come back from a new excursion into the country, with blue irises—do you remember how beautifully they grew in that little house with the trellis tower round by the rocks ?—and all sorts and kinds of sweet-smelling jonquils. . . . The room is very warm. I have a handful of fire, and the few little flames dance on the log and can't make up their minds to attack it. . . . There goes a train. Now it is quiet again except for my watch.

Monday : Have you read *Our Mutual Friend* ? Some of it is really *damned good*. The satire in it is first chop—all the Veneering business *par exemple* could not be better. I'd never read it before and I'm enjoying it immensely. Ma Wilfer is after my own heart. I have a huge capacity for seeing ' funny ' people, you know, and Dickens does fill it at all times quite amazingly.

As I write to you I am always wanting to fly off down little side paths and to stop suddenly and to lean down and peer at all kinds of odd things. My Grown-Up Self sees us like two little children who have been turned out into the garden. There we are hand in hand, while my G.U.S.

looks on through the window. And she sees us stop and touch the gummy bark of the trees, or lean over a flower and try to blow it open by breathing very close, or pick up a pebble and give it a rub and then hold it up to the sun to see if there is any gold in it.

As I write I feel so much nearer my writing self—my 'Pauline' writing self—than I have since I came. I suppose because what I said about the children had a 'little atom bit' of Kezia in it.

Tuesday
January 29, 1918

I feel greatly upset this morning because I realise for at least the millionth time that my letters to you are *not* arriving. I have taken great pains to write the address plainly on the envelopes. Are they safe when they arrive at the house ? Do they lie in the hall long ?

This has been brought home to me by your letter of last Friday in which you enclose Geoffroi's. You say you never heard from me that she had been here. Well, of course I wrote. And then I really cannot imagine that a great many other letters have not been lost. Did you get one with a telegram and a flower in it ? You see I have no notion which letters of mine have arrived, so I am quite in the dark as to whether you know it is warm here now. Your letters appear to turn up here quite safely, but mine obviously don't. However, I shall go on throwing them into the French dust-heap—but with I assure you, *beaucoup de chagrin.* . . . It is, I suppose, another of those innumerable mean dodges of which Life seems more or less composed.

Well, well . . . I wish I wasn't such a baby. The sun shines. It is almost hot. But if the sun were a reliable post-office I should much prefer it and would dispense with all its other devoirs.

I went for a walk yesterday, a little one. I can't take big ones yet. I got very much thinner those first days I

was here and I haven't recovered my lost weight yet.   Of
course, I shall.   I could not be more comfortable than I
am here now, and absolutely private and remote.   My
room feels miles away from the rest of the hotel and I
sometimes feel that Juliette and I are on an island, and
I row to the mainland for my meals and row back again.
I keep on with my fires.

I have a cold place, a little iceberg suddenly knocking
about in my heart where all was so warm and sunny.   I
will get it out before to-morrow.   But, looking out on to
the blue sea, the blue mountains and the boats with
yellow sails, I feel full of *hate*—hate for this awkward,
hideous world, these terrifying grimacing people who can
keep one's letters back.   I can't help it.


Thursday
January 31, 1918

Late Afternoon :  I decided when I went out this afternoon to buy the little coffee-pot and the coffee.   But first
I walked in the direction of the Hotel des Bains.   Yes, it
was beautiful, very—silver and gold light—old men
painting boats, old women winding wool or mending nets,
young girls making those gay wreaths of yellow flowers—
and a strange sweet smell came off the sea.   But I was
homesick.

I went to the paper shop to exchange a smile with
someone, and bought for three sous *The Paris Daily Mail*
and a smile.   A commercial traveller with a wooden leg
was in the shop taking orders.

" Toujours pas de chocolat ? " said Madame.

" Mon Dieu, Madame, if my poor leg était seulement de
vrai Menier, je serais millionaire ! "

Ha, ha !  Very good.  Very Typical.  Very French.
But I am faint with homesickness.  Although it is so goldy
warm, the tips of my fingers and my feet and lips and
inside my mouth—all are dead cold.  And so I walk along
until I come to the public wash-place, and there are the

women slipping about in the water in their clattering sabots, holding up those bright-coloured things, laughing, shouting, and not far away from them a travelling tinker with his fat woman sits on the ground beside his mule and cart. He has a little fire to heat his solder pan and a ring of old pots round him. It makes a good 'ensemble.' The washerwomen bawl after me " T'as remarqué les bas ! " but I do not care at all. I would not care if I had no stockings at all.

And here are those villas built up the hillside. Here is the one whose garden was always full of oranges and babies' clothes on a line. Still is. Also there is a dark woman in a wide hat holding a very tiny baby to her cheek and rocking it. The road is all glare and my shoes make a noise on it as though it were iron. I feel sick, sick, as though I were bleeding to death. I sit down on a mile-stone and take out *The Daily Mail*. I turn my back to the shimmering sea and the fishers all out in their little boats spearing the fish.

" Air Raid in London. Still in Progress."

A cart comes up full of chunks of hay. An old man in a blue blouse with great bushy eyebrows holds up his hand and cries " Il fait beau au soleil," and I smile. When he passes I shut my eyes. This must be borne. This must be lived through. . . .

Friday
February 1, 1918

This morning I got your Sunday night, Sunday morning and Monday night letter, all together, and they all seemed to be knocked off by such a steam engine that I wonder they didn't arrive sooner. . . .

I am rather diffident about telling you, because so many sham wolves have gone over the bridge, that I am working and have been for two days. It looks to me the real thing. But one never knows. I'll keep quiet about it until it is finished.

What extraordinary weather you have been having! As for to-day, here, at a quarter to nine it was hot in the sun, for I got up to pull the curtain over my dresses, thinking they would fade. The sea is like a silver lake, and the exquisite haze hangs over the coast. You can hear the fishermen from far, far away, the plash of oars and their talk to one another. Where there were 20 flowers, there seem to be 20 hundred everywhere : everything is in such abundant bloom. We never knew this place so warm. One could walk about in a cotton dress. Old men survey their villa gardens in cream alpaca jackets and swathed sun helmets !

My wing hurts me horribly this morning : I don't know why. And I don't care—really. As long as I can work— as long as I can work !

Good God ! There's some reckless bird trying over a note or two ! He'll be *en cocotte* within the hour. I simply loathe and abominate the French bourgeoisie. Let me put it on record again. There are a round dozen of them descended on this hotel and all, after a day or two, in each other's pockets, arms round each other, sniggering, confiding internal complaints, and " elle m'a dit " and " mon mari m'a dit," and the gentlemen with their " passez—mes*dames* "—God ! how I detest them. I must show it in some way. For they avoid me like pison, only breaking into the most *amused* laughter after I have passed (you know the style), and staring till their very eyes congeal while I take my food. It is the ugliness and the cruelty which hurts me so much, beneath all one's cool contemptuous manner. But I suppose a great part of the earth is peopled with these fry : only as a rule we don't see them. I do feel though that the Frenchies must be the lowest.

Would you send me *Nicholas Nickleby* ? (I am not reading Dickens *idly*).

The quiet day ! The air quivers and three tiny flies have just performed a very successful and highly intricate dance in my window space.

I bought such a nice little coffee pot. It will do for hot milk at home. It has a lid and is white with blue daisies on it. In fact, it's *charming* and only cost 65 centimes.

Sunday morning<br>
February 3, 1918

It is early for me to be up, but I had such a longing for a cigarette, and as I sit here in my pyjamas smoking a good one I'll begin your letter. . . .

I really feel I ought to send you some boughs and songs, for never was time nor place more suited, but to tell you the truth I am pretty well absorbed in what I am writing [1] and walk the blooming countryside with a 2d. notebook, shutting out *les amandiers*. But I don't want to discuss it in case it don't come off. . . .

I've two ' kick offs ' in the writing game. *One* is joy— real joy—the thing that made me write when we lived at Pauline, and that sort of writing I could only do in just that state of being, in some perfectly blissful way *at peace*. Then something delicate and lovely seems to open before my eyes, like a flower without thought of a frost or a cold breath, knowing that all about it is warm and tender and ' ready.' And *that* I try, ever so humbly, to express.

The other ' kick off ' is my old original one, and, had I not known love, it would have been my all. Not hate or destruction (both are beneath contempt as real motives) but an *extremely* deep sense of hopelessness, of everything doomed to disaster, almost wilfully, stupidly, like the almond tree and ' pas de nougat pour le noel.' [2] There ! as I took out a cigarette paper I got it exactly—*a cry against corruption*—that is *absolutely* the nail on the head. Not a protest—a *cry*. And I mean corruption in the widest sense of the word, of course.

[1] " Je ne parle pas francais," in *Bliss*.

[2] This a reference to a beautiful poem in Provençal by Henri Fabre, the naturalist, telling of the withering of the almond blossom by the cold.

I am at present fully launched, right out in the deep sea, with this second state. I may not be able to ' make my passage,' I may have to put back and have another try : that's why I don't want to talk about it, and have breath for so little more than a hail. But I must say the boat seems to be driving along the deep water as though it smelt port (no, better say harbour, or you'll think I am rushing into a public house).

After lunch.

Yes, I agree with you. Blow the old war. It's a toss up whether it don't get every one of us before it's done. Except for the first warm days here, when I really did seem to forget it, it's never been out of my mind—and everything is poisoned by it. It's *here in* me the whole time, eating me away, and I am simply terrified by it. It's at the root of my homesickness and anxiety and panic. I think it took being alone here and unable to work to make me fully, fully *accept* it. But now I don't think that even you would beat me. I have got the pull of you in a way because I am working, but I solemnly assure you that every moment away from my work is *misery*. And the human contact—just the pass the time away chat—distracts you, and that of course, I don't have at all. I miss it very much. Birds and flowers and dreaming seas don't do it. Being a biped, I must have a two-legged person to *talk* to. You can't imagine how I feel that I walk about in a black glittering case like a beetle. . . .

Queer business. . . .

I wonder what you will say to my ' important ' letter, and if you agree, will they let me thorough ? Can they keep me out of my own country ? These are a couple of refrains which are pretty persistent. They say here that after March this railway will probably be closed till June.

Sunday night
February 3, 1918

I don't dare to work any more to-night. I suffer so frightfully from insomnia here and from night terrors.

That is why I asked for another Dickens ; if I read him in
bed he diverts my mind. My work excites me so tremendously that I almost feel *insane* at night, and I have
been at it with hardly a break all day. A great deal is
copied and carefully addressed to you, in case any mis-
fortune should happen to me. Cheerful ! But there is a
great black bird flying over me, and I am so frightened it
will settle—so terrified. I don't know exactly what *kind*
he is.

If I were not working here, with war and anxiety I
should go mad, I think. My night terrors here are rather
complicated by packs and packs of growling, roaring,
ravening, prowl-and-prowl-around dogs.

God ! How tired I am !

Monday
February 4, 1918

No letter from you to-day. I had one from L.M.
written on *Friday*—so the posts have got a real grudge
against you and me. . . .

I am posting you the first chapter of my new work
to-day. I have been hard put to it to get it copied in
time to send it off, but I am so *exceedingly* anxious for
your opinion.

It needs perhaps some explanation. The subject, I
mean *lui qui parle*, is taken from F. and M., and God
knows who. It has been more or less in my mind ever since
first I felt strongly about the French. But I hope you'll
see (of course, you will) that I'm not writing with a sting.
I'm not indeed.

I read the fair copy just now and couldn't think where
the devil I had got the bloody thing from—I can't even
now. It's a mystery. There's so much less taken from
life than anybody would credit. The African laundress I
had a bone of—but only a bone—Dick Harmon, of course,
is partly, is—

Oh God ! Is it good ? I am frightened. For I stand
or fall by it. It's as far as I can get at present ; and I

have gone for it—bitten—deeper and deeper than ever I have before. You'll laugh a bit about the song. I could see Goodyear grin as he read that. . . . But what is it like ? Tell me—don't spare me. Is it the long breath, as I feel to my soul it is, or is it a false alarm ? You'll give me your dead honest opinion, won't you ?

If this gets lost I break my pen.

I am only, at the moment, a person who works, comes up to read newspapers, *and* to wait for postmen, goes down again, drinks tea. Outside the window is the scenic railway, all complete, and behind that pretty piece is the war.

Forgive an empty head. It rattled all night. I can't manage this sleeping business.

Monday night
February 4, 1918

I decided, after I posted your letter and MS. to-day and had my walk to try to forget work for an hour or two. So I have re-packed and re-sorted my box, gone through all my possessions, and generally behaved as though this were my last night on earth. Even to the extent of writing my address " *c/o you* to be communicated with in case of need," in French and English in my passport case.

And now all is fair. . . . What a fool I am !

The worst of REAL insomnia is one spends a great part of the day wondering if one is going to bring it off the coming night. Can I stand another last night ? Of course, I suppose I can. But must I ? Not to sleep and to be alone is a very neat example of HELL. But what isn't ? Ah, there you have me.

Tuesday.

I never had such a direct answer to prayer. Two letters, *real* letters, from you about our cottage and all that. This, of course, has given me the *salto mortale*, and I am a changed child. Also, I did manage by eating myself to death at dinner and only reading early poetry afterwards and taking 10 grains of aspirin to get to sleep.

God ! What it is to count on letters so !

Wednesday,
February 6, 1918.

I passed ' our house ' [1] again yesterday, and it looked so
heavenly fair with the white and red almond trees and the
mimosa attending that I went into a field hard by where
they were gathering the flowers and asked for information.
A big dark girl, with a great sheaf of flowers on one arm,
and the other arm raised, keeping her face from the sun,
said : " Ah, Madame, c'est une mauvaise maison.    Non,
elle pas louée.   Le propriétaire habite Marseille.   Mais,
vous savez, la maison est *ben* mauvaise ; elle se casse toujours.   On a fait de grandes réparations, il y a un an,
mais personne n'est venu pour la prendre.   Et, main-ten-
ant, elle est à moitié cassée encore.   On dit de cette
maison, qu'elle n' aime pas les gens." And then she bent
over the flowery fields again.

On my way home from my walk yesterday I met le père
de Marthe.   We shook hands.   He was very nice—you
remember, in a patent leather cap, rather like a drawing by
Gus Bofa.   Marthe is married and lives in Toulon.
" Son mari est à Gibralte."   Yes, he was the young man
who used to walk with her in the garden on Sunday.   I
said, " When you write, please remember me to her."
Said he, " J'écris *tous les soirs*.   Vous savez, elle était *ma
seule fille*."   This, of course, warmed my heart to an
extraordinary degree, and I wished C. hadn't given me
my furs so that I could have sent them to Marthe, etc.,
etc.

I worked a good deal yesterday, but I slept too.   It's
fatal for me to work late at night, when I am alone.   I
never realise unless I stop how *screwed up* I am.   Last
night, *petit enfant très sage*, I made myself another little
' front ' out of material I bought here—you know the
kind [drawing]—and it sent me into a fast sleep.

The widow here actually gave me two bunches of white
hyacinths yesterday.   What can it mean ?   They smell

[1] Not the Villa Pauline, but a beautiful cottage in an olive-yard,
about a mile away.

simply divine. And then Juliette still makes a garden of
my room. I have to put the flowers on the window sill
at night : *elles sentent si fort*. In the early morning when
I wake and see the row of little pots so *gentiment disposés* I
feel rather like the heroine of a German lyric poem. We
must grow all varieties of jonquils.

Have you got your meat card ? Of course, I think the
meat cards will stop the war. Nothing will be done but
*spot*-counting. And people will go mad, and butchers and
pork butchers will walk about with bones in their hair,
distracted. Talking of hair. Do you know those first
days I was here I went a bit *grey* over both temples. Real
grey hair—I know, I felt the very moment it came : but
it is a blow to see it.

Another thing I hate the French bourgeoisie for is their
absorbed interest in evacuation. What is constipating
and what not ? That is a real *criterion*. . . . Also the
people of the village have a habit of responding to their
serious needs (I suppose by night) down on the shore
round the palm trees. Perhaps it's the sailors. But my
English gorge rises and my English lips curl in contempt.
The other day one palm-tree had a placard nailed on it
" Chiens seulement." Was that funny ? It provided a
haw-haw for the day here. But on my life, I'd almost
rather, like that English lady, not know whether my
husband went to the lavatory or not, than be so unbuttoned.
No, this world, you know, this grown-up world everywhere, don't fit me.

Thursday
February 7, 1918

I am still *at it*. Oh ! can I hear about that MS. and
*what* are you going to say ? Now I'm up, now I'm down
—but I'm awfully frightened. The rest of the world can
take a 99 year lease of all the houses in Putney—but—
what do *you* think ?

I have such a passion, such a passion for life in the
country—for peace, for you lying on your back in the sun

looking up through wavy boughs, for you planting things that climb sticks—for me cutting things that have a sweet smell. Once the war is over, this is ours *on the spot*. For we shall live so remote that the rent won't cost much—and then you will become so dreadfully idle, with long curly hair like a pony that has been turned out to graze in a speckled field. . . .

Friday<br>February 8, 1918

Juliette is like a double stock—tufty, strong, very sweet, very gay. Yesterday she helped me wash my hair. Every service she makes a kind of ' party.' It was *fun* to heat and stagger in with two huge pots of water—to warm towels and keep them hot in folded newspapers—and the success of the operation was hers, too. She rejoiced over one's dry hair and ran away singing down the corridor. She sings nearly always as she works, and she has a friend, Madeleine, who pegs the linen on the line between the mimosa trees. When J. is doing the rooms M. calls from the garden, " Juli-*et-te* ! " And Juliette flies to the window. " Ah-hé ! C'est toi, ma belle ! "

What an enormous difference it makes to have her about rather than some poor foggy creature—or some bad-tempered one. But she could never be transplanted. She rises and sets with the sun, I am sure.

Saturday<br>February 9, 1918

I was just brushing my fringe when I heard a clumpety-clump in the passage that my heart seemed to recognise long before I did. It began to dance and beat. Yes, it was the Aged with your ADORABLE telegram :

" Sthry recewid mafnifiient Murly," I read, and of course this bowled me over so much that the pins won't keep in my hair and my buttons pop like fuchsia buds and my strings all squeak when they are pulled. Well, the

125

only response I *can* make is to send you the next chapter which I'll post, as before, on Monday. But oh dear, oh dear ! you have lighted such a candle ! Great beams will come out of my eyes at lunch and play like searchlights over the pommes de terre and terrify these insect children.

Now, of course, my only faint fear is : " Will he like the next chapter so much ? " Well, I must ' wait and see.' I must say when I wrote about the *tea* [1] last night—that's a funny little typical bit—I came all over and nearly cried a sort of sweet tears. . . . I say, haven't I got a *bit of you* ? Funny thing is I think you'll always come walking into my stories. . . . No, I must wait until I've had lunch before I go on with this letter. I am too much of a ' gash balloon ' altogether.

1.15. Well, I wish you had eaten my *tournedos* ; it was such a good 'un. The great thing here is the meat, which is superb. Oh, but now I am turned towards *home* everything is good. . . . Shall we really next month talk with Rib sitting in the fender playing on a minute comb and paper ?

How damned depressing and hideously inadequate that Versailles conference has been ! But what I do feel is— that handful can't stop the dyke from breaking now (is that true ?). I mean, there *is*—isn't there ?—perfectly immense pressure upon it, and L.G. and Co. may put their hands in the hole (like the little boy in *Great Deeds Done by Little People* that Grandma used to read me on Sundays) but it's no use. Oh, I *don't* know. When I think that I am not coming home and that ' all is over '— when that mood gets me, of course I don't believe it ever will end until we are all killed as surely as if we were in the trenches. . . .

> Sunday still and Monday after
> February 10-11, 1918

I have just done up in an envelope the rest of our story. . . . I don't want to exaggerate the importance of this

[1] See *Bliss*, p. 103 *sq.*

story or to harp upon it. . . . But what I felt so seriously as I wrote it was—ah ! I am in a way *grown up* as a writer—a sort of authority. Pray God you like it, now you've got it all.

I dreamed a short story last night, even down to its name, which was " Sun and Moon." It was very light. I dreamed it all—about children. I got up at 6.30 and wrote a note or two because I knew it would fade. I'll send it some time this week. It's so nice. I didn't dream that I read it. No, I was in it, part of it, and it played round invisible me. But the hero is not more than *five*. In my dream I saw a supper table with the eyes of *five*. It was awfully queer—especially a plate of half-melted ice-cream. . . . But I'll send it you. . . .

Monday. I wrote and finished the dream story yesterday, and dedicated it to Rib. I knew I would not write it at all if I didn't on the spot, and it kept me ' quiet.' . . .

Monday
February 11, 1918

About your letter about the first chapter [of *Je ne parle pas français*]. I read it and wept for joy. How can you so marvellously understand . . . I *did* feel (I do) that this story is the real thing and that I did not once (as far as I know) shirk it. Please God I'll do much better—but I felt : " There, I can lay down my pen now I've made that, and give it to him." But, Christ ! a devil about the size of a flea nips in my ear, " Suppose he's disappointed with the second half ? " . . .

I'll send you *Sun and Moon* to-day, registré, but, *of course*, don't *wire* about *it*.

Thursday
February 14, 1918

If you think I ought to stay till April, I stay and risk the offensive and the sous-marins without murmur. Voilà !

My health won't improve by being here : it's as good as it
ever will be—to ——'s rage, disgust and chagrin, of
course.  Oh, you should have seen her face drop when she
said, " I thought you were very ill."  My blood turned
ice with horror.

I went a great old walk yesterday, came in, screwed my
head tight, and thought myself nearly black in the face,
but got very little down.  Trouble is I feel I have found
an *approach* to a story now which I must apply to everything.  Is that nonsense ?  I read what I wrote before
that last and I feel : No, this is all *once removed* : it won't
do.  And it won't.  I've got to reconstruct everything.

If I do come in March I will come with her.  Frankly,
that *is* a relief—to feel I have some one to help me.  I
am not much good at this travelling alone. . . .

? Friday<br>
February 15, 1918

I haven't a puff in my sails to-day.  You never saw such
a head as mine must be within.  Nothing less than a
letter from you will do. . . .  It's also because I didn't
sleep, see ?  and couldn't find my place in the bed and
looked for it all night—*lashed* about in a hundred beds, I
should think, but no, didn't find my place to curl in.

Yesterday behind the hills at the back, I struck 3 divine
empty houses.  They have been empty for a long time,
and will be (till we take one).  I cannot tell you *how*
lovely they all are, or how exquisitely placed, with gardens,
terraces.  Ours had also a stone verandah and two
particularly heavenly trees embracing in front of it.  In
the cracks of the stone verandah little white hyacinths
were all in flower.  A sunny bank at the side was blue
with violets.  There was a baby tree that waited to be
hung with a poem.  And the approach !  The approach !
The colour of the house was a warm pink-yellow with a
red roof, the shape [here a drawing of the house].  Oh, I
can't make it, but it was, I think, flying with little loves.
It faces the city beyond the hills, which yesterday was

bathed in light.   But—I look, I see, I feel, and then I say
THE WAR, and it seems to disappear—to be taken off
like a film, and I am sitting in the dark. . . .

Saturday night<br>
February 17, 1918

My serious stories won't ever bring me anything, but
my ' child ' stories ought to and my light ones, once I find
a place. . . .

I am up early copying MSS for you.   When I get back
I'll work as regular as you (tho' with what a difference) but
I do seem to have broken through once and for all somehow, *and* I think there may be, if you hold me up by my
heels and rattle, some pennies in me.   Don't you ?   At
last ?   On my table are wild daffodils—Shakespeare
daffodils.   They are so lovely that each time I look up I
give them to you again.   We shall go expeditions in the
spring and write down all the *signs* and take a bastick and
a small trowel and bring back treasures.   Isn't that lovely
where Shelley speaks of the ' moonlight-coloured may ' ?

It's still (I think) very cold and I am in my wadded
jacket with the pink 'un round my legs.   But the sun is
out and I'll go for a big walk this afternoon and *warm up*.
I saw old Ma'am Gamel yesterday.   She is a nice old dear.
The way she speaks of you always makes me want to *hug*
her.   Yesterday she said I must pass by her before I go
back as she would send you a little souvenir—and then she
looked up at me and said, her blue eyes twinkling, " Il a
toujours ses beaux yeux, le jeune mari ? "   " Allez !
Allez !   On n'a pas honte ? " called Thérèse, who was
measuring biscuits for L. M.   I also saw (looking for a bit
of pumice stone : bought a bit for 1 sou) the old woman
from the droguerie.   She's got a new cat called Minne,
" un grand, un sauvage, un fou avec des moustaches which
would make a man pleurer d'envie."   In fact, she says, he
is " presqu'un homme—il *crache* absolument comme un
homme—et le soir il est toujours dans les rues."

I've just made myself a glass of boiling tea, very weak, with saxin. It's good. I drink it on and off all day. Do you remember that funny sort of scum that used to come on the water here ? It still does. I have to take it off with the point of my paper-knife. . . .

[" *February* 19. I woke up early this morning and when I opened the shutters the full round sun was just risen. I began to repeat that verse of Shakespeare's : ' Lo, here the gentle lark weary of rest,' and bounded back into bed. The bound made me cough—I spat—it tasted strange—it was bright red blood. Since then I've gone on spitting each time I cough a little more. . . . L. M. has gone for the doctor." *Journal*, p. 75.]

Wednesday
February 20, 1918

I feel much better to-day and the hæmorrhage is— hardly at all. Can't work much, or think very sensibly, but I am ever so much better than I was. . . .

Since this little attack I've had, a queer thing has happened. I feel that my love and longing for the external world—I mean the world of *nature*—has suddenly increased a million times. When I think of the little flowers that grow in grass, and little streams and places where we can lie and look up at the clouds—Oh, I simply ache for them—for them with you. Take you away and the answer to the sum is O. I feel so awfully like a tiny girl whom someone has locked up in the dark cupboard, even though it's daytime. I don't want to bang at the door or make a noise, but I want you to come with a key you've made yourself and let me out, and then we should tiptoe away together into a kinder place where everybody was more of our heart and size.

You mustn't think, as I write this, that I'm dreadfully sad. Yes, I am, but you know, at the back of it is *absolute faith* and *hope* and *love*. I've only to be frank, had a bit of a fright. See ? And I'm still 'trembling.' That just describes it.

To-morrow I shall write a gayer letter. Oh, just to forget me for a minute,—do you remember how the Fool in King Lear said : " 'Twas her brother who, in pure kindness, buttered his horse's hay." I thought that was a good phrase for nowadays. ' It is hardly the moment to butter the horse's hay ! ' Isn't it ? Pin it in the *Nation*.

Can I have another Dickens some time ? *Bleak House* or *Edwin Drood* ? Mrs. Gaskell positively fascinated me. I think she's an extremely good writer. The 2nd story in the Cranford book, *Moorland Cottage*, is really a little masterpiece. . . .

Wednesday night

That doctor is coming to-morrow, so I'll tell you what he says. He is a most awful fool, I am sure, but still I suppose he *is* a doctor, and that's a comfort. One thing he says, this south coast is no use for me—too relaxing— and I ought to have sat on a mountain. Fatal to stay here later than March. Well, that's perhaps true. I think it is, for every time the wind blows I shut up all my petals—even if it's only a breeze. . . .

I feel *chirpy* to-night. I don't care *what* happens, what pain I have, what I suffer, so long as my handkerchiefs don't look as though I were in the pork-butcher trade. That does knock your Wig *flat, flat, flat*. I feel as though the affair were out of my control then and that it's a nightmare. Last night was like that for me. Then this afternoon, when I sat reading Keats in the sun, I coughed and it wasn't red and I felt inclined to wave the fact to the whole world. . . .

No, to be in England, to see you, to see a good lung specialist—that's my affair and no other. But to be on alien shores with a very shady medicine man and a crimson lake hanky is about as near Hell as I want to be.

Thursday

" Pas de lettre encore.   Rien que le journal."

" Merci, Juliette."

Well, that often happens on this day.   Perhaps I'll get
2 to-morrow.   It may be those bloody raids which I see
have been on again.   I feel ever so much better again
to-day and *hungry*.   I should like to have a chicken *en
casserole* and a salad and good coffee.   It's a bit windy
to-day, so I'll take the air behind a screen of my daffodils
and not rush forth.   Do you remember, or have I mentioned lately, that poem of Shelley's, *The Question* ?   It
begins :

> I dreamed that as I wandered by the way
> Bare Winter suddenly was changed to Spring. . . .

I have learned it by heart since I am here ; it is very
exquisite, I think.   Shelley and Keats I get more and more
*attached to*.   Nay, to all ' poetry.'   I have such a passion
for it, and I feel such an understanding of it.   It's a great
part of my life. . . .

April ! April !

Friday
February 22, 1918

A Horn of Plenty !   Your Sunday letter and postcard
and your Monday letter.   Oh, *how* I have devoured them.
The Monday one which was written with swirling
twirley letters, made me a bit sad ; it was in answer to
mine saying *March* was definite, and now, alas ! our plans
are altered and I can't come before the swallow dares. . . .

I feel marvellously better to-day.   *No* temperature—
*vegetarian* [1]—and on the mend again.   But I have had
more than my share of alarums and tuckets, don't you
think ?   Great big black things lie in wait for me under
the trees and stretch their shadows across the road to
trip me.   You'll have to keep shouting, " Look out,

[1] i.e. no longer " in the pork-butcher trade," see p. 131.

Wig ! " when we walk together again.  The doctor has
been and says : If I use all his remedies, I'll be a well girl.
(I think he is such a fool.  Oh, I could write you reams
about him, but I'll *tell* you).  However, his remedies are
sound, I think—injections of some stuff called Goneol
and another called Kaikakilokicaiettus as far as I can make
out—*and* a tonic *and* fish to eat—whole fishes—fish *ad lib*.
If I am torpedoed on the way home I expect I shall burst
into fins and a mermaid tail as I enter the water and swim
to shore. . . .

There's a bit of wind to-day : it's a ¼ to 12.  I'm just
up.  L. M., I believe, ranges the mountains all the
mornings.  She comes back and I meet her at lunch,
with bright eyes and an Appetite which makes the hotel
*tremble*, and after having devoured the table-cloth, glasses
and spoons, she says, " What I miss is the puddings.
Don't you *ever* care for currant duff, *my dearie, or*— ? "
and then follows about 100 puddings as fast as they can
tear.  She keeps them all flying in the air like a conjuror,
and still like a conjurer, eats 'em.  What a strange type
she is !  But good to travel back with—

Saturday
February 23, 1918

Yesterday the woman at the paper-shop gave me a
bouquet of violets.  Here are some.  And Juliette has
filled my vases with yellow goldy wallflowers.  God !
how I love flowers.

After all my coming back is only delayed by a little
more than three weeks.  That's what I cling to for consolation.  Then I *shall* come back, for I can't stop here
any longer.  Even the doctor says not to stay here after
March.  So I must come.  Hooray !  Will my Rib be at
the window ?  What a throwing about he will get !
Does he ever walk up you ?  Never ?  Do you ever read
who made him on his tummy ?  Never ?  *Attend un tout
p'tit p'tit p'tit beau moment*, as they say here, and he'll
know these joys again. . . .

On Monday, P. G. I'll post more manuscript to you.
Would *The Nation* publish *Sun and Moon*? If they
publish that rubbish by S. I think they might. Have you
read any reviews of Yeats's book? And did you see his
remarks on Keats? There was a good story agin him
(though he didn't know it) in a quote I saw. He dreamed
once ' in meditations ' (! ?) that his head was circled with
a flaming sun. Went to sleep and dreamed of a woman
whose hair was afire, woke up, lighted a candle, and by
and bye discovered ' by the odour ' that he's set his own
hair ablaze. This *he* calls sort of prophetic. I think it's
wondrous apt. It's just as far as he and his crew can get
to set their hair afire—to set their lank forlorn locks
a-frizzle. God knows there's nothing else about them
that a cartload of sparks could put a light to. So he can
jolly well shut up about Keats. If you should ever have
the chance pull his nose for me. . . .

But oh! how *ignorant* these reviewers are, how far
away and barred out from all they write. There was a
review of Coleridge in *The Times*—so bad, so ill-informed.
But then, of course, I feel I have rather a corner in Coleridge and his circle. . . .

The sea is breaking restless and high on the coast
opposite. . . .

Monday<br>February 25, 1918

Isn't this nice paper? A biggish block of it costs 65 c.
I shall bring you one. There's fresh nougat here, too. I
must put a great lump of it in my box for you. You see
where *all* my thoughts turn to. Yesterday, *par exemple*,
it was as warm as summer. I sat on a bank under an olive
tree and fell a-dreaming. Now I came back as a surprise
and just sent you a wire to the office : " Look here she's
back Rib," and then I lighted the lamp and arranged the
flowers and your presents were on the table. And at last
your steps—your key in the door. . . . *Or* I came again
as a surprise and phoned you from the station. " Is that

you, Jack ? I've just arrived," I sat there thinking like this until I nearly wept for joy. It seemed *too good to be true*. Will it really happen . . . really and truly ?

I'm so subdued to-day. I expected N.Z. letters and got none, and it's very windy and cold, and my work is *thick*, absolutely *thick*, for the moment. Under it all is : Will the offensive prevent me coming back ? Will the Channel be closed ? You know this mood. Your letter to-morrow will start the wheels going round again, and I'll be a gay girl and write more. But I don't seem to have seen anything to tell you of. I feel in a sort of quiet *daze* of *anxiety*. I tell you so you will understand the tone of this letter. *All is well really*. But I'd like to call out your name very loudly until you answer and I begin to run. . . .

Tuesday
February 26, 1918

When I read about B. R. being carried shoulder high, I felt quite *sick*—for such a silly, an incredibly stupid thing. How humiliated he ought to feel ! It would be for me like if I was a burglar and was caught after having burgled the potato knife. I expect if he goes to prison he'll get immensely fat in there : in fact, he's so blown already that I shudder. . . .

Last night after a full moon and a sea like velvet a huge thunderstorm burst over the town. Rain, bright lightning, loud wind. I was sitting up in bed writing, for thank God ! I've managed to stave off the werewolf a bit, and the storm was wonderful. I had forgotten what it sounded like. . . .

Trust L. M. for knocking then—a low ominous knock. I think she hoped I had been struck by lightning. (I always feel her dream is to bury me here and bring back a few bulbs from Katie's grave to plant in a window-box for you.) She asked if she might lie on the floor (you know these *tile floors*) till it was over, as it was so very agitating.

We must have plenty of gillyflowers in our garden. They smell so sweet.

How shall we spend the day ?
With what delights
Sweeten the nights ?
When from this tumult we are got secure,
Where mirth with all her freedom goes
Yet shall no finger lose,
Where every word is thought and every thought is
        pure ;
There from the tree
We'll cherries pluck, and pick the strawberry. . . .

Don't you like that ?

I shan't go out to-day because it rains. I'll read *Le P'tit* this afternoon and *Nausicaa* and write you about them, and I'll make no END of an effort to finish this story called *Bliss*. I hope you'll like it. It's different again.

I was thinking last night that I must not let L. M. obsess me. After all, she is a trial, but I must get over her. Dosty would have. She adds to the struggle, yes, but the struggle is always there—I mean if one don't feel very strong and so on. But they have nearly all had to fight against *just this*. So must I and so will I. I hope I've not been a coward in my last letter or two. At any rate, my loins are girded up no end to-day, and I spent the morning in bed full steam ahead.

Queer the effect people have on one. Juliette is a positive help to writing. She is so independent and so full in herself—I want to say fulfilled, but it's a dangerous word. I love to feel she is near and to meet her. She *rests* me positively. She'll make some man tremendously happy one day. Yes, she's really important to me. As to all the other *swine* with which the hotel is full—well, they are swine.

Unhappy ! Shall we never more
That sweet militia restore

When gardens only had their towers
And all the garrisons were flowers ;
When roses only arms might bear
And men did rosy garlands wear ?

I *keep* (as you see) wanting to quote poetry to-day. When I get back I shall be like a sort of little private automatic machine in the home : you wind me up and a poem will come, I've learned so many here while I lie awake. . . .

I shall make Rib a wedding-dress of blue jersey, sailor-knot, full blue trousers and p'raps a very tiny *whistle* on a cord—if I can find one. . . .

Wednesday
February 27, 1918

Your Saturday letter has come—the one about the Eye and about my wings. Now I am being an absolute old *coddler* for your sake and doing *everything* and feeling ever such a great deal better, SO do you do the same. We are the most awful pair I've ever heard of. We'll have to pin notices in our hats and on our chests saying what we've got and then get a couple of walking sticks and tin mugs if this goes on. . . —Oh dear, you oughtn't to look at anything smaller than a cow.

I have read *Le P'tit*. It's *very* good — very well done. I think it's got one fault, or perhaps I am too ready to be offended by this. I think the physical part of Le P'tit's feeling for Lama, is unnecessarily accentuated. I think if I'd written it I wouldn't have put it in at all—not on his side. On hers, yes. But never once on his. Am I wrong, do you think ? Yes, of course, I agree it's well done, that part, but I would have left it more mysterious. Lama must do all she does, and Le P'tit must say : " Si tu savais comme je t'aime ! " But " lorsqu'un spontané baiser dans l'affolement furieuse de l'instinct chez le jeune homme . . . " that I don't like.

But the ' way ' it is done, the ' method,' I do very much. Nausicaa has got something very charming too. If he wasn't a Frenchman he'd be a *most* interesting chap. But I do find the French language, style, attack, point of view, hard to stomach at present. It's all tainted. It all seems to me to lead to dishonesty—Dishonesty Made Easy—made superbly easy. All these *half*-words, these words which have never really been born and seen the light, like " me trouble," " vague," " tiède," " blottant," " inexprimable " (these are bad examples, but you know the kinds I mean) and the phrases and whole paragraphs that go with them—they won't, at the last moment, *do* at all. Some of them are charming and one is loth to do without them, but they are like certain plants—once they are in your garden they spread and spread and spread, and make a show perhaps, but they are *weeds*. No, I get up hungry from the French language. I have too great an appetite for the real thing to be put off with pretty little kickshaws, and I am offended intellectually that ' ces gens ' think they can so take me in.

It's the result of Shakespeare, I think. The English language is damned difficult, but it's also damned rich, and so clear and bright that you can search out the darkest places with it. Also it's *heavenly* simple and true. Do you remember where Paulina says :

> I, an old turtle,
> Will wing me to some withered bough
> And there my mate that's never to be found again
> Lament till I am lost.

You can't beat that. I *adore* the English language, and that's a fact.

Thursday
February 28, 1918

It's three o'clock. I've just finished this new story, *Bliss*, and am sending it to you. But though, my God ! I *have* enjoyed writing it, I am an absolute rag for the rest of the day and you must forgive no letter at all. I will write at length to-morrow. Oh, tell me what you think of *our* new story (that's quite sincere). Please try and like it, and I am now free to start another. One extraordinary thing has happened to me since I came out here! Once I start them they haunt me, pursue me and plague me until they are finished and as good as I can do. . . .

I walked to a little valley yesterday that I longed to show you. I sat on a warm stone there. All the almond flowers are gone, but the trees are in new leaf and they were full of loving, mating birds—quarrelling, you know, about whether to turn the stair-carpet under or to cut it off straight. And the trees were playing ball with a little breeze, tossing it to each other.

I sat a long time on my stone, then scratched your initials with a pin and came away. . . .

You can feel how I'm wheeling this old letter along in a creaking barrow. My head is *gone*. I'll send a long one (letter, not head) to-morrow.

Saturday
March 2, 1918

I sent that wire yesterday, but when the Mayor asked to translate " Hay for Heron " [1] I was rather up a tree! So I said, " tout va très très bien." That was true, wasn't it ? But if the wire is stopped, what a roundabout I and the censor would sit in before I explained !

It is so Bitterly Cold to-day that no amount of clothes, food or fire can stop spider-webs of ice flying all over one's skin. Juliette says I am like a little cat, and I feel like one, because I am always by my own fire or, as I go along the corridor, purring round any stove that is lighted there. And there was " pas de poste aujourd'hui." I didn't really expect any letters. Look here ! Did you know you sent me 2 copies of *Master Humphrey's Clock* ? It was in the back of *Edwin Drood* as well as in the separate volume. I thought I'd just tell you.

[1] The Heron Farm was the name of the farmhouse in which we planned to spend the rest of our days.

What an old wind-bag G. K. C. is ! His preface to the
Everyman book is simply disgraceful.

I must talk a bit about the Heron. We must find a
place where it is warm and at the same time *bracing, i.e.,*
*abrité* and yet rather high. But, to be absolutely frank,
I am beginning to change my mind about this place for
the winter. I won't come here again. If it is calm, it is
perfect, but there is *nearly always* " un pue de vent " and
that " vent " is like an iced knife. One would be much
snugger in a thoroughly snug cottage with doors and
windows that fit, a good fire, etc. *And* I don't want to
have two homes. No one can. If we have the money
and the desire we shall always be able to cut off together
for a bit *irgendwohin*. But one home, with all the books,
all the flowers, is enough and can't be beat.

If I talk about my own physical health—well, I know I
ought to be in the air a lot. Well, if we have a garden,
that's what I call being decently in the air, to plant things
and dig up things, not to hang pegged on a clothes line and
be blown about like a forlorn *pantalon*. Also, I want to
range about with you, BUT ALWAYS with our own
cottage to come back to and its thread of smoke to see
from far away.[1] That's life, that's the warm south,
wherever it is.

My God ! how we shall talk when I get back, planning
all this and saying, " Yes, I think so, too."

I don't think I can wait much longer for a garden—for
fruit trees and vegetables. The thought of knocking
lumps of earth off a freshly pulled carrot fills me with
emotion ; " je suis tout émue," as these crawly froggies
say, at the idea. Another—plums with the bloom on
them, in a basket—and you and I making jam—and your
Mother coming to stay with us—and—and—everything.

L. M. has made me perfectly sick to-day. She's
skittish. " Dearie, I'm very proud. I remember the
word for candle—*bougie*. That's right, isn't it ? I'm
not really very stupid, you know. It's only when I am

[1] See *Odyssey*, Bk. I.

with you, because you are so many millions miles ahead of
all the rest of mankind— " and so on.  I *squirm*, try to
hold my tongue, and then—*bang*! and again I shoot her
dead, and up she comes again.

I've begun my new story.  It's nice.

Monday
March 4, 1918

I am writing to you, as yesterday, after my early breakfast, and still tucked up.  Immensely tucked to-day, just
a fringe and two fingers showing because outside it is all
white with SNOW.  And icy cold within.  These houses
are not made for such rude times.  There seem to be a
thousand knife-like airs that draw upon each other and do
battle even unto th' extremities o' the floor.

*J.*: You are very silly.

*W.*: My breakfast crumbs have gone to my brain.

But it is very silly of the Lion to come in like this.  I
expected him to be a rough rude tumbling monster, but
not with a mane of icicles!

*Bang* at the door.  " Une dépêche, Madame."  Cinq
sous for the Aged.  I open it. . . .

Good God!  How I love telegrams!

And now I see you handing it across the counter and
counting out the pennies.  But the telegraph form,
feeling awfully gay, flies off while the girl hands you the
change, and begins to buzz and flap round the gas-jet and
against the window-pane—UNTIL, finally, you have to
make a butterfly net out of a postman's bag and climb on
to the counter and on to that iron rail (a Lovely Fair
holding your grey ankles the while) and do the most awful
terrifying balancing feats before you snare it.  Then you
go out, quite exhausted, saying, ' I shan't have time for
any lunch now ! '  But at that moment Wig appears riding
on a cloud with a little heavenly hot-pot tied up in a
celestial handkerchief.  No, I must put this letter away
to cool until the postman has been. . . .

Later, but no calmer. A Wednesday and a Thursday letter came. Quick March is the best joke of the year, I think.

Monday night
March 4, 1918

It is very late. The winds are howling, the rain is pouring down, I have just read Wordsworth's poem, *To Duty, and* a description in a N.Z. letter of how to grow that neglected vegetable, the Kohl-rabi. I never heard a wilder, fiercer night : but it can't quench my desire—my burning desire to grow this *angenehme* vegetable, with its fringe of outside leathery leaves, and its heart which is shaped and formed and of the same size as the *heart* of a *turnip*. It is of a reddish purple colour, will grow where there have been carrots or peas. Of course, I can see *our* Kohl-rabi—the most extraordinary looking thing—and W. and J. staring at it.

Do you think it ought to look like that ?
No. Do you ?
No. I think it's done it on purpose.
Shall I show it to somebody and ask ?
No, they'll laugh.

And as they turn away the Kohl-rabi wags and flaps its outside leathery leaves at them. . . .

Tuesday. Thunderstorms all night and to-day torrents of rain and wind and iciness. It is impossible to keep warm—with fires, woollies, food or anything, and one is a succession of shivers. The DRAUGHTS are really infernal. How I despise them for not being able to fit a window ! Or a door ! And how my passion for solidity and honesty in all things grows ! Our house must be honest and solid like our work. Everything we buy must be the same. Everything we wear, even. I can't stand anything false. Everything must ring like Elizabethan English and like those gentlemen I always seem to be mentioning " The Poets." There is a light upon them, especially upon the Elizabethans and our ' special ' set—

142

Keats, W. W., Coleridge, Shelley, De Quincey and Co.,
which I feel is like the bright shining star which must hang
in the sky above the Heron as we drive home.   Those are
the people with whom I want to live, those are the men
I feel are our brothers, and the queer thing is that I feel
there is a great golden loop linking them to Shakespeare's
time. . . .   If you knew what a queer feeling I have about
all this as I write.   Is it just because I am so steeped in
Shakespeare ?   I can't think of jam-making even, without

> And if you come hether
> When Damsines I gether
> I will part them all you among.

And you know, if ever I read anything about *our* men, you
should see how arrogant I feel, and how inclined to say,
' Child, child ! '   And dreadfully inclined to say to the
poor creature who makes a mild observation about *my*
S. T. C.   " You really must not expect to understand ! "
Yes, I am a funny woman—and a year or two at the Heron
will make me a great deal funnier, I expect.

I do long to see you again and talk BOOKS.   For your
Worm is the greatest bookworm unturned.   It grows on
me.   I always was a bit that way, but now—and with the
Heron before us—well—Do you feel the same ?   My
Shakespeare is full of notes for my children to light on.
Likewise the Oxford Book.   I feel they will like to find
these remarks, just as I would have. . . .

Wednesday
March 6, 1918

Oh ! Madame G. is here with her husband, and she is
nearly doing for me, I can't think or write or escape.   She
is a dear and generous and all that, but a most APPALLING
bore, and I haven't the physical strength for her.   I feel
as though all my blood goes dead pale, and with a slight
grin.   When she goes on Friday I shall spend Saturday in
bed *with the door locked*.   I hate people, I loathe G.—

unlimited, tearing, worrying G.—saying the same things, staring at me. If only I were *bien portante*, I suppose I should not feel like this at all, but as it is, wave after wave of real sickness seems to ebb through me and I dissolve with misery ... I can't say her nay. " Nous sommes venus exprès pour vous voir." And she brought me books and *berlingots pour Monsieur*, etc.

It's not the slightest use pretending I can stand people : I can't. . . . This " grande femme, forte et belle, me parlant du midi, des poèmes ravissantes d'Albert Samain ... *et* de Keats ! " and Monsieur who dogs me, saying that I ought to pick up " pour me donner les belles joues roses " ! I said faintly, clinging hold of a rosemary bush finally, and aching to cry, " La santé est une question de l'esprit tranquille chez moi, Monsieur, et pas de bouillon gras," and the darling rosemary bush squeezed my hand and left its fragrance there and said, " I know, my dear ! "

Aid me, ye powers. Oh, my poets, make a ring round little me and hide me. Oh, I must find a daisy for an umbrella and sit under it, but then, down would come L. M.'s shoe just for the pleasure of raising up " cette plante, si frêle, si délicate " ... Everybody is too big— too crude—too ugly.

Thursday
March 7, 1918

This is my little moment of quiet before I am thrown to the Three Bears again. (Fancy *Southey* being the author of the Three Bears !) I am in bed. It's ten o'clock. The post hasn't come, but at break of day the Aged brought me your telegram, a particularly nice one, and so with that smiling on my knee I feel almost as though I'd had a letter. . . . It's a blue and white day, very fair and warm and calm. The sort of day that *fowls* enjoy, keeping up a soft faraway cackle—you know the kind ? Were I alone I should dive into my new story. It's so plain before me.

But I don't dare to. They'd see me, they'd look over the fence and call. No, darling new story, you'll have to wait till Friday night.

Poor old Carpentrassienne! If she knew how she offends me—how the sight of her binding up her balloon-like bosom preparatory to " la fête de la soupe " makes me *frissonne*! If she mentions another book that she's going to make me eat when I go and stay with her, I think I may—fly into bits! And this French language! Well, of course, she always did caricature it, but in my clean, pink Elizabethan ears it sounds the most absolute *drivel*! And poor old L. M.'s contributions! " En anglais mange les poudings c'est très bien."

Hours and hours and hours of it! Are you wondering where Wig has left her sense of humour? Oh, my sense of humour won't take his head from between his paws for it—won't wag his tail or *twirk* an ear.

It's a comfort that the cold has gone again *pour le moment*. I hope it has in London, too. Here to-day it feels very quick March indeed. We shall have to send our telegrams all the same, you know. The man at Havre said : " Of course, if you have urgent family affairs which recall you to England before the time is up, it can doubt-less be arranged." I think he meant that I should do wisely to have *evidence*—like a telegram. So, unless you think the How is Mother telegram with its answer, ' Mother is worse operation necessary come soon possible,' too extreme, that will be the one we shall send. I'll be *most awfully frightened* till I am on English shore. And even then it will be no good for you to attempt to meet me because the trains are hours late—or perhaps nearly a day late, and we'd both suffer *too* cruelly. You know what I'd feel like thinking you were waiting and I couldn't get out and push the engine. No, I'll have to (*a*) phone you at the office, (*b*) go home by taxi if it's not office hours. Voilà !

My poetry book opened this morning upon " The Wish " by old Father Abraham Cowley.

Ah, yet, ere I descend into the grave,
May I a small house and large garden have,
And a few friends and many books, both true,
Both wise and both delightful, too !

Pride and ambition here
Only in far-fetched metaphors appear ;
Here nought but winds can hurtful murmurs
    scatter
And nought but Echo flatter.
The gods, when they descended, hither
From heaven did always choose their way :
And therefore we may boldly say
That 'tis the way, too, thither.

This gaiety is the result of absolute desperation. I've
such a headache that everything *pounds*, even the flowers I
look at, everything beats and drums. I feel absolutely
*bled white* and it still goes on till to-morrow evening 8 p.m.
Insufferable monsters ! They have just snapped up a
whole half-pound of biscuits (2 francs) bought by L. M.
for me (I *said* a quarter !) In consequence, I never
touched one, and watched them dip the half-pound in
their tea—" les sucreries de la guerre épouvantable." My
knees tremble, and where my little belly was there is only
a cave. If they were not going to-morrow, I'd leave,
myself, with a hand-bag. *Or* die and have L. M. plus the
G.'s at my *pompes funèbres*. " C'était une femme tellement douce ! ! ! " No, madness lies this way. I'll stop
and try to get calm. Oh God ! these monsters ! !

On Saturday D.V. after a whole day alone I will be
again at least a gasping Wig—not a Wig in utter despair.
DAMN PEOPLE !


Friday
March 8, 1918

My last day of Three in Hell and Hell in Three.

In bed. Breakfast over. The window open, the airs
waving through and a great beam of sun shining on a

double stock. . . . But I'm blind till to-morrow. The
G.'s go by a train at 8 o'clock to-night and to-morrow I'll
be myself again.

I feel horribly weak and frail and exhausted, I must
confess, and if they stayed a day longer, should take to my
bed. But once the *great pressure* is gone, I will perk up, as
you know, ever so quick again. But don't ever worry
about not replying to the G. and don't feel under the
least obligation to her. She's so blown that not even the
ox could brake her belly—and she's a damned underbred
female. All that she has done or was to have done for me
is the purest conceit on her part, because I am English and
you write *pour le Times* and we have been innocent enough
to flatter her vanity. She said yesterday : " Mais,
qu'est-ce que c'est, mon amie ! Même quand vous
n'êtes pas très bien portante, c'est seulement avec vous
que j'ai le sens de la vie ! " And I thought of L. M.'s
" Even if you are nervy, Katie, it is only when I am with
you that I feel full of life." And H. L.'s " *So* strange—
the divine sense of *inflation* that I have when I come near
you." Oh, if you are a little warrior in times of peace, *do*
keep me from harpies and ghouls ! ! !

I write those three remarks out of horror, you understand, because they do terrify me. . . .

The lines of the poem I quoted were, alas ! not mine.
They were writ by Thomas Randolph (1605-1635) and
were part of an ode to Master Anthony Stafford to hasten
him into the country.

> Come, spur away.
> I have no patience for a longer stay,
> But must go down
> And leave the changeable noise of this great town :
> I will the country see. . . .

And the verse ends with this line :

> Tis time that we grow wise, when all the world
> grows mad.

It's altogether a most delightful poem. I wish I knew what else he had written. There's another line charms me :

>    If I a poem leave, that poem is my son.

I feel he is a man we both should have known—that he is, most decidedly, one of the Heron Men.

And did Sir Thomas Wyatt write a great many poems ? He seems to me extraordinarily good ! Do you know a poem of his : *Vixi puellis nuper idoneus* ? My strike ! It's a rare good 'un.

Saturday
March 9, 1918

A cold wild day, almost dark, with loud complaining winds, and no post. That's the devil ! None yesterday, none to-day ! I should at least have had your Monday. I am very disappointed. . . .

However, the Monsters have gone. A darling brown horse dragged them away at 8 o'clock last night. For the last time I, shuddering, wrung M.'s little half-pound of swollen sausages, and Madame's voice rang out, " J'ai eu entre mes mains *cinq mille* lettres de Mistral," and then they were gone, and I crept up to my room, ordered a boiling coffee, locked the door and simply sat and smoked till midnight. I'll shut up about them now. I feel better physically already. Isn't it awful to mind things so ?

Oh, why haven't I got a letter ? I want one *now, now*— this minute—not to-morrow ! ! And I believe it's there and the Post Office just won't deliver it, to spite me. I believe that *quite seriously*.

' By the way ' *re* President Wilson. Monsieur G. says he is not at all liked in France. And why ? . . . It's all very well for him to stand on a mountain and " dire de belles choses." He's never suffered. He only came into the war because he saw that the Allies were going to be beaten and realised that if they were, Germany would attack America with fleets and fleets of " sous-marins puissants." America's entry and " retard " were both on purely commercial grounds. Wilson held out to collect as much war-profits as he could—came in to avoid having those war-profits taken from him by Germany. So *the* men are L. G. and Clemenceau. They do understand that you can never " traiter avec ces gens-là," that we must go on until—" bien sûr "—England and France bleed again, but equally " bien sûr " Germany is in the hands of whoever is left " en Angleterre ou la France " to do whatever they please with. Their pleasure, of course, being to make strings of sausages out of the whole country.

" Goûtez-vous ! C'est du Boche. Pas mauvais ! "

God ! if you knew how sick to death I am of all this and how I long for home and peace. I'll not stick this much longer, and I shall very soon ask for news of Mother. . . . They will kill me between them all.

Sunday morning
March 10, 1918

Another *jour glacé*—so cold indeed that the country might be under deep, deep snow. It's very quiet, and through the white curtains the sea shows white as milk. I am still in my bye, for I have just had mon petit déjeuner. It *was* good. I made it boiling in my tommy cooker. I really think that Maman must have gone to see a fire-eater or been frightened by one before I was born. Why else should I always demand of my boissons that they be in a ' perfeck bladge " before I drink 'em ? And now I am waiting for the courier.

Alas ! the same light quick steps won't carry it to me any more—for Juliette is gone. She came into my room last evening in an ugly stiff black dress without an apron. I noticed she had her boots on and that she was very thickly powdered.

She leaned against a chair, looking at the floor, and then suddenly she said, with a fling of her arm, " Alors je pars—

pour toujours. . . . J'ai reçu des mauvaises nouvelles . . .
une dépêche . . .mère gravement malade viens de suite . . .
alors ! eh ben, voilà . . . y a rien à faire." And then
suddenly she took a deep sobbing breath. " J'ai bien de
la peine ! " I was so sorry that I wanted to put my arms
round her. I could only hold her warm soft hand and
say, "Ah, ma fille, je le regrette, je le regrette de tout
cœur."

She lives on the coast of Corsica. The idea of the
journey, of course, *terrifies* her. And then she was so
happy—" si bien bien bien ici ! " and the *beau temps* is just
coming and she did not know how she could pack her
things, for she came here " avec toutes mes affaires
enveloppées d'un grand mouchoir de maman." But
she'd never saved and always spent. " Il me faut acheter
un grand *panier sérieux* pour les emballer."

Of course she thinks she'll never come back here again ;
she's in the desperate state of mind that one would expect
of her, and she wept when we said Goodbye. " Qui vous
donnerait les fleurs main-ten-ant, Madame, vous qui les
aimez tant ? C'était mon grand plaisir—mon grand
plaisir ! " I saw her in the hall before she left wearing a
hideous hat and clasping her umbrella and *panier sérieux*
as though they had cried " To the Boats ! " already.

I must not write any more about her, for after all, she
can't mean much to you. She *has* meant an enormous lot
to me. I have really loved her—and her songs, her ways,
her kneeling in front of the fire and gronding the *bois vert*
—her rushes into the room with the big bouquets and her
way of greeting me in the morning as though she loved the
day, and also the fact that she distinguished your letters
from others. " Ce n'est pas *la* lettre—malheur ! "
Goodbye Juliette, my charming double stock in flower.
I'll never forget you. You were a real being. You had
roots.

This morning it was Madeleine, the laundrymaid,
Juliette's friend, promoted, who brought me *mon déjeuner.*
*Très fière,* in consequence. With her fringe combed down

into her big eyes, a dark red blouse and a scalloped apron—
I could write about these two girls for ever, I feel to-day.
Yes, I'll write just a bit of a story about them, and spare
you any more.

You remember writing to me in your criticism of " Je
ne parle pas français " that Dick Harmon seemed to have
roots ? It struck me then and the sound of it has gone
echoing in me. That's really the one thing I ask of people
and the one thing I can't do without. I feel so immensely
conscious of my own roots. You could pull and pull and
pull at me—I'll not come out. You could cut off my
flowers—others will grow . . . And I could divide up the
people with or without them in a jiffy. And although
one may be sometimes deceived—sometimes they are so
clever, the bad ones : they plant themselves and look so
fair that those two little children we know so well stand
hand in hand admiring them and giving them drops of
water out of the tin watering-can—they fade at the going
down of the sun and the two little children are perfectly
disgusted with them for being such cheats, and they *hurl*
them over the garden wall before going back to their house
for the night.

Well, well ! The heap of dead ones that we have thrown
over. But ah, the ones that remain ! All the English
poets. I see Wordsworth, par exemple, so *honest* and
*living* and *pure*.

Here's the courier.

Good God ! Your Tuesday letter, and I read " Wordsworth—so honest and so pure." And remember my
letter yesterday, and here is yours in answer—just the
same !

Monday
March 11, 1918

Bytwene Mershe and Averil
When spray beginneth to spring
The litel foul hath hire wyl
On hire lud to synge.

I can see her out of my window on a branch so fine that every time she sings it bends in delight. Oh, it is such a sweet sound. It is an early morning Heron bird. . . .

And now you must wake up and leap and fly out of bed. There is a smell of coffee from downstairs and I run on to the landing and call " Mrs. Buttercup! Will you please put the breakfast in the garden." And I come back to find you dressed already and a *staggering* beauty in corduroy trousers and a flannel shirt with a cramoisie necktie! And then Richard comes up from the field with a big bright celandine in his buttonhole. And you say as we go down, " My God, there's a terrific lot to be done to-day "—but not as if you minded. While I pour out the coffee you cut up the bread, and Richard says, " I say, Jack, couldn't you make a fine thing of the house from here with the sun on it like that." And just at that moment Mrs. Buttercup hangs a strip of carpet out of an upper window which gives it the finishing touch. We are going to drive over to a sale to-day in our funny little painted cart to see if we can buy some ducks and we have to call at the station on the way back for a parcel of paper. . . .

*Knock :* " C'est la blanchisseuse, Madame. Je suis très matinale. Il fait beau, n'est-ce pas ? "

Well, it's a good thing she did come. I might have gone on for ever. . . .

Funny you should have mentioned a cow. I was *worrying madly* over a nice name for a cow in bed last night. I wanted first to call it " Chaucer " : then I thought " Edmund Spenser "—and only after I had ranged up and down for a long time did I remember that a cow was *feminine* ! ! and would kick over the pail and give you a swish in the face and then stalk off if she were so insulted.

There is a certain little white pink, striped with dark red, called " sops-in-wine." *We must grow it.*

I have also a feeling too deep for sound or foam for all kinds of *salads.*

Tuesday
March 12, 1918

L. M. has heard from Gwynne's that she is to come back
as soon as possible.   That being so, and I wishing to travel
with her, I wired you as arranged to-day.   I shall not be
able to tell *when* we start, until I hear from Cook's as to
what sort of chance we have of getting places in the Paris
train.   But, of course, I'll wire you as soon as anything
definite occurs.

I feel (as you may imagine) on the wing already—oh,
ever so on the wing!! And now just having sent your
telegram and been to the mairie with it and so on, I feel
very empty in the head, and it's hard to write.   I'll calm
down and be more fluent to-morrow.   But to really have
despatched my pigeon!   Pretty thrilling!   Don't let
Rib answer.   He'd say " *She's* all right," and do us in the
eye.   I hope Rib does post me a card.   I rather see him
tagging along the Redcliffe Road with a ladder to prop
against the pillar-box made of dead matches. . . .

By the way, I am afraid the English colour ' maroon '
was a corruption of the French *marron.*   I've just thought
of it.   However, that is no reason why it should not be
orange-tawny.   But the English maroon—I had once a
maroon sash I remember, and it was not gay.

It's such a vile day here—cold, dark, the sea almost red,
very sinister, with bursts of thunder.   And dogs are
barking in the wrong way, and doors bang in the hotel,
and all that is pale looks too white—blanched. I must get
the idiot to give me a handful of wet leaves or so to light
my fire with.   And then I must try not to pack and re-
pack my trunk for the rest of the evening (in my head, I
mean).   But you know the feeling.   Think of it !   No,
I just can't.   I wish the Channel wasn't between us.   I
am very frightened of being torpedoed.   I'd be sure to
sink, and oh, until I have been potted out and grown in a
garden, I don't want to be either drowned or otherwise
finitoed.   So wear something crossed over your heart for
a good omen.   No, I can't write to-day.   My heart is

wrapped up in that telegram.  I feel almost serious, too
—anxious, you know.

Wednesday
March 13, 1918

There's such a sad widower here with four little boys,
all in black—all the family in black—as though they were
flies that had dropped into milk.  There was a tiny girl,
too, but she was not fished out again soon enough, and she
died.  They are *silly*, so *stupid* : that's what makes me
sad to see them.  Like a Dostoevsky 6th floor family to
whom this has happened.  The man can't quite make up
his mind whether his little boys can walk or if they must
be carried, so he does half and half, and sometimes during
meals he feels one of them and dashes up, his eyes rolling,—
dashes out of the *salle à manger* to get a coat or a black
shawl. . . .

I read in my *Daily Mail* to-day that the double daffodils
are out in English gardens and red wall-flowers.  I have
been to Gamel's also to-day and asked her to put in
reserve for me 1 lb. of butter.  That makes me feel
*presque là*.  The tulips are coming out here, but I shan't
dare to bring them because of the journey.

Oh God ! this pathetic widower !  One of the little
boys has just begun to make a sort of weak sick bird-piping
and to jump up and down—and he is *radiant*.  He is sure
they are well already.

To-morrow I shall hear from Cook's, I hope, and then
I'll feel more settled.  You know, I am already ' on the
wing ' and have been making up my *marvellous accounts*—
you know, pages and pages where everything is reduced
and then turned back again—and the simplest sum seems
to be thousands.

Thursday
March 14, 1918

I received your telegram this afternoon.  I had also a
letter from Cook's to-day saying that one must engage a

place a week in advance for the *rapide*. So I am sending
L. M. to Marseilles to-morrow to spy out the land, and
she will get the seats for as soon as possible. In the mean-
time I will wire you my delay. I must try *at all costs* to
get across before Easter. That means, however, that I
can't possibly leave here before the 20th at earliest, and it
may be a day or two later. It will be as soon as I can. I
shall have much more to go upon once L. M. has been to
Cook's and if possible to the Consul's. Your telegram, of
course, made me feel I must *rush* even to-night.

I was amused because it had been opened, read and
translated by these people (for it was still wet) and they
gathered in *force* to see me receive it, with their hands and
eyes all ready to be lifted proper. You see your little
Briton casting a moonlight beam upon it and saying, as
she read, " Voulez-vous me monter un thé simple à
quatre heures, s'il vous plaît ? " They were very cool
upon that. So was the tea. From a sort of ' ice to ice '
principle, I suppose.

Saturday—no Friday<br>
March 16, 1918.

Charles [Lamb's letters] came and a perfectly heavenly
letter which simply bore him on rosy wings to my bedside
—also the papers that bound him. I am going to make
him a very thick coat with a velvet collar and ten buttons
a side for the journey. For I cannot resist such a companion across France.

Your letter has made my coming *real again*. It keeps
flashing in and out, now light, now dark, like a revolving
lighthouse (not your letter—my coming). Sometimes I
do see—but sometimes there's nought but wavy dark.

L. M. is gone. A great mistral is roaring. It's a
*brutal* day, and my room is only just done, 4 p.m., and I
spent the night hunting and hallooing after a flea. I saw
it once—a pox on it !—sitting on the edge of my navel and
looking into that organ through a telescope of its front

legs as though it were an explorer on the crater of an extinct volcano. But when *I* hopped, it hopped and beat me. Now it is still roaring in this room somewhere. It was a very wild savage specimen of a monster—the size of a large China tea-leaf—and tore mouthfuls out of me while I slept. I shall hang out a little sign to-night: " No butter, no margarine, no meat." But I'm not hopeful.

*The Sunday Evening Telegram,* which was Lamb's under-vest as it were, gave me a Great Shock. In this little time, and even with *The Paris Daily Mail* occasionally, I had almost forgotten that appalling abyss of vulgarity which does exist. I had to ring for a fork and have it took away. Did you read Lamb on Rousseau ?

So you have got Thomas Wyatt. Well—I suppose that is quite natural. The poem I meant begins

> They flee from me who sometimes did me seek
> With naked foot stalking within my chamber. . . .

and what especially caught me was the second verse which I can't now read calmly. It's marvellous, I think.[1] I could say why, but I must take this to the post before the wind blows *too* loud and *too* cold.

[1] The first two verses of this beautiful poem are :

> They flee from me that sometime did me seek,
>   With naked foot stalking within my chamber :
> Once have I seen them gentle, tame and meek,
>   That now are wild, and do not once remember
>   That sometime they have put themselves in danger
> To take bread at my hand ; and now they range
> Busily seeking in continual change.
>
> Thanked be fortune, it hath been otherwise
>   Twenty times better ; but once especial—
> In thin array, after a pleasant guise,
>   When her loose gown did from her shoulders fall,
>   And she me caught in her arms long and small,
> And therewithal so sweetly did me kiss
> And softly said, ' *Dear Heart, how like you this ?* '

*To Lady Ottoline Morrell*                     March 1918

I have taken this tiny piece of paper in the slender hope that I may still be able to hide behind it and try (ah ! try) to explain my inexplicable silence without falling into too dread a panick at sight of your stern looks of anger and dismay. . . .

Would to God I were *not* this fickle, faithless, intolerable, devilishly uncomfortable creature whom you must, a thousand times, have whistled down the wind !

But Lady ! Pity her—Alas—poor soul ! Katherine is curst !

All goes well. She makes merry. She delights in sweet talk and laughter. She runs in the field with her darling companions filling their wicker arks and hers with a thousand pretties. She hugs the ' black but beautiful ' fire with her dearest and is not last in gossip of those who are not there. And then, quite suddenly, without a wing-shadow of warning, without even the little moment in which to tie up the door knocker with a white kid glove or a chaste crape bow, she is shut up in her dark house, and the blinds are pulled down and even the postman who hangs upon the door bell might hang there like fruit, my soul, till the door rot—she could not answer him.

The real, tragic part of the affair is that what happens to her while she is so wickedly *out* yet dreadfully *in* she cannot tell or explain. And though her enemies may see her at those times dressed in a little snake weskit and supping off toads' livers with fiends wild and slee, she dares sometimes to dream that her friends (can she *hope* for friends—accursed one ?) will perhaps be kinder, and even beckon her to her stool by the chimney corner—and even hand her the custard cup of Hot Purl or Dogs Nose that was her share aforetime—

A curse on my pen ! It twing-twangs away but my heart is heavy. Why aren't I true as steel—firm as rock ? I am—I am—but in my way, Ottoline—in my way. And yes I agree. It is no end of a rum way—

I wish you were *here*. Dark England is so far and this room smells spicy and sweet from the carnations—pink and red and wonderful yellow. The hyacinths, in a big jar are put on the window sill for the night for my little maid says they give you not only sore throats but *dreams* as well! It is very quiet. I can just hear the sea breathe —a fine warm night after a hot day.

Spring, this year, is so beautiful, that watching it unfold one is filled with a sort of anguish. Why—O Lord, why? I have spent days just walking about or sitting on a stone in the sun and listening to the bees in the almond trees and the wild pear bushes and coming home in the evening with rosemary on my fingers and wild thyme on my toes—tired out with the loveliness of the world.

It has made the War so awfully real, and not only the war—Ah, Ottoline—it has made me realise so deeply and finally the *corruption* of the world. I have such a horror of the present day men and women that I mean never to go among them again. They are thieves, spies, janglours all—and the only possible life is remote—remote—with books—with *all* the poets and a large garden full of flowers and fruits—*And* a cow (kept for *butter only* !).

What have you been reading lately? Shelley? Have you read *The Question* lately?

> I dreamed that as I wandered by the way
> Bare winter suddenly was changed to spring.

Oh, do read it—this moment—it's so marvellous—

Why aren't I talking to you instead of writing. I shall come back to dark England soon. It's a trouble you know to have *two* Souths of France, as I have. But a sweet trouble—and I'd not be without it.

No, there's nobody to talk to. I have written a great deal. I think the Woolves must have eaten *The Aloe* root and branch or made jam of it.[1]

---

[1] *The Aloe* was the name of the original version of *Prelude*.

*To J. M. Murry*      At the Café Noailles, Marseilles,
                       Thursday, March 21, 1918.

The train goes to-night at 7.5.

Tea, orange-flower water, fever, a pain in my stomach, tablettes hypnotiques (" ne pas dépasser huit tablettes dans les 24 heures "), sun, dust, a great coloured—a dreaming swaying balloon of balloons out side—yellow, red orange, purple. (A little boy has just had it bought for him and he's terrified of it. He thinks it means to carry him away. What's the good of being cross with him ? But she *is* cross. She shakes him and drags him along.)

L. M. has lost all her luggage, but *all*, and has had to buy it all over again with a rucksack to put it in. She can't think how it disappeared. " Will you see about it at Cook's for me *and* write to the hotel and explain ? " I've done that. But she is good otherwise, quieter now that she is *en voyage*, and she has bought, oh, such *good* figs.

I feel so ill—such a belly ache and a back ache and a head ache. The tablettes hypnotiques cost 7.50. What do you think of that ? But they are the same things that good old Doctor Martin gave Mother to give me. That being the case, I bought them, just as Mother would have, and felt a *mysterious well-being* all through me as I swallowed one. I couldn't have gone off to-night if I had not bought them. I should have had to go to an hotel and lie there.

Cook's seemed to take a perfect joy in giving me the £5, and long beams of light came from my fingers as I took it and tucked it away.

It is so hot, so very, very hot. One feels as though some fiend had seized one by the hair and then peppered one all over with dust and sand. (Rotten sentence !)

I had an omelette for lunch—2 francs—and then thought some cauliflower, because it was only 20 c. and very harmless. So I had that and then some stewed fruit. God ! The cauliflower was 2 francs instead ! And you can buy whole ones at Bandol for 35 centimes ! Can you see my

face ? And L. M. comforting me : " It's not as if it is
for every day but only for one day."

Paris to-morrow, and then the offensive at the Consul's.
Shall I arrive before this letter ? And will Rib make
fringe papers of it under my very eyes—what he will call
" les petits frissons " ? Or does it mean I am going to be
torpedoed and that's why I keep on writing ? Oh, I *hope*
not. I am very frightened of the journey on the sea,
because my wings are so sinkable.

(Deux citronades—deux ! That gives you the day.)

This place seems to me *infected*. I mean in the fire and
brimstone way. It ought to be destroyed and all the
people in it. It is a filthy place. And the actor next to
me, who is holding out the promise of a part to a poor little
woman *while* he eats her sweets and drinks her chocolate—
on him I would let fall the biggest brimstone of all.

God help us !

[On the same day that Katherine Mansfield arrived in
Paris, very dangerously ill, the long-range bombardment
of the city began, and all civilian traffic was suspended.
She did not reach London until April 11th, three weeks
later. Her letters during this period of illness and
anxiety are too painful and intimate to be published.]

> Friday night
> Select Hotel, Place de la Sorbonne,
> Paris, March 22, 1918

You know, somehow I couldn't altogether believe that I
*would* be home on Sunday. . . . It is not the worst that
has happened. That would have been to be tied up in
Bandol till May. I think, from the manner of the man at
the Military Permit Office to-day, that there is no doubt
the 19 Bedford Square people will give me a permit. The
only trouble is the time it takes and the horrible worry it
entails here with the police. For Paris is guarded against
strangers with hoops of steel. However, all can be
arranged. And having written and sent my doctor's

chit to No. 19 and gone to the Commissaire for permission to remain here and permission to depart as early as possible, I must just see it through.

This has been a *bad* day—looking for a hotel all day— with " Do let us take a taxi, Katie ! " and strange desires on M. L.'s part to go to hotels at about £1,000 a bed and £500 petit déjeuner. Finally, late this afternoon I was passing along the Boulevard St. Michel and saw this, at the end, next door to the Sorbonne. It is very quiet— trees outside, you know, and an extremely pleasant chiming clock on the Sorbonne *même*. Also next door there is the best looking bookshop I have ever seen—the best set out, with exquisite printing on all the window cards and so on. The hotel seems just what is wanted. Six francs for my room with déjeuner—a big square room with 2 windows, a writing table, waste-paper basket, two arm chairs, de l'eau courante, a low wooden bed with a head piece of two lions facing each other, but separated for ever, kept apart for eternity by a vase of *tender flowers*. There is also a white clock with three towers. It stands at six. But this is a fine room to work in. Immediately I came in I *felt* it and took it.

The people are quiet and simple, too, and the maid is pretty. The two armchairs, I have just observed, are very like pug-dogs, but that can't be helped.

Very well, until they let me come home I shall stay here and write. All the back of my mind is *numbed*. The fact that this *can* happen seems to me so dreadful. . . .

Saturday
March 23, 1918

It is simply horrible, but it can't be helped and I must just go on, trusting that they will finally let me through. . . . I have written to Bedford Square, applied at the Police for permission to return and now there is nothing to do but wait.

This place is in a queer frame of mind. I came out of

the restaurant last night into *plein noir*—all the cafés shut, all the houses. Couldn't understand it. Looked up and saw a very lovely aeroplane with blue lights ("couleur d'espoir," said an old man, pointing to it) and at the door of the hotel was met by the manager and made to descend to the *caves*. There had been an *alerte*. About 50 people came, and there we stayed more than long enough. It was a cold place and I was tired. At eight this morning as I lay in bed—bang! whizz!—off they went again. I washed and dressed and just had time to get downstairs before the cannons started. Well, that *alerte n'est pas encore finie*. It's now 3.45! Most of the shops are shut —all the post offices—the shops that are not quite have a hole in the shutters, and you put your arms over your head and *dive* through. The *curse* is the post office, as I have to register my letter to Bedford Square, and now I've lost a whole day. I have gone out, between the showers, to the police and fixed all *that* up, thank goodness—and now, as soon as I can post this letter, there will be rien à faire qu'attendre. C'est joliment assez!

I look out at the lovely day and think: I might have been at Havre by now. . . . This *waste* of life here. Why should the Lord treat us so. It's not fair.

[K. M. did not arrive in London until April 11th.]

*To Mrs. Virginia Woolf*                     Tuesday
47 Redcliffe Road, S.W.
Early May, 1918

I have been 'kept in' ever since the sunset I spent with you last week. And I thought you were leaving for Asheham sooner. That was why, missing one day, I did not send the drawings the next.[1] I gave Murry the notices to have printed for me and I thought as they were going to adorn picture galleries it would be a good idea to

---

[1] J. D. Fergusson's designs for the cover of *Prelude*, which appear on certain rare copies of the first edition.

have the pictures on 'em. They ought to be ready by
to-morrow. He will send you some, together with the
blocks. *Your* notice looks awfully nice.

I hope to go away to-morrow. Curse! I feel damned
ill in body these last few days. " My wings are cut and
I *can*-not fly I *can*-not fly I *can*-not fly."

But Virginia dear—how I enjoyed my day with you ;
it's such a lovely memory. I shall think of you a great
deal while I am away—and then I must look out for your
Tchehov article.

Well, I was going to end off at the end of this page—
but before I do I want to tell you that I re-read *The Mark
on the Wall* yesterday and liked it tre-*mend*ously. So
there !

I hope Asheham is lovely.


*To Lady Ottoline Morrell*                          Sunday
                                               May 12, 1918

I am so sorry, we cannot come to Garsington. I am
leaving London again on Friday for—I don't know in the
least how long—and Murry is tied by every leg to his office
stool. The country must be divine. I am going to *Looe*
which is full of pigs and bluebells, cabbages and butterflies
and fishermen's orange shirts flung out to dry on pink
apricot trees. It sounds un printemps bien solide !

Life feels to me so full at present—simply *charged* with
marvellous exciting things. Is it the spring that won't
be denied even at my age ?

Yes, I know that God is a monster and there are moments
when one *realises* the war, but there *are* other moments
when one rebels in spite of oneself and then—the flood-
gates are open and one is swept away on this heavenly tide.
Do you feel that—or do you think I'm *too* heartless ?
But what is to be done ? How can one remain *calm* when
even the barrel organ seems to put forth new leaves and
buds and laburnum is in full flower on the Redcliffe Road.
It is all—as M. would say—*too difficult*.

*To the Hon. Dorothy Brett*

Sunday
May 12, 1918

If you are passing through on your way to Scotland don't forget to let me know. I am not going to Looe until the end of this week. . . .

Hurrah! it's begun to hail. Vive le joli Printemps! Murry is lying down upon the shell shaped 1840 sofa reading a book. He is wearing a mauve shirt and pinkish socks, and above his head on the black marble mantelpiece there is a bowl of dying lilacs.

I saw Virginia on Thursday. She was very nice. She's the only one of them I shall ever see, but she *does* take the writing business seriously and she *is* honest about it and thrilled by it. One can't ask more. My poor dear *Prelude* is still piping away in their little cage and not out yet. I read some pages of it and scarcely knew it again, it all seems so once upon a time. But I am having some notices printed and they say it will be ready by June. And won't the "Intellectuals" just hate it. They'll think it's a New Primer for Infant Readers. Let 'em.

Curse this letter writing. If only we were together. I've such a deal to say and this fool of a pen won't say it. *Will* it keep.

Each time I dip it into the honey pot a very exquisite little bee with a message under its wing flies out and off in the direction of Garsington. Don't frighten it away. It is a guaranteed non-stingless or anti-stinging bee.

Now God in His Infinite Wisdom hath made the sky blue again.

Oh dear, oh dear—people are vile but Life *is* thrilling— There is a man who plays the flute in this street on these faint evenings. . . . Well—Well—

*To J. M. Murry*

Friday
Looe, Cornwall
May 17, 1918

I have been sitting in a big armchair by the *three* open windows of my room wondering how I shall group or

164

arrange events so that I may present them to you more or
less coherently. But I can't. They *won't* group or
arrange themselves. I am like a photographer in front of
ever such a funny crowd whom I've orders to photograph
but who won't be still to be photographed—but get up,
change their position, slink away at the back, pop up in
front, take their hats off and on. . . . Who *is* the most
Important One ? Who *is* Front Middle Seated ?

I had a very comfortable journey. The country in the
bright morning light was simply bowed down with beauty
—heavy, weighed down with treasure. Shelley's moonlight may glittered everywhere ; the wild flowers are in
such a profusion that it's almost an agony to see them and
know that they are there. I have never seen anything
more solemn and splendid than England in May—and I
have never seen a spring with less of the *jeune fille* in it.
God ! why are you caged up there ? Why is our youth
passing while the world renews itself in its glory ?

I must confess, of course, that, standing in the middle
of the goldy fields, hanging from every tree, floating in
every little river and perched on top of every hill, there
was a Thermos flask filled with boiling coffee. I have
so often seen people in trains armed with these affairs,
*appearing* to uncork them and pretending that real steam
and real heat flows, but—but I've never believed them
until today. At Plymouth I got out and bought two
wheat-meal bigglechiks from the scrupulously clean
refreshment room (fresh hot meat and potato pasties still
for sale !) and made an excellent tea. But indeed I had
such constant recourse to the bottle that some soldiers in
the carriage could not quite believe my exquisite signs of
satisfaction were tout à fait sober. But 'twas nectar.
And, of course, we shall never be without one again.
Only think for a moment. One need never want again for
a cup of tea at one of those ' odd ' moments which always
come on journeys to us.

A. and D. were at Liskeard. A. just as I had imagined,
*bronze*-coloured with light periwinkle eyes carrying a huge

white bag bulging with *her* Thermos flask and a vest of D.'s
(I didn't find where *it* came from or how) and a box of
paints and a handful of hedge flowers and "the most
beautiful lemon." D. was awfully kind: he did everything. We featherstitched off to Looe. It was very hot
—all glowing and quiet with loud birds singing and the
blue-bells smelled like honey. The approach to Looe is
amazing, it's not English, certainly not French or German.
I must wait to describe it. The hotel buggy met us
driven by a white-haired very independent boy who drove
the horse as though it were a terribly fierce ramping white
dragon—just to impress us, you know. We drove through
lanes like great flowery loops with the sea below and huge
gulls sailing over or preening themselves upon the roof
tiles, until we came to this hotel which stands in its
garden facing the open sea. It could not be a more
enchanting position. The hotel is large, "utterly first-
class," *dreadfully expensive*. It has a glassed-in winter
garden for bad weather with long chairs, a verandah—the
garden hung between the sun and the sea. A. had taken
for me a really vast room with three windows all south;
the sun comes in first thing in the morning until 3 in the
afternoon. It is clean as a pin, gay, with a deep armchair,
a bed with two mattresses. . . . For everything (except
the cream) for four meals a day served in my room, breakfast in bed, the extra meat and so on, it is 4½ guineas.
There! I know it's dreadful. I can't possibly live here
under £5 a week alors, and I've only just four. But I
think I ought to stay here at least till I'm strong enough
to look for another, because for a cure it could not be
better.

The old servant unpacked for me, gave me hot water,
took away my hot water bottle just now on her own and
filled it. Don't you think I ought to stay here, just at
first, and get a strong girl? I know it's hugely dear, but
I feel it is right—that I will get well quicker here than
elsewhere. All is so clean and attended to. A. had
arranged everything of course and filled the room with

flowers. She has just walked across to say Goodnight.
She really *is* wonderful down here—like part of the spring,
radiant with life. It's ten o'clock. I am going to bed.
My room has all the sea spread before it. Now with the
blinds down there floats in the old, old sound, which really
makes me very sad. It makes me feel what a blind
dreadful losing and finding affair life has been just lately,
with how few golden moments, how little little rest . . .
I find it *so* hard to be ill.

10.30 Saturday morning.   In bed
May 18, 1918

Having ' slept in it ' I am convinced that this place is
what the South of France should have been—so still and
warm and bright. The early sun woke me pouring into
the room and I looked out and there were the little
fishing boats with red sails, and row boats in which the
rower *stood*—in the familiar way. Rib was wide awake.
He looks such a grub down here—poor darling—after his
long dip in filthy London.

The old woman who looks after me is about 106, nimble
and small, with the loveliest *skin*—pink rubbed over cream
—and she has blue eyes and white hair and *one tooth*, a
sort of family monument to all the 31 departed ones.
Her soft Cornish cream voice is a delight, and when she
told me " There do be a *handsome* hot bath for eë," I felt
that I had given a little bit of myself to Cornwall, after
all, and that little bit was a traveller returned. I had the
hot bath and slipped back into bed for breakfast. (I
should have brought Charles [1] rather than Dorothy.[2])

Breakfast was—porridge, a grilled mackerel—most
excellent—four bits of toast, butter, home-made winter-
crack jam, cream *ad lib* and coffee with $\frac{1}{2}$ pint hot milk—
all on a winking bright tray. So there !

I shan't get up till 12 any day, and then I shall just sit

---

[1] Charles Lamb's *Letters*.     [2] Dorothy Wordsworth's *Journal*.

in the sun and read. The Three Windows are wide
open now : one is almost *on* the sea.

This is only a note. Do you know what guelder roses
are ? Big sumptuous white clusters with a green light
upon them. We must grow them. . . .

Sunday morning
May 19, 1918

When I got up yesterday I sat in my long chair in a kind
of pleasant daze—never moved—*slept* and really did not
wake until tea when I opened Dorothy Wordsworth and
read on steadily for a long time. The air is heavenly, but
don't imagine I walk or lift anything or even move more
than I need. I can't even if I would—for the least effort
makes me cough, and coughing is such fiendish, devilish
pain that I'd lie like a mummy to avoid it. However—
the divine sea is here, the haze and brightness mingled. I
stare at that and wonder about the gulls, and wonder why
I must be ill. All the people who pass are so well, so
ruddy. They walk or run if they have a mind, or row past
in little boats. Perhaps the curse will lift one day.

This place is very good for *just now*. You see I am going
to stay in bed all day, not going to move, and all is done
for me so pleasantly by the old 'un. She came in early
and threw open my windows at the bottom, and said the
air was better than medicine—which it is—and yesterday
she patted my cushion and said I must try and gather up a
little *harn*ful of strength. I am always *astonished,amazed*
that people should be kind. It makes me want to weep.
You know. It's dreadfully upsetting. What ! Can it be
that they have a *heart* ! They are not playing a trick on
me, not ' having me on ' not ready to burst their sides at
my innocence ?

A. and D. came in last evening with an armful of those
yellow irises that grew in the Marsh near Hocking's Farm.
They had been picnicking in the woods all day among the
blue-bells and were very burnt and happy. A. must be

doing *some* kind of good work, for I can feel her state of mind—a sort of *still* radiant joy which sits in her bosom.

There pipes a blackbird, and the waves chime. Would that you were here! Yet—perhaps—better not.

Monday
May 20, 1918

Monday : a gorgeous day. I really might be *on* the sea. Certainly yesterday had a Big Black Cap on it, but here is dawning another blue day and I feel better—really better. Yesterday this *pain* was very dreadful and then I had the most trying fits of weeping. I was simply swept away by them. I think it was the fever made me so feeble and wretched. Just as I had written you another *farewell* letter A. came in with a picture for me. And she, thereupon, took charge, and soon the whole hotel seemed to be off. My bed was made, boiling bottles appeared, hot milk, a shade out of an orange bag she put on the gas, and sent for the doctor—all in the most ideal cheerful manner.

The doctor came at 11 p.m. The whole place shut up of course. He is—or appeared to be—about 19, but I am sure 19 times as intelligent as L. A wild Irish boy with curly hair and eyes which still remember what the world looked like at 9. He spent about an hour walking over the worn old battlefield with his stethoscope and saying, like Gordon, "*Wait now*." Finally decided my left lung is pleuritic again for the present and that is what gives it the pain. I must stay in bed, but I could not be in a better place. A man came down here in precisely my condition and in a month he had gained a *stone* and was a changed creature in every way.

A., poor darling, was waiting downstairs to hear the verdict. It was midnight before she left, and the manageress left me the Thermos flask full of boiling milk for the night. In fact, they are one and all amazingly kind. So here I am, in bed again, but breathing the sea and the sun and A. The baby doctor is coming again to-day. He made me feel like an old writing woman—a sort of old George Sand tossed up by the tide last night. Once I can get over this attack of pleurisy I know I shall get really well. I feel it, and I keep hearing all about the wonders in the woods and fields.

This is an appallingly *dull* little note. But you know what one feels like. My skull and crossbones effusion of yesterday I have destroyed. . . . As soon as I am well enough I am going out sailing with those fishermen that I see from the window. So different from France. Here one longs to be *on* the *sea*.

I have still got the feeling that this place is absolutely marvellous even though I haven't seen it.

P.S.—You know the last three days I was in London I had pleurisy. This doctor says I have got over the worst of the attack and have only to lie still to-day and to-morrow, and I shall feel *much better* again. I believe that.

Monday
May 20, 1918

What—of all other things—seems so hard is how we swore *not* to let each other go again . . . and then how soon . . . we were gone. Yesterday, thinking of all this in the afternoon, I wept so. I could not bear it : I thought I must come back and *die* there rather than always this living apart. But now that I am stronger to-day I feel that all may *yet* be well, and the Heron, now that I am away from London, is so clear and perfect.

I opened this letter to say A. and D. have both been here, and the doctor, too. He says I am getting on all right. I must stay in bed for the present, and I must take cod liver oil and iron mixed ! ! He is just like a student in a Tchehov book. But he promises me that as soon as my left lung calms down I can go out and drive and sit on the beach. Oh, such glorious prospecks ! A. is being perfect. I am *eating* all I see and milk 4 times a day *and* butter *and* cream. Bacon for breakfast : new laid egg-wegs. The food is excellent. . . .

But you know, *I shall always be homesick.*

Tuesday morning
May 21, 1918

I am to get up to-day, and I feel there is going to be
a letter from you. (How dangerous these glad feelings
are !)

I am incredibly better really, for all this complete rest
and food and sleep. I must have slept more than I've
been awake by a long chalk. To-morrow, the little young
larned gentleman, as the old 'un calls the doctor, says I
may go for a drive with A. and see all the butterflies and
the hedges. Oh, she brings me bright bouquets that take
the breath ! We must have our Heron soon. You have
no idea of all the treasure that still lies in England's
bosom. . . .

Queer—I can't write letters any more. No, I can't. I
have written *too* many, you know. I think it is *infernal*
that we should be apart. But we *must* not be together.
What an impasse ! Sometimes I am so bewildered,
utterly bewildered, as though I were caught in a cloud of
rushing birds.

But I understand Wordsworth, and his sister and Coleridge. They're fixed, they're true, they're calm.

And there you live, wearing yourself out in that bloody
office, wearing yourself out in your rooms. No, it's
*unbearable*.

Tuesday afternoon.   May 21, 1918
(See that ' t.' It means it is dancing.)

This afternoon came your two letters. My pen—it's
as though the ink flows through its veins again—just that.
I will stay here then for the present. It is truly ideal—
perfect room, bed, food, and all arranged for me and
served so decently and punctually, perfect attendance.
Also I think my young doctor is about the best I could
possibly get anywhere. He's absolutely our generation,
you see, tremendously keen on this business, and takes
my case so intensely that A. now feels he's the only man
who *could* have such a grasp of it. She won't let me move

or open a window without just running round to the surgery and asking. . . .

I confess I feel better to-day than I have for MONTHS and I can breathe more easily. I have been up and out in the sun for half an hour. As soon as I am well enough the doctor is going to take me driving, on his rounds. But he won't let me drive at all yet or do anything but sit in the sun. " Wait now ! " he says. " I can see the kind of woman you are. There's nothing but a pain like a knife that will put a stop to you."

This place out in the sun to-day was a miracle of beauty. The sea and the coast line remind me curiously of New Zealand, and my old servant is like an old woman down the Pelorus Sounds. (My dream N. Z. and dream old woman, of course.)

A. has just brought me oranges and caramels and smiles and such a lovely flower picture.

" My dear," she said. " The idea just came to me— sharp, like a bit in a plate, you see—This is the place for Mansfield ! " Can't you hear her ?

Don't send Lamb. But if I could have any anthology of English poetry, p. ex. *A Pageant of English Poetry*, or any other. *At your leisure. No hurry*.

I burn to review books. I shall do them well and promptly here and post the books back to you.

I'll write every day, of course, and tell you when I see more. I have only really opened my eyes wide after reading those two letters of yours.

I won't climb a hill without a permit.

Rib sends a kiss, and if you can find him some orange and white striped bathing drawers he'll be obliged.

I suppose Harrison won't take my story.[1] Wish he would.

As to the Armenian cushion—I shall be known by it. I feel I'll never go out without it. It's so dark and bright and perfect. I can see people at the Heron taking

[1] *Bliss.* It had been sent to *The English Review*, which published it

cushions into the garden and our children saying, " No, you can't take that one. It's *hers*. *He* gave it to her."

There is a haze on the sea to-day from the heat, and a slow rocking swell. The fishing boats have hung out the fine tarred nets between their two masts. They look very exquisite.

You see I am just like a plant revived by your letters. I have just had *tea*,—thin bread and butter, gooseberry jam, cream, and two fresh buns with SUGAR on top. I must ask these people where they got the tea-pot. It's very beautiful.

Wednesday<br>May 22, 1918

Another tropical morning : all the fishing boats out. I feel *extraordinarily* better, grâce à cod liver oil and iron. (You've got to take it, you know, or *I* shall stop.)

The people here, the ' management,' are awfully decent to me. I mean far more than they need be. I give a lot of trouble—well, it's true, I pay for it—but still that don't account for their thoughtfulness. Coming in every morning at about 7 to open my windows wide, and heating my last glass of milk at night, and always leaving me biscuits. The old 'un made me feel about four last night, when she said, as she put my hot water down and I was going to bed, " Come here while I unbutton eë."

A. and I have been sitting outside, she talking about the spring. She can't mention the flowers without her eyes just *cry over*, as she says. She brought me masses of pink lupins—terrifying flowers, but beautiful. This garden is so gay with real purple columbines and gillyflowers and marigolds and early roses. At night a procession passes along the coast road of fine old sailors, each with an enormous cabbage under his arm—It looks to be a sea cabbage—grown on their new allotments. They are beautiful, hale old men.

[A drawing of a boat.]

She has just come outside my window. I wish I could

draw her. She's a little beauty. See that queer kite-shaped sail ? Oh, God, how I love boats !

Everybody has a boat here. Little babies leap out of their mothers' arms into sail-boats instead of peram-bulators.

May 1918

The Old 'Un says : she has been working for this hotel these three years now. " When they get busy I go out to kitchen, but while it's quiet like, I keeps upstairs. Missus says it do be wunnerful the way I climb upstairs at my age. I'm sixty-eight gone—and my husband, he's seventy-eight. We've had eight children, but they're all away and scattered, except my youngest darter. She died when she was 25 and left a baby eight months old. So I took her and she has been my little maidy ever since then. I say sometimes she do seem the only child I ever had, the others are so away and scattered—two in Wales, two in Canada, one is a parish nurse in London, and they're all married. I have two sisters living here, they are both up and above me in years—one is 78 and one is 74, but they are *two spry maidens* with it all. Then my husband's brother—he's eighty-four, but he still works in garden and used to clean the lamps before this awful war. I've never had an illness except once : I had a fall in my garden and was under doctor in hospital for eight months. He said : ' You've hurt your kidney and it's floating, but we can't do any-thing, for there's no fat to you, and you'll not work again.' ' Well,' I told him, ' I don't know where it has floated to, but I must work. I love work. I shan't be idle till I come to churchyard (and then my old husband says I will be getting up to tend my own flowers).' And that's three years since. My darter from Canada sent me a parcel the other week—lard and currants and *some tea they'd grown themselves*. Rare beautiful flavour it had, too, so fresh and all. She's got a handsome little lad, but he can't walk. He's got infantile paralysis—like all the children get out there. . . . "

Thursday afternoon
May 23, 1918

It's a windy *fluid* day. I can't walk in it, but I have
started working—another member of the " Je ne parle
pas " family, I fondly dream—It's a devastating idea.
However, I am only, so to say at the Heads, at Pencarron
Light House, with it, yet—not even *in* Cook's Straits,
and they look par-tic-u-larly rough and choppy. . . .

It's such strange weather, not warm, with big sighing
puffs of wind, and the sea a steady glitter. At four o'clock
I got up and looked out of window. It was not dark.
Oh, so wonderful. I had forgotten such things.

The old 'un has just brought the morning post—letters
from C. and M. and W. D. I expect yours will come this
afternoon. I didn't expect it this morning. God! I
feel so hard-hearted. I don't care a button for C.'s letter
and yet—it was so charming. In fact, I only want to
*drop* all those people and *disappear* from their lives—
utterly disappear. . . .

I must get up. I am afraid there are no flowers in this
letter. I haven't any. I'm shorn of them to-day. When
I ' see ' again, I'll show you, too. I feel extraordinarily
better and stronger with no pain at all. But I can't
write you the letters I should like to, because my ' vagrant
self ' is uppermost, and you don't really know her or want
to know her.

I wonder what *is* going to happen—if the war will end
in our lives. But even if it does end, human beings will
still be as vile as ever. I think there is something in the
idea that children are born in sin, judging from the hateful
little wretches who ' play ' under my window—somehow
horrible little toads, just as evil as slum children. I
believe if they were left to themselves the strong ones
would kill the weak 'uns—torture them and jump on them
until they were flat ! Well, that's excusable in grown-up
people, but in children . . . !

Oh, people are ugly. I have such a contempt for them.
How hideous they are, and what a mess they have made of

everything! It can never be cleared up, and I haven't the least desire to take even a feather duster to it. Let it be, and let it kill them—which it *won't* do. But oh (without conceit) where are one's playfellows? Who's going to call out and say: I *want* you. Come and see what I've made? No, one must have an iron shutter over one's heart.

Now I *will* get up.

*To Lady Ottoline Morrell*                          May 24, 1918

I have been walking up and down this huge, bright, bare hotel bedroom, really, if one had looked through the 'spiritual' keyhole,—wringing my hands, quite overcome, for the *n*th time by the *horror of life*—the sense that something is almost hopelessly wrong. What might be so divine is out of tune—or the instruments are all silent and nobody is going to play again. There *is* no concert for us. Isn't there? Is it all over? Is our desire and longing and eagerness, quite all that's left? Shall we sit here for ever in this immense wretched hall—waiting for the lights to go up—which will never go up.

Heavens! the hysterical joy with which I'd greet the first faint squeakings of a tuning up—the lovely relief with which one would lean back and give oneself up and up to it. But no—I don't hear a sound.

It's all very well to say like Koteliansky: "I am dead," but what the devil is the good of that with all this *fury* of living burning away in my bosom—with God knows nothing to feed it or fan it—just burning away.

But the ugliness—the ugliness of life—the intolerable corruption of it all—How is it to be borne? To-day for the first time since I arrived, I went for a walk. Anne Rice has been telling me of the beauty of the Spring— all the hedges one great flower—of the beauty of these little 'solid' white houses set in their blazing gardens— and the lovely hale old fishermen. But—the sea stank— great grey crabs scuttled over the rocks—all the little

private paths and nooks had been fouled by human cattle
—there were rags of newspaper in the hedges—the village
is paved with *concrete* and as you pass the " tiny solid white
houses " a female voice yells : " You stop it or I'll lay a
rope end across eë."

And then—*hotels*, you know, strange hotels ! The
horror of them—The grimace for service rendered, the
perpetual " Would you please bring up my letters as soon
as the post arrives ? "—another *strange bed*, and the
mysterious people whom one always passes going to or
coming from the lavatory. . . .

Oh—how I *loathe* hotels. I know I shall die in one. I
shall stand in front of a *crochet dressing table cover*, pick up a
long invisible hairpin left by the last ' lady ' and die with
disgust. It's almost funny—loving as I do, loving
passionately, beautiful rooms, the shape of furniture,
colours, quiet, I find myself wandering eternally in rooms
papered with birds, chrysanthemums in urns and bunches
of ribbons, and furnished with fumed oak and lace curtains—
and that *glare* from the windows—that dreadful gape which
reaches to every corner—that sense of nowhere to hide !

But all that is only part of the other, greater curse which
is upon life—the curse of *loneliness*—I am quite certain
that it is all wrong to live isolated and shut away as we do—
never exchanging and renewing and giving AND receiving
—There ought to be something fine and *gay* that we
tossed about among us—and kept ever so thrillingly in the
air, as it were, and never let fall—a *spirit*. But where is it,
and who wants it ? . . . I am in despair. In such despair,
that sometimes I begin weeping like a green girl—but that
is no use, either. My tiny world tinkles : " Of course,
with all that sea and air outside and all that butter, milk,
and cream *in* you'll be as fit as a fiddle in no time."

Which is altogether too simple.

Write to me—will you ? I shall be here another week
at any rate. Then I must wander somewhere else I think.
This place is grotesquely expensive, too. But *write* to me
—if you can.

*To J. M. Murry*

Saturday morning<br>May 25, 1918

Yesterday on my way to the post I met Pagello and went off with him to the surgery. Such a queer place, so absolutely ' Russian '—I mean as Tchehov has described. It will walk into a story one day. It was warm windy weather, I made a tour of the town. I pretend to A. I like it, and I do in so far that it satisfies my literary sense. It is very compact—ugly—the side streets are concreted over. There is a sense of black railings, and out of that *dear* little white house with the flowers comes a female voice : " You stop thaät or I lay a rope across eë." Which is just what I expect of Cornwall. But I'll stay, I am determined to stay here for the present, until the end of June at any rate. And then I shall only go off to some other country place, perhaps—*certainly* not to London.

I shan't stay at this hotel after my fortnight is up. A. and I are going to look for two rooms. For many reasons. This place is perfect when you are ill, but it's frightfully *bald* when you are not. It's too ladylike for me, too, and I'm not a lady. And I want a sitting room. I can't work, can't concentrate in this bedroom. It's too big and too glaring. Also that great blue gape at the windows don't mean anything to me. Perhaps it would if I looked at it from my cottage door. But A. says (she agrees with me) there are excellent rooms to be had with women who cook extremely well, etc. I shall go looking this next week. This place has been perfect for its purpose, but j'en ai assez. I want to WORK and it's too hard here. Each time I light a cigarette I feel a refined shudder come over this hotel. I will find something first chop, sunny, with a view over the snug little town as well as the sea. It would be worth staring at—this little town. . . .

Sunday<br>May 26, 1918

It's true the melancholy fit is on me, at present. But, as I told you in the S. of F. (seemed always to be telling

poor you) that to be alone (*i.e.*, without you) and to be
utterly homeless, just uprooted, as it were, and tossed about
on any old strange tide, is utterly horrible to me and always
will be, even though I were twelve stone and a prize-
fighter—though I own my horror would be a bit ridiculous
then. However, I fully, freely acknowledge that it's *got
to be* for the present and my only salvation lies in drowning
my melancholy fit in a flood of work.

But what about A. ? you ask. Oh, yes, of course I see
A. occasionally, as much as both of us want to, for an hour
at a time perhaps ; but you know it's all on the *awfully
jolly* surface. I can't really talk to A. at all. Still, it's
nice to have her here and she's a distraction and " too kind
for words. . . . "

Passons oultre.

It's Sunday. Cornwall in black with black thread gloves
promenades on the edge of the sea : little tin bells ring and
the Midday Joint is in the air. Pas de soleil. Low tide
and the sea sounds to have got up very late and not found
its voice yet.

Damned queer thing. I have dreamed for two nights
in succession of the name of a street *rue Maidoc*. " Not
rue Medoc," says Chummie, " but rue Maidoc." There is
an exhibition of pictures there and Chummie is showing 3
—" two landscapes and a portrait by Leslie H. Beau-
champ." We idled down the street afterwards arm in arm.
It was very hot. He fanned himself with the catalogue.
And he kept saying, " Look, dear," and then we stopped,
as one person, and looked for about 100 years, and then
went on again. I woke and heard the sea sounding in the
dark, and my little watch raced round and round, and the
watch was like a symbol of infinite existence. . . .

There is a circulating library here. Not quite bare.
It's got *In a German Pension* and *Eve's Ransom* by Gissing.
I took out the second yesterday. Although, like all poor
Gissing's, it's written with cold wet feet under a wet
umbrella, I do feel that if his feet had been dry and the
umbrella furled, it would have been extremely good. As

it is, the woman of the book is quite a little creation. The whole is badly put together, and there is so much that is entirely irrelevant. He's very clumsy, very stiff, and, alas, poor wretch! almost all his ' richness ' is eaten up by fogs, catarrh, Gower Street, landladies with a suspicious eye, wet doorsteps, Euston Station. He must have had an infernal time.

I'll send you back D. W.'s *Journal* in a day or two, just in case you have a moment to glance into them—to refresh yourself with the sight of W. sticking peas and D. lying in the orchard with the linnets fluttering round her. Oh, they *did* have a good life.

Well, I'm going to work now till lunch.

P.S.—Please don't forget to tell me the moment Harrison sends my story [*Bliss*] back. Back it will come, of course. But I want to know *at once*.

> Monday
> May 27, 1918

You see, I was in the S. of F. from December till April. What was it like on the whole ? Just HELL. As you know it nearly killed me. Then I came back to rest with you. All my longing, all my desires, all my dreams and hopes had been just to be with you, and—to come back to my home. Bien! I came. Heard how ill I was, scarcely seem to have seen you, except through a mist of anxiety, felt that *all* your idea was for me to get away into the country again. Well, I understood that. Although, please try to realise the appalling blow it was to me to uproot again—and so soon, with hardly a word spoken. Please do try to realise that. Plus the knowledge that I was more ill than I'd thought, and that all my precious ' privacy,' my love of ' self-contained ' life, doing all for myself in my own way . . . was to be taken away from me, was ' bad ' for me, enfin.

However, it was only for a month or six weeks that I was to be alone. Then you came down for your holiday and we went back together. I arrived, and found I was to be here (without a word explaining why this change had been) at *least* 4 months, until the *late* autumn. No word of your coming, no word of anything else. It was a sort of ultimate *comble*. It knocked me back onto my own lonely self. I was in despair, as you know, and I saw Life quite differently. I felt that I could endure no more, and I fell into the dark hollow which waits for me always—the old one—and I wrote from there. . . .

Now about the Elephant.[1] Get it if you can, and we will make it a Singing Elephant with all our hearts.

As I wired you this morning, I am not going to leave this hotel after all. I cannot explain to another landlady that my lungs are weak. Also the fag of wondering what I shall order to eat would mean I'd order nothing. Here, it comes, and one eats it, and it's over. And they know me here, now, and are more than kind to me. The old un,' Mrs. Honey, is ' pure Heron.' Bless her! I can always hear her and my gran'ma talking as they put the linen away. So here I shall remain. . . . You must try to come here, as we did once arrange, even for a week, and we'll have a sail-boat and go " whiffing for pollocks." I am working hard and Pagello says I have made remarkable progress.

Tuesday
May 28, 1918

It's windy this morning and sunny and there's such a loud noise of gunfire : it sounds like a bombardment : the house is shaking.

I wrote a great deal yesterday. I'm fairly out at sea with my new story. The same difficulties plague me as they did before, but it certainly ' goes.' Will you please ask F. for " Je ne parle pas " and put it with my other MSS. ? He don't want to read it. Why should he ?

[1] The name given to a singularly tall grey house in Hampstead, which we took in July 1918.

God ! I do want to know so much that I can't know yet. About the Elephant, about your flat. How soon is it to be taken over ? What will happen to our things ? How can I wait to hear all this ? If you are not too tired, try to tell me all, won't you ?

I sat up in bed last night writing till after one o'clock. This new story has taken possession, and now, of course, I can't go out without my notebook and I lean against rocks and stones taking notes. I expect I shall be arrested in the course of a day or two. I think these people have an idea that darling A. and I are spies. And you should have heard the postmistress yesterday asking if the word was *Elephant*.

It's a good thing you are not here. I'd be a perfect plague. But are these feelings the result of a hot bath, a big pink rose I'm wearing, a grenade (the strongest cigarette—heavy-weight Spanish champion—I've ever smoked) and a sunny wind ? For in the course of this letter I've got up and now I'm wearing Feltie and just off to the post.

Wednesday
May 29, 1918

This is absolute Heronian weather, and I think our Heron must be somewhere near here, because it is so amazingly open and healthy. And now that the black monkeys have folded up their little tents (I see *and* hear them) I am beginning to feel like A. does about this place. Also, now that I *can* walk and look over the walls. . . . Forty-nine sailing boats sailed ' into the roads ' yesterday. I counted them for you. There they all were skimming about. . . . This place is 4 miles from Polperro, 10 from Fowey. You can go across country to Fowey in a jingle. A. and I mean to do it one day.

I have heard from V—— who dislikes the drawings very much. So does L. Well, it's their press. I suppose they'd better not use them. Just a plain blue cover with " Prelude " on it. Don't bother to type

*Carnation.* Let it be. You've enough to do. I am, of course, in heaven that you liked it, cos I did too. And you ' understood.' I meant it to be ' delicate '—just that.

A. is painting me and old Rib. Rib, of course, is violently flattered and keeps flattening down his fringe at the thought. He is getting very brown. He is going to bring a tame shrimp HOME, please, he says.

*To Mrs. Virginia Woolf*                         May 29, 1918

It's of course for you and Leonard to use 'em or not, and as you don't like 'em—why there's an end on't. But the blue paper with just the title on it would be nice : I hope you use that. Six or seven orders—what extreme minginess ! I blush at the idea. I shall have to come back and persuade you and L. to let me sell it on a barrow —customers to bring their own wrappings. I thought of you at Asheham : I am glad it was so lovely. Don't forget that you have asked us for later—will you ?

I really don't know anything about this place. While the Lord continues allowing his sun to shine in this superb fashion—its heavenly—heavenly. To my drunk eyes it seems all Cornwall, not at all Devonshire—far better than the South of France—*the* place for great artists like ourselves to wander in—and so on. But I'm frankly not sober. The tide comes in very big and brimming, goes out leaving heavy, weedy rocks and pools and little creeks and long sands and winkles. There are tiny islands covered with thick forest, valleys dipping down to the sea with marshes yellow with kingcups and irises. Then there is the little town, built on both banks of a deep river and joined by an extremely ' paintable ' bridge. And sea-gulls, and flowers—and *so on*. (I wish I didn't keep saying and *so on*. I loathe the phrase.) Well—Virginia if you would ask the Belgians to post me 4 packets of those Blue cigarettes, cut my throat I will send you a postal order by return.

I wish I could send you something in this letter. . . . There's that tiny little horse shoe I found yesterday—it

would go into an envelope. No, you'd think it absurd—
No, I've nothing. Oh, did I say before how very greatly
we enjoyed your Tchehov review ?

*To J. M. Murry*                                    Friday
                                               May 31, 1918

No post. Bin and gone. I understand *why* there's
none, all right. I got your Wednesday letter yesterday,
see ? But all the same.... Oh, it is so *hot*, too. Why
aren't you here ? Why didn't you arrive last night, so
that we could have a pig-nig to-day. These are not real
complaints, you understand, only laments for the impossible. A. and I are going off for the day, she with her
sketch book and I with my writing book—and our *flasks*
and sangwiches. She is going to bathe. The people here
even are bouleversé by the weather and lovely day.
[A long wavy line across the page.]
That is one immense wave which lifted me right up into
the sun and down again. Mrs. Honey brought me a letter
after all ! And the moment when I got it and saw your
black writing on the blue—oh dear, does anyone know the
meaning of rapture but me ?
I'll send the first long chapitre of my story this week.
Your letter has so *fired* me that I know I'll write like billy-o
to-day.
I must answer your ' news.' I still sigh for a Definite
Elephant. They ought to let you know this week.
Do please send me Frank Harris's letter. I like him for
that. But then I don't *hate* him at all. Now that I see
all round him, he astonishes me, and I like and pity him—
and he does enormously feed one's literary appetite.
How he beats that man in *Raw Youth*, par exemple, and
yet what a man he'd be in that espèce de livre !
I am getting so dreadfully young—a sort of Pelorus
Sound Wig. Rib and I seem about the same age again.
He is wearing my coral necklace to-day.
There is my bath coming. Mrs. Honey says I must get up.

Saturday
June 1, 1918

It is another day the spit of yesterday. I think it is the end of the world—but not a Sullivan end. No, the planet will fry rather than grow cold. . . . Nine o'clock. The room is bathed in sun. I've just had bregglechick and I am *so hot* that I pine for a *cold shower*. Is it hot like this in London?

Yesterday A. and I took our lunch and tea and went off for the day. We found an ideal beach, really ideal. And the flowers on the way! Every blade, every twig has come into flower. Right down by the sea there are the foxgloves, sea pinks, dog daisies—I even found violets—and yellow irises every where. It was really almost too hot—exhausting. I crawled into a cavern and lived there a long time. Then I went among the deep sea pools and watched the anemones and the frilled seaweed, and a limpet family on the march! By lunch time our sang-wiches were frizzling, and A. kept wishing her Thermos flask had a great platter of ice cream in it, *my dear*!

We had intended to work and we tried to, but it wasn't possible. This is the most astounding place. Where we were was absolutely deserted—it might have been an island—and just behind us there were great woods and fields and may hedges. I got fearfully burned and tired, too. I simply had to lie down with a stone for a pillow at one point; but in the cool of the evening when we came home I felt refreshed again. Only I wanted to come back to a cottage instead of a big hotel. It was still light, pale, wonderful at ten o'clock last night and *very* warm.

This heat—in this place, you see, the water and the country—is absolutely the ideal weather, I think. And, as A. says, that terrible dust you get down South isn't here. All is *intensely* clean, dazzling, the seagulls glitter even when you are close to them down at the ferry, and all the old men are clean and fine as sailors are.

A. has just been here to ask me to go whiffing all day. But I can't stand another of those days just yet. I am sitting on the balcony all day now under my parachute, feeling tre-mendously well and fit and eating away and getting browner and browner—and I want to ' work ' to-day. She of course says : " If you've got your health and you feel good, to Hell with art ! " But, elle est plus simple et rude que moi.

What about this Billingsgate trial ? Is it going to topsy-turvy England into the sea ? What ultimate Cinema is this ? It is very nauseating. I feel great sympathy for Maud Allan. But I have not seen much of the trial—only *Daily News* without tears.

P.S.—This letter is badly written and expressed : it's the dancing light. Forgive it.

P.P.S.—4.30. I've not moved from my balcony all day. If you could see the water, half green, half a tender violet, and just moving. It is unbelievably exquisite.

June, 1918

This weather can't go on. It will stop just before you come. That's my awful fear. I've never *never* known anything like it. And then I feel so well—eat, walk— went out to sea yesterday with an aged boy in a blue jersey and a straw hat with some sea pinks round the crown. His name was Pearrrrrn. Rib, of course, when I got home started walking on his hands and bursting with laughter. " What's the matter, Ribni ? " " Your nose is peeling, now," said he. It's true. I am as brown as a half-caste. I do wish the Elephant would take our bun that we're offering it so awfully anxiously, don't you ? Why does it go on waving its trunk in the air ? Blessings on thee, my beast. Do let us go for a ride on you,—I with what the old 'un calls my red silk *parachute* hiding us both from the world.

If you do come down here and I do meet you at the station I think the Heavens will open. I don't want to think about it. No, I hide the thought away, and just

occasionally open the door a tiny bit, just enough to let
a beam of light out. But oh, even *that's* so blinding.
You see, we'll go for picnics. Yesterday, I saw you,
suddenly, lying on the grass and basking. And then I saw
us sitting together on the rocks here with our feet in a pool
—or perhaps two pools.

I'll do Gus Bofa and Paul Margueritte on Sunday and
post them on Monday. I can't go out on Sundays
because I haven't a Prayer Book and Hymn Book to carry.
The people would stone me.

Did I tell you they are building a lugger here ? To the
side of the bridge ? To be launched in July. The
carpenter and the carpenter's boy think I am so funny, that
now when they see " 'tis herr again," they become
comedians and pretend to pour tar on each other's heads
or to swallow immense long nails and then take them out
of their ears. You know the sort of thing. But this
boat-building is always a sort of *profession d'amour* for me.
It's our boat, and I am just keeping an eye on the workmen
until the King comes down in a jersey and he and the
Queen and Ribni the Infanta sail away and away with a
silk carpet for a sail.

There is a saw mill here, too, which maketh a pleasant
noise.

I hope I see Anne to-day, for last night, after I came in,
I wrote 4 of those " Poems " for our book. I rediscovered
the form and the style, I think. They are not in verse,
nor in vers libre. I can't do these things. They are in
prose.

> (1) To a Butterfly.
> (2) Foils.
> (3) Le Regard.
> (4) Paddlers.

You would like them. They are very light. Like Heron
feathers, so to say.

God ! God ! This sun and air. What is one to do ?
The walls of the Heron are so warm. But the pantry is
very cool, and the milk stands in a shallow pan. I went in

there just **now**. How *can* there be a War Office and
MI7d ? [1]

I've found a little tiny horse shoe which I am going to
nail on one of our doors. Shall I send it you ? No.

Sunday<br>June 2, 1918

Voilà ! Encore un ! Il fait plus chaud que jamais, et
je suis décidée de ne pas sortir. Je reste alors sur le
balcon. . . . Avez-vous l'idée de venir ici ? Dites-moi.
Parce que, depuis votre télégramme, vaguement, chaque
soir je vous attends, et quoique je peux attendre pour
toujours, tout de même, c'est inquiétant de ne pas savoir
vos projets.

I don't know why I am writing pidgin French : perhaps
because the English in the dining-room sounds so *remote*
from any tongue of mine. It's a cursed nuisance. Since
this hotel has filled a bit, they cannot serve my repasts,
except breakfast, in my room, and I have to descend to
the common feeding ground. Dead serious—there's not
a single person there under 65 and the oldest and most
garrulous is 84 ! A more revolting, loathsome set of old
guzzlers I can't imagine. Not only with their blown-out
old bellies and clicking false teeth have they the appetites of
proud, fierce lions, but oh ! and oh ! and oh !—I'd better
not talk about them.

I sit at a table pushed up against the window, and try
not to look on or to HEAR. They'll make a good story
one of these days, but that's grim comfort. I can *smell*
them all up and down the passages now. But they are
just as bad as the Frenchies were, in the room next to mine
at Bandol. In fact, they are just exactly the same, and in
the same state of pourriture.

I know what they are like. They are exactly like blow-
flies—but exactly, in every way. They have unsettled

[1] The Department of Military Intelligence in which I was serving.

me so.   It is so infinitely hard for me to go among them,
don't you know ? and of course, being the particular kind of
silly that I am I cannot help but listen and look.   Instead
of splendidly ignoring them, I simply quiver with horror.

Late last evening I went off to the village to look for
(vain quest) an orange or an apple or any kind of fruit.
Neither are there any cigarettes except 2/1 for 25.   Will
you send me a few cigarettes or (better) ask L. M. to get
another box of those Grenades ?

No, I am not what you call a good girl to-day.   I am
sad.   I have seen another *horror* this feed time, and I can't
quite *fly*, after it, but have to hang on a flower and try to
forget it before my wings will spread again.

Monday evening
June 3, 1918

This is just a line because I feel lonely and want to talk.
It is ' close on dinner ' as Mrs. H. says, so I'll soon have to
sit among the fuzzies again.   I've solved the tea problem,
which I really could not stick (tea en famille : one big
pot).   I give my flask to the cook and then she pours mine
in and leaves it for me to descend for.   I feel awfully like
a spider going down for a fly and tearing off to eat in
solitude.   But it is a great idea.   I could not see those
awful old claws among the bread and butter again.   Why
do I *mind* uglies so ?   Mrs. H.—funnily enough—seems
quite to understand that I do, and talks as though she
' tended ' them in their cages.   Well, I wish she did.   My
bregglechick in bed has become a kind of gay feast—
without 'em.   I saw A. to-day who wanted me to go out,
but no, I've spent the day up here resting in my chair and
looking at the sea which has got quite rough.   Now you
can hear the boats *creaking* in the roads and the waves
sound eager.

Oh God !   Suddenly it sweeps over me again.   We are
writers !   You are a poet and I write stories.   But how
this knowledge makes me *ache* for us to be together.

I wonder what it meant—your telling me the story of

Strawberry Heart.[1] For me it was something like this. We lay down together and it grew dark, and while we were there we wandered away to that country you told me about. But curiously there were moments when this wandering was almost intolerably painful to me. I wanted to implore you to stop. I felt I'd *faint* if you went on, and you went on and on. I lost absolutely all sense of time and place until it was like dying, like the years one must go through before one dies. . . . And then quite suddenly the front door came back, and there stood an old sniggering crone with long, long grey curls, curls past her waist, fumbling at the keyhole with a bunch of keys and come to *spy* on us.

### GONG.

Well, that's over, and I waylaid the waitress and took my coffee up here. Perhaps they think I've got a deserter sewed up in the mattress. And now it's cloudy and almost cold and all the ships have gone.

No, I'll write no more to-night. I want to pull up the tent pegs. I don't like this ground any more. *Something smells.*

Tuesday. (A New Nib.) If you could have known what an inspiration your little ' chit ' was. The post was late. I argued that I couldn't hear from you this morning, and then down this fluttered. I had been awake nearly all night, too. It was all so noisy and at 2 o'clock my French windows burst open—out popped the candle—the blinds flapped like sails. As I rushed to the rescue I thought of that Appalling Moment when Kirillov rushed at Pyotr Stepanovitch.[2] There's a big Gale blowing this morning, but it's sunny.

For some curious reason (I can't explain) this is ' over ' for me. I mean, my being here by myself. It's finished, done with. It don't interest me a pin. It's a marvellous

[1] *Cœur de Fraise*, a story by the late J. P. Toulet, which I had re-told in a letter.

[2] In Dostoevsky's *The Possessed*.

place really, an incredible place, but I've got cold to it
again. And this continual uncertainty about the
Elephant ! Not that I want it hurried. Good God, no !
But I do wish they would say Yea or Nay. I want to put
myself in it, and I'm afraid to, in case they throw me out.
By myself it's understood that I mean US with every
single one of our possessions.

Note. (*a*) Need we *rush* into stair carpets ? Foreigners
don't. C-C.'s stairs were delightful in their bones.

(*b*) Why buy a geyser ? A big sort of stock-pot with a
tap on a gas ring (like those things in Lyons) would surely
cost a deal less and do the job.

(*c*) You're not to buy things without ME, and please,
oh please, don't let L. choose ANYTHING. Her idea of
me is so utterly absurd : it's always humiliating.

" Are you disagreeable to-day ? "

No, but I feel that I am shut behind so many doors.
And I'm sad and exasperated—and the wind throws everything about. Everything is flapping, even my thoughts
and ideas.

But if we get into a quiet place—a rabbit burrow—or
creep under a giant rhubarb leaf, I'll lie still and look at
you, and you will find I am really warm and loving. . . .

P.S.—Has Harrison returned *Bliss* ? I bet £100
Massingham won't print *Carnation* : that's just ' by the
way.' I *know* he would hate my mind.

Wednesday,
June 5, 1918.

Mittwoch. Die Hitze ist zurückgekommen.
I'm much less depressed to-day. Oh God ! I *do* get
black. I simply go dark as though I were a sort of landscape, and the sun does not send one beam to me—only
immense dark rolling clouds above that I am *sure* will never
lift. It is terrible—terrible. How terrible I could only
' put into writing ' and never say in a letter. This afternoon I am going to Polperro with A. and we shall " boire

du thé sur l'herbe fraîche." She came up to see me last night. She has quite the right idea about the country and living in it. I explained to her last night what I meant by *religion*. I feel awfully like a preacher sometimes, I really have a gospel : this seemed rather to startle her.

Last night (this letter is like kalter aufschnitt, please forgive it) I read *The Well-Beloved* by Thomas Hardy. It really is *appallingly bad, simply rotten*—withered, bony and pretentious. This is very distressing. I thought it was going to be such a find and hugged it home from the library as though I were a girl of fifteen. Of course, I wouldn't say this about it to another human being but you, c'est entendu. The style is so PREPOSTEROUS, too. I've noticed that before in Hardy occasionally—a pretentious, snobbish, schoolmaster vein (Lawrence echoes it), an " all about Berkeley Square-ishness," too. And then to think, as he does, that it is the study of a temperament ! I hope to God he's ashamed of it now at any rate. You won't like me writing like this about him. But don't you know the feeling ? If a man is ' wonderful ' you want to fling up your arms and cry " Oh, do *go on* being wonderful. Don't be less wonderful." (Which is unreasonable, of course.)

This happened yesterday.

(Wig gets up from the table and is followed by old white-bearded monkey, with bruised eyes and false teeth.)

Excuse me Moddom, is thaat a New Zealand stone you are wearing ?

*W*. Yes.

*O. M*. Do you come from New Zealand, may I ask ?

*W*. Yes, I do.

*O. M*. Reely ! What part, may I enquire ?

*W*. Wellington.

*O. M*. I know Wellington. (Shows false teeth.) Do you know a Mr. Charles William Smith, a cousin of mine, who was residing there in 1869 ?

*W*. . . . .

*O. M*. But perhaaps you were not born then.

*W*. (very faintly) No, I don't think I was.
Voilà for my grey hairs !

Oh, how lovely these Chinese poems are ! [1] I shall carry
them about with me as a kind of wavy branch all day to
hide behind—a fan.

It's good, I think, that I didn't meet Massingham, who,
I am sure, will not print *Carnation*. And please don't
forget to tell me when *Bliss* comes back. I feel it is come.
That's why.

Thursday
June 6, 1918

I have just eaten a juicy, meaty orange that *hasn't* riped
among soup squares and blotting paper like the ones down
here. And they're not only food for the body, they
positively *flash* in my room, a pyramid of them, with on
either side attending, a jar of the brightest vividest
marigolds I've ever seen. (Yesterday on m'a fait cadeau
from Mr. Palliser's cliff garden of Spanish irises and
marigolds—a boatload full.)

It's *very* warm. I have a letter from you saying the
Elephant seems to want us,—as did your telegram. (God,
how I love telegrams. I could live on them, with oranges
and eggs en supplément.) But I have so much to say that
I can't begin. Let me dance my way through the
flowery mazes of your letter again—until I get to (what's
the place called in the middle of a maze, where you stand
on a little platform and look round ?) Well, I'm there
now and standing on the top.

(1) They say there are superb *sales* here. We might
jingle off to them when you're here. Chairs, par exemple,
eh ?

(2) I saw Pagello yesterday, who gave me more cod and
iron. He's satisfied with me and he says I'll always be a
Light Weight Champion. So don't expect me to be a

[1] Mr. Arthur Waley's translations.

Heavy One. Jimmy Wilde is more my size than Jack Johnson.

(3) Rib is glad you liked his letter. He was, very incommoded by a pen. He writes with a brush made of mouse's whiskers as a rule, but you can't get them while the war's on.

(4) Nice look-out for Art when Pemberton-Billing is pelted with flowers and Lord A. D. our conquering hero. I feel very sorry for poor Maud Allan.

(5) Which is a very nice age.

I am sending you some of my notebook to-day. Please let me know what you think of it. I've been keeping it since I was here. Do you think *The New Witness* might ? . . . Or am I getting a little ' fresh ' ? Here's a letter I got from V., too, which is nice. . . .

Well, yesterday, A. and I went to Polperro. It's all my I, you know, to go to places like Étaples and so on while these spots are here. Polperro is *amazing*, a bit spoilt by " artists " who have pitched garden-suburb tents in and out among the lovely little black and white and grey houses—houses that might have been built *by* sea-gulls *for* sea-gulls. But you must see this yourself. You'll *not* believe it. I didn't, and can't even now. It was a divine afternoon, foxgloves out everywhere, AND we found the most SUPERB fresh strawberries.

A. was a darling yesterday. You can imagine both of us—our excitement at finding these. We each bought a basket and had a basket put by for us to bring home *and* arranged for the carrier (for 2d.) to bring us fresh berries 3 times a week.

*Wig* (feverishly) : Will they last till the 20th of this month ?

*Strawberry Woman :* " Why, bless eë, they be just a coming on."

They are grown there in gardens overhanging the sea. A. and I took ours and ate them on the cliffs—ate a basket each (½ lb., 8d.) and then each ate and drank our propre

thé and became ' quite hysterical,' as she says.   We could
hardly move and stayed much longer than we had meant
to.   The whole afternoon in my memory is hung with
swags of strawberries.   We carried home our second
baskets (just having ' one more occasionally ') and talked
about raspberries and cherries and plums.

Looe is much more beautiful than Polperro.   Polperro
smells—like those Italian places do, and the people
(families who have been there since the Armada : that's
true) are dark, swarthy, rather slovenly creatures.   Looe
is brilliantly clean.   But it really is, you know, a place to
have in one's inward eye.   I saw H. W.'s cottage, but went
no furder.

As I wrote that I have kept up a running fire with Mrs.
Honey.   *She* says I ought to have children.   " It might
maäke eë a deal stronger, and they do be such taking little
souls."   I agreed and asked her to order me a half-dozen.
The other night her husband ' waited ' for her outside,
and she asked me to " come and look at him on the
bal-*coney*."   A fine, neat old man, walking a bit shaky.
She said, " He don't look his age, do eë ?   He wur a rare
*haandsome* lad."   There is still love between those two :
that's what attracts me to Mrs. Honey.

*To Mrs. Virginia Woolf*                              Thursday
                                                     June 6, 1918

It was extraordinarily kind in you to have heard my
prayer.   Here (if it's not stolen) is the P.O.   That is
right—isn't it ?   And now I have their address for next
time.   Admirable cigarettes !   I am very sorry to hear
about your throat.   What a very great bore for you—not
being able to smoke *or* talk.   Oh dear—what's left in this
lovely languorous weather ?   Do you sit at the window
and sip cups of wine all day ?   I hope you'll " get better
soon."   How jolly about the blue paper and Trystan
Edwards,[1] too.   Perhaps he will sail up the river to get his

[1] A sailor, who was one of the few advanced subscribers for *Prelude*.

copy in a three-masted brigantine with eleven sails. But I am afraid not.

This place is still exquisite. I wish I felt more of a little lion than I do. However, it's nice to sit on one's balcony under a campion-pink sunshade and stare at the sea and think what a wonderful business this writing business is. I've been keeping a note book too. That's fun, but it's rather lonely fun and it makes one feel a bit spinsterish, too. It's a form of Patience—almost.

Truth is—I miss M. terribly, but he is coming down on the 20th for ten days and then I shall come back to London with him, *and* come and see you, if I may. (But please don't think I'm a " sad old creature." I'm not.) Wish you were here. We'd have strawberries for tea. They come from Polperro, from little gardens overhanging the sea.

*To J. M. Murry*                             Saturday
                                          June 7, 1918

God knows, my ' blackness ' does not come from anything in your letters. Truthfully, I think it comes from my health : it's a part of my illness—just that. I feel ' ill ' and I feel a longing, longing for you : for our home, our life, and for a little baby. A very dark, obscure, frightening thing seems to rise up in my soul and *threaten* these desires . . . that is all. I know this will recur and when it is there I cannot put it away or even say : This is *temporary*, this is just because of so and so. No, again I am enveloped and powerless to withstand it. So please try and understand it when it comes. It's a queer affair—rather horrible. . . .

I have just been to the post and sent you a " quite unnecessary " telegram. I had to, otherwise my heart would have flown away. My room feels awfully quiet, but the worm has gone off for the week-end with A. She fetched him this morning. She is doing a Still Life of him surrounded with marigolds. It *ought* to be lovely. She thinks he is " too perfect for worlds, *my dear*."

196

We are to have a sketch. Of course, Rib was so flattered that he left me without a pang. He's coming back on Monday. A. is more than good to me, brings me fruit, flowers, and this morning a bottle of cider, and last evening some very superior chocolates that D. had sent her. She is infinitely generous, too, in looking after me.

Monday
June 9, 1918

Here's my *third* letter. I've torn up one attempt, kept another as ' interesting evidence,' and this one I'll send. It's a process of clarifying . . . you know.

Truth is—it is one of my très mauvais jours, as bad as can be. I'm jetty black. But what's the use of saying so ? No use at all. It only confirms me though in my deter- mination not to spend another day here after you are gone. I could NOT stand it. That's as much as I'll stay. I'll try and stick until Friday week, and no doubt I shall. But not a day more ! !

I shan't buy anything on my own. No energy. I shall buy a bottle of Beaune, however, because I feel I must take some stimulant regular, plus the milk, cod liver oil, iron, etc. Wine that maketh glad the heart of man. What heavenly words ! Are they true, do you think ? Then I shall be a drunkard. But they are not true.

Addio. I am in despair, you see. Laissez-moi. Let me wave my jade-white hand and go. . . .

Tuesday
June 10, 1918

It is quite obvious upon this morning's showing that *several* of my letters have been lost in the post and especi- ally (1) the one with the tour of the Elephant interior in it, (2) my (I'll confess) rather precious ' Note Book,' of which I don't possess anything like another copy.[1]

[1] The Note Book was lost.

What has happened, at its very brightest and best, is that the post has been—that these treasures have been perhaps ' over-weight '—there's been a 1d. to pay and naturally no one to pay it. So the postman has chucked them away. On the other hand, some person in the house, either tops or bottoms, may have stolen 'em. That's just as possible, in fact, very much more so.

This ' sort of thing,' familiar, oh, ever so familiar as one is with it, is still devilishly wearing. So if they *do* turn up WILL YOU PLEASE LET ME KNOW.

I mourn the Note Book. Yes, I *do* mourn that.

Perhaps you will understand *if if if* you get my letter this morning why I sent my so unreasonable wire. That was the only explanation—Impatience. A profound dismay at the idea of holding out so long, a feeling that I'd get cramp or the waves would go over my head too often or the rope would break. So, though I *know* and do absolutely realise you're hurrying as fast as your boat will sail you, I yet—simply couldn't help lifting up my cowardly little voice and saying, " Oh please do try to come faster."

You see a fortnight in London is so broken up into little bits, so shaken and scattered that it can be gathered up and held tight in the smallest little bag.

(*Bolo :* ' What, Monsieur, is a million ? A little pile like that ! ')

But a fortnight in MY world (into which you will never enter, even loving each other as we do) is a thing quite without beginning or end. You see 14 nights or 12 nights or 2 nights *can* be up the gathered meadow of Eternity and down again.

There are hours, moments, glimpses, when one can't face it, when one wants to stand with one's face in one's sleeves and just WAIL. . . .

I have torn up and chucked in the waste-paper basket all the work I have done these last few days. It was *hectic*.

Mrs. Honey brings me the afternoon post. Hides it behind her apron and says, " I thought you'd be wanting

a caändle," and then suddenly just like a girl shows me the
letter.  " There's nought so good for eë."

Your letter has just lifted me from under the appalling
umbrella . . . I can't write to-day.  I am going off to the
plage to watch the waves. . . .

Wednesday<br>June 12, 1918

No letter by this morning's post, so the day sets in very
quiet.  It's rather like waiting for a clock to strike.  Is it
going to strike ?  Is it *not* going to strike ?  No, it's well
past the hour now. . . .  Still, ' thanks be to Fortune,'
I've the afternoon to look forward to—two chances a day :
that beats France.

*Re* Jam.  Mrs. Honey has got a nice little lot of goose-
berries coming soon—they are called ' golden drops ' and
do make haändsome jam.  She's keeping them for us.
BUT do you like gooseberry jam ?  I do, awfully, if it's
home made, and yet it's not (which really *is* a point in
these days) *too* alluring.  I am become, since I arrived
here, a Gluttonous Fiend sur le sujet de marmelade d'
oranges.  It really does seem to me one of the superb dis-
coveries, eaten early in the morning—and so prettie
withal.

Yesterday afternoon, on the rocks, among the babies and
family parties (*too* near me for my taste), each of us with
our tea and trimmings and cigarettes, Anne and I sat.
And SHE talked and I added :

" A—— ! "
" Really ! "
" How extraordinary ! "
" Yes, I can imagine it."

ringing the changes on this little chime, which somehow
wonderfully was enough to bring *all* her thought rushing
to me in a little urgent troop until I really (if you will
please conceive of me as a kind of little warm dim temple)
couldn't have held another.

But oh—they *really* were—some of them—no end " interesting."

Why didn't I have a letter !

All the same I am a nice little thing this morning. If you were here I think you'd like my ways.

I fell fast in love with you last night at about 12.30. I was going to bed, dropping my velvet coat and velvet shoes on the bank before I took a header into what I was afraid was going to be a dark little pool, and suddenly I saw you in the ' garden room ' making something, with a packing case, a hammer, a plane, nails. . . .

" Hold this for me." I held it, and you banged away.

" Half a minute. I'll just put a paper down to catch the sawdust."

And later you put a little pot of glue in a saucepan of boiling water, where it *bumped* away while it melted.

This was so Ineffably Heavenly that I tied a love word to the leg of my very best and fastest pigeon and sent it off to you, to perch on the end of the grey bed and give the top of your head the gentlest possible peck so that you'd wake and get the message. Did you ?

I must go out out out into the world.

Friday
June 14, 1918

King of the Turnip Heads !

I hasten to throw this letter into the wall to tell you (in case you do ' see your way ') (and my D. N. says there is a ' glut ' of them au moment présent dans notre Londres) the way to make Strawberry Jam. As far as I remember it's like this.

¾ lb. of sugar to each
1 lb. of fruit.

Put the fruit and the sugar in a pan overnight. Turn, before leaving, ever so gently with a wooden spoon. (Turn the fruit, I mean. Don't *waltz* round it.) By the next day the berries will have ' sweated.' Boil, without adding any water, (gently again) for ¾ of an hour. And then apply the Saucer Test. (During the $\frac{3}{4}$ of an hour, Christian, you must *not* seek repose.)

God! as I write I freeze, I burn, I desire, with a passion that is peign, to be there all in my little bib and tucker.

" Yes, Rib dear, you should have a taste on your own little dish! . . . " But I think this receipt is right.

If you feel there ought to be water added—well, you know our high courage on former occasions. And it's always been triumphant.

The time for boiling given here is for a lot. Perhaps it needs less for a little. That's a point I have never yet decided.

Sunday
June 16, 1918

The weather has changed: it's really more lovely than ever, but showery—immense clapping showers of rain, castles and mountains in the sky and reflected in the purple sea, the air smelling of elder flower and seaweed. But alas! for my bones. It's brought on a devilish fit of spinal rheumatism, and I walk like little Nell's grandfather—and spent until four o'clock this morning—literally—wondering whether people my age could have paralysis. If not, how account for being cold-stone to the knees and so on and so on. The pain is devilish, devilish, devilish. . . .

Yesterday morning I went into Looe and met Mr. P. and had a talk about chickens, tulips and boats. He is a *huge* man, a positive Titan. I came home to find another huge bouquet from his garden—mixed sweet williams, superb great velvet flowers. My room looks full of them and Ribni's dark head shines out of velvet bows. A. has made such an exquisite painting of mon fils chéri *and* given it me.

This morning when I woke up Mrs. Honey was particularly honeycomb. Dear old soul—in her black Sunday dress. She said "You've not slept. Thaät's bad. I'll see to it that you haäve your coffee right hot." And she brought me boiling coffee and "a fried egg with bacon fried for a relish." When I had done up all my buttons and was having a small sit down she said, looking at me with her kind old eyes, "Shall I recite you some verses I learned when I was a girl? Will eë haäve *The Death of Moses* or *A Mother's Memories*?" I said I'd have both. Down she sat. Each had, I should think, about 40 verses to it. She never hesitated for a word. She folded her hands and on and on went her soft old voice telling of the "crested waves"—telling of "the lion the King of Beasts" who sat under the mountain where Moses was buried and "forgot to roar."

> "Yea, from the monster's golden eyes
>   The golden tears dropped down. . . ."

I listened and suddenly I thought of Wordsworth and his 'faith' in these people—and again, in spite of everything, I believed in England. Not only in England—in mankind. You will understand me when I tell you that I wanted to weep, to cry, Father, forgive them, they know not what they do.

Oh, the beauty of the human soul—the Beauty of it—the Beauty of it. Don't let us *ever* forget!

Duhamel knows it. There will be others. We will build an altar.

No, I've not written half what I meant to, and I *can't*. My back has got the upper hand. I'm off to bed with a hot water bottle. It's no good, Betsy. But don't worry. I'll be better to-morrow. It's only *body*, *not* heart, *not* head. Those are all I've got intact.

Monday
June 17, 1918

I do feel to-day that Friday is—oh, so near. I keep making preparations . . . and speculations. Will my

flowers last till then ?　Shall Rib wear his new dress or
the old one his father loves ?

I feel ever so greatly better to-day (can't write or spell
tho'). I had a good night. Oh, a *good* one ! A. came
early and began the great painting—me in that red,
brick red frock with flowers everywhere. It's awfully
interesting even now. I painted her in my way as she
painted me in hers : her eyes . . . " little blue flowers
plucked this morning . . . "

The reason why I have been so very quiet about my
weight is I was only 7.10 when I weighed last, so I didn't
tell you. For I had lost a couple of pounds. I know
when and why. It was when I had one of my blackest
moods—I felt very dreadful ; but by next Wednesday I
ought to have found them again and I will wire you the
good tidings. . . . Bother—wasn't it ? I wish you
would whisper C. to send me ½ lb. of good chocolates. I
*pine* for that sweet toothful, and there is nothing here just
now but chewing gum. Everybody in this hotel has told
me how much better I am to-day than I was yesterday—
which is very nice of them.

I say—what about Thursday ! I told Rib who became
a shocking boy on the spot, absolutely too much for any
woman to deal with. I threatened him finally with the
Children's Court and said I'd tell the magistrate he was
incorrigible. But he pays no attention, only asks the
empty air : " Well why does she keep on kissing me while
she says all this ? "

You're not to think I bullied you about this large suit
case. (You do.) Really and truly I have only gone into
the affair in such detail to make you feel comfortably
disguised—camouflaged—in the presence of the chim-
panzees. For, tho' they don't bite, their chatter is the
hell of a bore, don't you think ? You must not bring
anything but a coloured handkerchief and a tommyhawk
if you don't want to.

Thursday
June 20, 1918

To-morrow, to-morrow, to-morrow. That is at full gallop.

The wardrobe " thrills me through and through " (to be sung con amore.)

Don't fall out of the train. Perhaps you had better tie a label on your top button. I don't trust you *at all*.

Rib says : " Parentchik, I shall be there to meet, on the stopping of the chariot, the August Emergence." He says he is going " to write a book now called *Fan Tales*."

Now. Oh, *please* hurry. But *don't* rush.

*To Lady Ottoline Morrell*                              Tuesday
47 Redcliffe Road
June 1918

It is simply dreadful that you should suffer so much and that doctors should be such useless fools. . . . What can one say ? I know so devilishly well the agony of feeling perpetually ill and the longing—the immense longing just to have what everybody else takes so easily as their portion —health—a body that isn't an enemy—a body that isn't fiendishly engaged in the old, old ' necessary ' torture of— breaking one's spirit—

" Why won't you consent to having your spirit broken ?" it wonderingly asks. " Everybody else yields without a murmur. And if you'd only realise the comfortable, boundless numbness that you would enjoy for ever after—" I wonder sometimes how it will end. One will never give in and so—All the same it would be more tolerable if only people understood—ever so little—but *subtly*—not with a sort of bread jelly sympathy—but with exquisite, rare friendship. (Oh, dear, I *still* believe in such a thing and *still* long for it.)

You see, I cannot help it. My secret belief—the inner-most ' credo ' by which I live is—that *although* Life is loathsomely ugly and people are terribly often vile and cruel and base, nevertheless there is something at the back of it all—which if only I were great enough to understand would make *everything*, everything, indescribably beautiful. One just has glimpses, divine warnings—signs— Do you remember the day we cut the lavender? And do you remember when the Russian music sounded in that half-empty hall? Oh, those memories compensate for more than I can say—

*To Mrs. Virginia Woolf*  
Tuesday  
July 2, 1918

I love to hear of Lytton's success. It seems quite measureless to man. I put my head out of window at night and expect to find his name pricked upon the heavens in real stars. I feel he is become already a sort of myth, a kind of legend. Modern princelings are hushed to sleep with tales of him and grave young duchesses disguise themselves at their Fairs and Pageants with . . . the delicate beard, the moonlight hat, the shy, reluctant umbrella. . . .

Yes, I am very sorry that we shall not see each other this week. Your Pearl of a Letter made me realise what an infinite deal I want to talk about with you. But it will keep. I have spent the last two days lying on the sommier, with a temperature for doux ami. But writing seems a great labour and every book I want out of reach—the topmost leaf of the tallest tree. But I like to listen to this street. There is a piano in it, a parrot, and a man who cries feather-brooms—all excellent in their way.

*To Lady Ottoline Morrell*  
Tuesday  
August 1918

It's a divine morning, quiet and hot. The watercart has just gone down the road and now the piano opposite is braiding its hair in swift, intricate braids. I cannot help feeling, to-day, that the world, at any rate, is the 'friend of man' and longs for us to walk upon lawns and idle in gardens and wear shady hats and dabble our feet in pools, and lie in grass and lose ourselves in forests and watch the light and the air shaking tall trees. . . .

Oh—these misunderstandings! great ones and little ones—do let us drive them all into the sea. Why do we allow them to rush at us and snap and hurt us all so *horribly*? God knows we have all of us had reason enough to suspect and to mistrust . . . but "is it too late?"

*To the Hon. Dorothy Brett*                      Friday
                                             July 19, 1918

When are you coming to London again? And if you *do* come do not forget to let us know. Our last interview was so hung with drops of rain and cups of tea—I should love a longer, dryer one. And what are you doing? And how are you feeling? And are you painting? Or do you feel like I feel just at present. . . . Another slice of this loaf I cannot and will not eat. I want to change the baker—the bread—everything—everything—I want to sit at an entirely new table, in fact, with new hands to pour out strange wines—and unfamiliar music playing. . . .

No, that ain't enough either—Change the country— the climate, too. Let's all put on velvet masks and have our fortunes told by Chinese wizards.

July 20, 1918

I went to see the Naval Photographs to-day. They are wonderful. And all the middle of the gallery is occupied by a Naval *Band* which, at the first beat carries you far, far out into the open sea, my dear, so that you positively bob up and down in an open boat upon huge immense waves of sound, gasping, breathless, holding on to ropes and trying to bale out your mind with the catalogue before you are swept on again. When I reached the final room I really *did* give way and was floated down the stairs and into the kind air by two Waacs and a Wren who seemed to

206

despise me **very** much (but couldn't have as much as I did myself). They asked me, when I had drunk after a glass of the most dispassionate water, whether I had *lost* anybody in the Navy—as though it were nothing but a kind of gigantic salt-water laundry—

*To Lady Ottoline Morrell*                    Saturday afternoon
                                              July 1918

I was simply enchanted with your letter. It came, after a dreadfully bad night, an age-long night which leaves one at the mercy of first impressions next morning. You know the feeling ? One lies in a kind of daze, feeling so sensitive—so unbearably sensitive to the exterior world and longing for something ' lovely ' to happen. The something lovely *did* happen to me—with your letter. I longed to get up and send you a telegram to your Hotel— just to say how wonderful it had been—but could not get up all day. So, tied to the sofa leg, I thought about it and you.

I am so thankful that the raid is over and that we shan't have another. Oh, don't let us ! They *are* so exhausting, and so wretched, and then when outsiders come in and start boasting on their own account I want to fly into the wilderness and like the dove in that hideous anthem " Bui-ild me a ne-e-est and remain there for Ever at rest." But *otherwise* I hate the idea of perpetual wilderness and the dove idea of rest don't appeal to me at all.

We are supposed to have fought our way over to Asheham to-day—hung with our own meat and butter, but I couldn't face it. There seemed to have been so many things to catch and so many changes to make—a sort of government controlled game of musical chairs without any music, very grim. No, I couldn't. So instead I am sitting squeezed up in a corner of this formless room while a man cuts new pinnies for the armchairs and the sommier—lemon yellow ones with dashes of palm trees on them and parrots simply clinging to the branches.

The parrots have, I think, a quite extraordinary resemblance to M. The tide is very low—at the ebb—in the Redcliffe Road and the sky is the colour of weak cocoa. I wish I could simply disappear—become invisible and find myself somewhere where the light was kinder with a superb new book to read by someone I'd never heard of before. But these are dreams and I must, when this scissor man goes—take my filet to the Fulham Road and do *shopping*. Oh! Oh! Why hasn't M. £2,500 a year? It would be so lovely to bask in money for a little.

I have a story called " Bliss " in this month's *English Review*. If you should see it will you really tell me what you think? Is that terre dangereuse? No, not really.

I will send you a cardboard box. I'd adore some flowers. But I think I have several boxes, so I shall send them all—in case they are still as rare at Garsington.

*To Mrs. Virginia Woolf* July 1918

I do not want to leave your letter unanswered. I do hope we can come later, we were awfully disappointed, too. Forgive me—I've nothing to say. This is just a friendly way I love to think of you at Asheham.

My mother has died. I can't think of anything else. Ah, Virginia, she was such an exquisite little being, far too fragile and lovely to be dead for ever more.

*To Lady Ottoline Morrell* Sunday
July 21, 1918

Will you pass through London on your way to the sea? If you do—*please* let me know. I long to see you. I was so glad to hear from you yesterday. I wish I were with you now—not on the lawn but sitting under some tree with all the dazzling, silent brightness just beyond— where we could talk and be alone.

I heard the *infinitely* sad news yesterday that my darling little mother is dead. She was the most exquisite,

perfect little being—something between a star and a flower
—I simply cannot *bear* the thought that I shall not see her
again—

We move to Hampstead on the 25th.

Monday
July 22, 1918

I have been condemned to the sommier for the last few
days, and not able to walk at all. There is nothing I
should have loved more than to walk in your garden—
otherwise.

But the King of the Hanky-Pankies is coming this
morning to electrify me and I hope to have new legs—
arms—wings—everything—in a week or two.

I can't go on like this ; even a caterpillar would turn.

We leave here next Monday for :

2 Portland Villas,
East Heath Road,
Hampstead.

Portland Villas !—it sounds like one of those houses
where a " few guests are taken slightly mental not objected
to. Firm home-like treatment."

But inside it is going to be a vision—a sort of spring
perpetual with delicate little flowery poems on the top
floor window boxes and short stories, very rich and gay on
the first floor sills. In the garden ' the Mountain '
dreams of African trees—violet trees covered with bunches
of violets and assegai trees with leaves like spears. But I
don't believe in *them*.

It's such a strange morning here—puffs of silver cloud
blowing over the roofs and Indian gentlemen in mustard-
coloured turbans prancing up and down the pavement,
and now here's the electric man with his little box. He
has a waxed moustache and we are beginning to ask if it is
*lumber* or *ribs*. Oh dear !

Thursday
July 25, 1918

Yes, my mother's death is a terrible sorrow to me. I feel—do you know what I mean—the *silence* of it so. She was more alive than anyone I have ever known.

How are you ? And are you going to the sea ? Brett said you thought of it. Garsington must be divine in this weather, though. I hope that we shall see each other soon. I am longing to be in my new house—out of this *common* passage way—*common* door. I sit in front of these three windows and feel that I am sitting in a shop—with nothing whatever to sell. M. is, as usual, working a hundred times too hard—but he cannot stop himself and I cannot stop him. I can only look on and deplore it. However, like a little forlorn Ibsen hero the ' miracle ' is going to happen for him when he gets into his new house. His study has lemon-yellow walls and orange curtains. I have an idea that I shall hang a parrot in it . . . as well.

Oh, I long for gaiety—for a high spirit—for gracious ways and kindness and happy love. Life without these is not worth living. But they *must be*. We have—the few of us—got wings—real wings—beauties—to fly with and not to always hide under—

*To the Hon. Dorothy Brett*
Wednesday
2 Portland Villas, Hampstead
August 14, 1918

I was so glad of your letter to-day. Yes, it is an *immense* blow. She was the most precious, lovely little being, even so far away, you know, and writing me such long, long letters about the garden and the house and her conversations in bed with Father, and of how she loved sudden, unexpected cups of tea " out of the air, brought by faithful ravens in aprons "—and letters beginning " Darling child, it is the most exquisite day "—She *lived* every moment of life more fully and completely than anyone I've ever known—and her gaiety wasn't any less real for being *high courage*—courage to meet anything with.

Ever since I heard of her death my memories of her come flying back into my heart—and there are moments when it's unbearable to receive them. But it has made me realise more fully than ever before that I love *courage*—spirit—poise (do you know what I mean ? all these words are too little) more than anything. And I feel inclined to say (not to anybody in particular) " Let us love each other. Let us be *kind* and rejoice in one another and leave all squabbles and ugliness to the dull dogs who only become articulate when they bark and growl. The world is so dreadful in many ways. Do let us be tender with each other."

*To Lady Ottoline Morrell*                   Thursday
                                     2 Portland Villas, Hampstead
                                          August 22, 1918

Yesterday afternoon, when the flowers came I felt quite overwhelmed—I felt as I took them out of the box : " Unless I mention every single flower to her how can I tell her how I *saw* them ? "—the black poppy, the two pale sunflowers—all the different yellow ones—and then, above all, these round bright beauties. My sea-side lodging is a bower and even M., who is, at the moment, like the bathing dress, perpetually hanging out to dry after a *sad, sad* wetting—gave a great gasp of delight.

Oh, but I sigh for happiness—for a world which isn't always ' out of joint.' This constant living on the defensive—how tiring it is ! Why *won't* people live more freely and more widely. But no, there they are—*smug*—like little plants in little pots—that ought to have been put out in a garden years ago—years ago. But they prefer their life on a shelf—out of the " full force " of the sun and wind—each one tight in itself and away from its companions. But Fear, Distrust, Cowardice, Smugness—surely they are more horrid worms than one would find in any garden. But I don't give up hope—I can't, and here is this divine, cloudless day waiting for something more to flower. Remember me when you lean over the tobacco plant—I can see it and breathe it now—how exquisite it is ! There must be fields of tobacco plant in the moon—

*Isn't* David Copperfield adorable ? I like even the Dora part, and that friend of Dora's—Julia—somebody, who was ' blighted.' She is such a joy to me. Yes—doesn't Charley D. make our little men smaller than ever —and such *pencil sharpeners*—

I have discovered nothing to read, and do not know how the days pass. The electric man is still filling me with sparks, every day for ¾ of an hour ; it is very comforting, and I think it is going to beat the rheumatiz. How are your headaches ?

October 1918

I love to think you are going to the Ballet, and I *wish* I were with you, in that warm light place where there's music and dancing. (It sounds as though I were meaning Heaven ; except that I am *sure* Heaven will be infernally chilly.)

I am lying in my basket with a spiritual flannel round my chaps. Occasionally the Mountain (8000 feet high) swoops over me and says : " Shall I *steam* it and put the custard *round* or—— " and occasionally Murry drops an *Evening News* on to me, as a sort of sign from the great world beyond—I have read *War and Peace* again—and then *War and Peace* again—and then I feel inclined to positively sing to it :

" If You were the Only Book in the World ! "

*To the Hon. Dorothy Brett*      Saturday afternoon
October 12, 1918

Your letter came by itself with a special loud great knock at the door for it. I fancied it had been carried in the bosom of some hielan' drover, *and* saw him at the door with his dirk showing in the folds of his plaid and his ram's horn of whisky. Outside all his shaggy beasts munched the wet willows. . . .

I was awfully glad to hear from you. It all sounds so far away like a novel of Turgenev—so far away from Hampstead and London. I wish you would come back soon and have a fixed pied-à-terre of your own.

It must be very difficult to live in one's family when one has flown out of the nest. What can I do with my wings now I am back ? There is no room for wings in the largest nest imaginable—and it's no use pretending that I haven't got 'em. They have carried me ever so far up and away—That is the sort of pipe that I should make— yet, of course, *not* having that nest to fly to—I imagine it the softest loveliest place to *rest* oneself *out* in, as the Germans say.

Why isn't there some exquisite city where we all have our palaces—and hear music—and walk in heavenly landscape and look at pictures and where all the people are beauties—moving in the streets as it were to a dance. I am quite serious. I *pine* for lavishness. For the real fruits of the earth tumbling out of a brimming horn (perhaps it is four years of Khaki.).

No, I didn't see the Doctor. I saw a big Gun on my own—who was very intelligent. He says I have got this disease in both lungs that I can get better in London but I must go off to some mountain peak to be cured. " Serious but recoverable," said he. I see M. and I climbing up some peak after this war and finding a tiny house at the top with windows like spectacles, and living in it—all nicely dressed in big rabbit skins—specially rabbit-skin gloves—which we shall never take off until we have gradually eaten them off with our bread and butter—as one does.

I am full of new ideas for work. Rather held up at moment by my wretched machinery which creaks and groans and lets me down. But I mean to get it in good enough order to be able to ignore it and plunge into the REAL LIFE.

*To Anne Estelle Rice*                    October 13, 1918

Your letter went to the cockles of my heart—bless you
for it—*and* curiously enough I had been thinking over the
Spring Book only yesterday—seeing it and hoping that
we would bring it off.  Shall us ?  Let's.

I will send you a Bud or a Leaf as they pop out and if
you like 'em—ça ira.  I have a very definite idea at this
distance, at this temperature, and with the willow leaves
flying in at the windows, what Spring felt like to me—
and it's so mixed with lobsters, winkles, the smell of the
sea—weedy pools, it *ought* with the help of the Lord to
have enough Body.  I shall get down to it—bang off—
especially as I am tied to the Sofa leg until Thursday week.
That means I can't come and spend the delightful day
with you until after then—Hélas.  But ask me again,
won't you, and I'll come along with my slippers in a satin
bag and my Plain Knitting.  I long to see the studio.  I
love the Quality of your Fine Feeling for Decoration.  One
feels immensely *rested* and *stimulated* at the same time—a
sort of fruitful Basking, if you know what I mean.  I'm
sending you to-day a snippet of home-made Cake from my
home.  Birthday cake (I was 30 yesterday !).  I hope it
arrives in good order.  You are to eat every crumb yourself !

My house is rather a joy when I can forget that the
tooth glass is out of proportion with the lotion bottle,
etc., etc., etc.  My Papa sent a specialist to see me yesterday, who said that if I didn't go into a sanatorium I had
not a Dog's Chance.  Blast his eyes !  Je m'en f—.  I
feel full of fire and buck.

I am sure Peace is coming—aren't you ?  Oh, I have
such a longing for France.  Can you hear that street cry
Marchand d'habits ?  It sounds like *Chand abi* and is said
or *sung* with a sort of jump in the middle.

Well—God bless us all—and you expecially—your
' Hedge ' [1] nods and waves as I write, with orange butterflies fanning their wings over the campions.

[1] A drawing by Anne Estelle Rice.

Really, in spite of all England shrieking and imploring
everybody not to make Peace until they've had a rare kick
at him and a rare nose-in-the-mud rubbing one does feel
that Peace is in the Air.

> " It is all about, my sister
> Yet it is unborn "—

(Those lines struck me suddenly and seemed suddenly
mysteriously lovely.)   They took my breath away.   It was
like listening at the door and hearing the winter steal away
leaving Spring, Spring, in a basket on the doorstep of the
world.

Oh, Brett—let there be no more War.

I have been spending all my days gradually fitting into
a smaller and smaller hole as my puff gets less.   Now I'm
in bed—and here I must stay for a bit.   This is very
cursed : in fact, it's HELL, but I shall get out of it and
once we have lain down our knife and fork and agreed to
eat no more German I'll be well again—But England !
What !  *Peace !*  It's like suddenly snatching away all
their next coupons—What did my son die for, Sir ?   To
keep the war going or to end it, Sir ?   To keep it going,
Sir, until everybody else's son is as dead as he !   They, the
old gentlemen over 70, who write to *The Times* would like
to have *such* a Peace that they could plant a campstool in
any corner of Europe, sit down, throw their handkerchiefs
over their faces and go to sleep there without being dis-
turbed by *one single solitary* soul.   But they won't get
their way—

Lawrence and Frieda have been in town.   Frieda was
ill and in bed but I saw a very great deal of Lawrence—
For me, at least, the dove brooded over him, too.   I
loved him.   He was just his old, merry, rich self, laughing,
describing things, giving you pictures, full of enthusiasm
and joy in a future where we become all ' vagabonds '—
we simply did not talk about people.   We kept to things
like nuts and cowslips and fires in woods and his black self

*was* not. Oh, there is something so loveable about him and his eagerness, his passionate eagerness for life—that is what one loves so. Now he is gone back to the country.

*To Mrs. Virginia Woolf*　　　　　　　November 1, 1918

I meant to answer your letter sooner but my strong right arm refused to obey me. I should *love* to see you one afternoon next week. Would Wednesday suit you ? I am a very dull dog, and in bed, but I try to look as though I were there for pleasure and not for necessity. But do come—There is a power of things to be talked over. M. will send you a very pretty, delicate, little flowery map of the way. It's extremely easy to find and I swear to God it's not more than 8 minutes from the Tube station.

I am awfully glad that *Prelude* has given a little pleasure. I have felt guilty towards you on its account, as a matter of fact, for I thought it had been a Bad Failure and you cursed the day. . . .

Well, Virginia dear. . . .

THEY have tied a bunch of beech leaves to my bed post. What lovely things they are—so full of life. The cold, reluctant air blows in, the fire streams up the chimney and a little clock outside strikes *three* in a way that raises your eyebrows. ' My dear child—I am perfectly prepared to believe you, there is no earthly need to insist on it.' *I hate* that clock. Now, in France, a little clock like that would strike as though it were all astonishment and amusement at finding itself at *three* or *four* or *five*, but —however, it's no matter.

*To Lady Ottoline Morrell*　　　　　　　November 4, 1918

I have been quite unable to write these last few days— with acute neuritis in my arm and shoulder—Another New Dish. That's the worst of illness. If one could only choose one dish à la carte—eat it—make a grimace over it

and throw the plate away. But it's this infernally boring
table d'hôte with all these little side dishes and kickshaws
that you're simply not allowed to refuse—It is distracting
and sometimes I feel it never will end—

I have felt so cut off from the world without a pen. I
lay and read *The Egoist*. It seemed to me marvellously
good in its way—and I had quite forgotten how much
Meredith enjoyed writing. It's delightful how this
enjoyment comes through—he shares your laugh, catches
your eye, sees the point just as you do. But really a
very difficult book for Englishmen to read without
*twinging*.

But when I read *Rhoda Fleming*, and that seemed to me
so *false*, so preposterous—one could only groan for it—
and it's so odious. All this lingering over the idea of a
lily white, white as snow jeune fille in the embrace of an
ugly, vicious, little old man made me want to cry like
Lawrence that " His sex was all wrong "—But he is a big
man, and he *can* write wonders.

These strange, wild evenings shaken with wind and rain
have something of Spring in them. One can't help feeling
that to-morrow the first green will be there, and perhaps
you will meet a little child with a fist of wan daffodils—
It does not matter dreadfully that it is not true. If Peace
comes I really do feel that the winter will not be real
winter, it can't be cold and dark and malignant. A
miracle will happen.

But I wish the horrible old knitting women at Versailles
would *hurry, hurry*—Do you see that President Wilson is
coming to attend the Conference in Person—Already—I
fondly dream of—Oh, such a meeting ! A sort of glorified
Christina Pontifex interview between us. I am afraid I
am staying in bed too long !

Lawrence has sent me to-day a new play of his —very
long, just written. I must read it. I have glanced inside
and it looks *black* with miners.

Oh, what *shall* I do to celebrate the end of the war ?

November 13, 1918

My thoughts *flew* to you immediately the guns sounded. I opened the window and it really *did* seem—just in those first few moments that a wonderful change happened—not in human creatures hearts—no—but in the *air*, there seemed just for a breath of time—a silence, like the silence that comes after the last drop of rain has fallen—you know ?

It was so wonderful—and I saw that in our garden a lilac bush had believed in the South wind and was covered in buds—

Oh, why is the world so ugly—so corrupt and *stupid* ? When I heard the drunks passing the house on Monday night, singing the good old pre-war drunken rubbish, I felt cold with horror. *They* are not changed—and then the loathsome press about Germany's cry for food.

My baby longing for people to "kiss and be friends"—

How horrid they are *not* to—Why don't they fly at each other, kiss and cry and share everything. One feels that about nations—but alas ! about individuals, too. Why do people hide and withdraw and suspect—as they do ? I don't think it is just shyness. . . . I used to. I think it is *lack of heart* : a sort of blight on them which will not let them ever come to full flower.

And the worst of it is I can't just accept that, calmly, like M., for instance, and say—" Very well—Let them go then." No *still* I feel full of love—still I desire lovely friends—and it will always be so, I think. But Life is so short I want them *here now at once* before Next Christmas —radiant beings—bursting open my door—

I suppose it's great nonsense.

I have been translating Maxim Gorki's Journal of the Revolution all last week. I find Gorki wonderfully sympathetic—— This journal is dreadful. It makes you feel, *anything anything* rather than revolution.

November 1918

If I have not written before it is not my fault, really not my fault—it is this confounded weather which puts me so out of tune I hate to send such a jangle—Here I sit, staring at the writing-table like some sea-sick traveller who dares not lift his eyes to the waves outside but he will be quite undone. *If* I do—there is the grey cloud chasing the black cloud and the trees in their dark, ugly green tossing their branches like old crones at a weak-tea party telling how that Autumn has come back—unexpected and has turned Summer into the street and Summer has gone off dear knows where without even her flowery shawl poor lamb, and Autumn has wired to Winter to curtail his journey and start for home—*home*. This desperate news makes one's flesh creep again. I heard a coalman pass this morning and was half inclined to put a black cross on our door.

Do not think I am not grateful for the exquisite, sweet-scented basket. All my flowers this year have come from you. I never shall forget them. It's so strange I feel I have spent almost a whole summer at Garsington : each of these flowers is a remembrance. I love your garden. I often walk in it invisible. How long *is* it since we have really walked there together ? Why does it seem so long ? My heart aches at the thought.

These preparations for Festivity are too odious. In addition to my money complex I have a food complex. When I read of the preparations that are being made in all the workhouses throughout the land—when I think of all those toothless old jaws guzzling for the day—and then of all that beautiful youth feeding the fields of France—Life is almost too ignoble to be borne. Truly one must hate humankind in the mass, hate them as passionately as one loves the few, the very few. Ticklers, squirts, portraits eight times as large as life of Lloyd George and Beatty blazing against the sky—and drunkenness and brawling and destruction. I keep seeing all these horrors, bathing in them again and again (God knows I don't want to) and then my mind fills with the wretched little picture I have of my brother's grave. What is the meaning of it all ?

One ought to harden one's heart until it is all over. But Oh—Life might be so wonderful—There's the unforgetable rub ! And we've only one life and I cannot believe in immortality. I wish I could. To arrive at the gates of Heaven, to hear some grim old angel cry, " Consumptives to the right—up the airy mountain, past the flower field and the boronia trees—sufferers from gravel, stone and fatty degeneration to the left to the Eternal Restaurant smelling of Beef Eternal." How one would skip through ! But I see nothing but black men, black boxes, black holes, and poor darling M. splitting a very expensive black kid glove his Mama had made him buy. . . . One must get out of this country.

Did you read about Mrs. Atherton ? It was a strange peep through the windows. I wanted very much to write to the Earl of March and thank him for his evidence —How queer it all was ! There were touches positively Shakespearian. When she said to her maid : " This is the last time you will brush my hair " and " please hold my hand a little," it was like Desdemona and Emilia at 47 Curzon Street.

*To the Hon. Dorothy Brett*                Tuesday
                                  December 18, 1918

Oh—the cold ! My feet are ice—my fingers and nose —ice, too. And shiver after shiver goes down my spine— I cannot konker it with clothes. Where did your lamb come from ? Is it one of the Jaeger flock ? I think I shall have to buy an immense tea-cosy and wear it and crawl under it as a snail does its shell—I go to Switzerland in early April. The cows ought to be laying properly by then—It's no good before then. My plan is to let this house furnished for a year—then Murry will come back, find a tiny farm in a remote spot and put the furniture into it and live there. I shall make my General Head-Quarters abroad—a little house and a big maid on some mountain top—Italy, I think.

When I have found a cuckoo clock you will come and stay with me—won't you—and draw mountains ? At present I feel with you that Life is ugly. I am hardly alive. I have not been out for months and cannot walk up and down the stairs with any success. But apart from that—I feel in my heart as though I have died—as far as personal life goes. I don't even want to live again. All that is over—I am a writer who cares for nothing but writing—that's how I feel. When I am with people I feel like a doctor with his patients—very sympathetic—very interested in the case ! very anxious for them to tell me all they can—but as regards myself—quite alone, quite isolated—a queer state.

*To Anne Estelle Rice*              December 1918

No go. Not a single Peasant's cart will take me. They will neither come to me *here* nor call for me *there*. We have 'phoned every garage and stable in the neighbourhood. It's a cursed disappointment, but I shall just have to ' wait a bit.'

I wish we were all in France with a real Xmas party in prospect—snow, huge fire, a feast, wine, old, old French tunes on a guitar, fancy dresses, a Tree, and everybody too happy for words. Instead we are wondering whether to give the postman 5 shillings, *or*, since we have only been here since August, will 3 be enough ? Etc. Etc. Etc. This cursed country would take the spirit out of a Brandied Cherry.

*To the Hon. Dorothy Brett*          Wednesday
                                      January 1, 1919

We had a superb Xmas—stockings—a tree, decorations, crackers, pudding, drink—most potent and plentiful—parcels pouring in and out. Murry seemed to wear a paper hat (a large red and yellow butterfly) from Xmas

Eve until after Boxing Day—We gradually, under the influence of wine and chinese mottoes gave a party— Charades—Kot, Gertler, Campbell, etc. Oh, I did *love* it so—loved everybody. They were all fluttering and twinkling like candles in the darkest, most mysterious Tree of all—I wanted to say to everybody—Let us stay forever just as we are—Don't let us ever wake up and find it is all over.

It made me realise all over again how thrilling and enchanting life can be, and that we are not old—the blood still flows in our veins. We still laugh. The red chairs became a pirate ship. Koteliansky wore a muff on his head and Campbell a doormat tied under the chin—can't this happen more often ? Ought not Life to be divided into work and PLAY—real play ? We ought not to have to sit in corners when our work is over. I feel that I have a thirst for Happiness, that never will be quenched again.

My prison doors have been opened at last—I'm allowed to go out—I have found a man who is going to *cure* me. But he says I must not go to Switzerland but to a tropical climate in the Spring—like Majorca or Corsica. So when I am surer than ever that I shall be able to tempt you to come and visit me in a little house with a fig and a date by the door—Hurrah for Life ! But this isn't a letter. It is a hail—and so do let us spend a part of a Very New Year indeed together.

*To Anne Estelle Rice*                          Monday
                                              January 13, 1919

> My darling Anne
> After my Plan
> For New Year's Day fell through,
> I gave up hope
> Of catching a rope
> Which would land me down near you.
> Since then I've been
> (Pulse one sixteen
> Temperature one o three)

> Lying in bed
> With a wandering head
> And a weak, weak cup of tea.
> Injections, chère
> In my derrière
> Driven into a muscular wad
> With a needle thick
> As a walking stick—
> How *can* one believe in God !
> Plus—pleurisy
> And je vous dis
> A head that went off on its own
> Rode a circular race
> That embraced every place
> I ever shall know or have known.
>
> I landed in Spain
> Went to China by train
> And rounded Cape Horn in a gale
> Ate an ice in New York
> Caught the boat for Majourke
> And went up the Nile for a sail. . . .

Light refreshments, bouillon, raw eggs and orange juice were served on the journey. M. came in, fell over the screen, went out again, came back, dropped a candle, groaned, and went again, and the Faithful One changed the hot water bottles so marvellously often that you never had a hot water bottle at all. It was always being taken or brought back.

All this, Anne darling, is a new treatment that my new doctor has started—a treatment by injections. He is a wonderful man. In April he says I ought to go to a place like Corsica. Switzerland is impossible, tank de Lord. So I think I shall. . . . Well, Anne dearest, I'll keep on thinking and thinking about you, and wishing you all the luck there is. I shall be no good after to-day till the end of this week for I have another consignment shipped into me to-morrow. But I'll write again then. Quelle vie !

*To Mrs. Virginia Woolf*                    February 1919

Alas—I have just had another inoculation and by tea-
time to-morrow I shall be sailing on tropic seas—I am
trying a new treatment which gives me a high temperature
for 48 hours each time it is applied. I wonder if you
could and would come next Monday ? I want *very* much
to see you. You know M. has been made editor of *The
Athenæum* ; he was wondering whether you'd write for it.
I wish you would. . . . There's a deal to talk over ; I
wish I were more physically stable—it's dreadful misery.

*To Lady Ottoline Morrell*                    February 1919

I feel that winter, cruel forbidding winter is content to
leave nothing unfrozen—not one heart or one bud of a
soul to escape ! If only one did not feel that it is all so
wrong—so wrong. It would be much happier if one
could feel—like M.—mankind is born to suffer. But I do
feel that is so wrong—so wrong. It is like saying : mankind is born to walk about in goloshes under an umbrella.
Oh dear—I should like to put a great notice over England,
*closed* during the winter months. Perhaps if everybody
were shipped off to blue skies and big bright flowers they
would change. But I don't know. The miracle is that
one goes on hoping and believing *through it all* just as
passionately as ever one did—

This is a grey, grim, pavement of a day, with slow
dropping rain. When the Mountain brought me my
early-morning tea this morning she whispered, tenderly :
" Do you think it would be a good idea to change one ton
of coal for two of large anthracite ? I don't think we
require a special permit and even if we do I think it is
worth it." My bed turned into a railway truck, shuffled
off to the pit head, and two tons of large anthracite were
tumbled on it . . . a very lourd paquet to begin the day
with. . . .

*To J. M. Murry*                              March 7, 1919

At about 4.30 this afternoon there sounded the smallest
possible knock on the door—so faint that nobody but
Ribni could hear it.   He waved his fan at me, presented
arms with it, and said DOOR.   So I went.

Opened it, looked

        down

           down

               down

to a minute young gentleman whose boots were just seen,
who was as it were, extinguished under a stained-glass
halo.   I realised immediately that this was an angelic
visitation.   (The darling had 2 very small *black* wings
sprinkled with diamonds and stars.)   But when he handed
me the bouquet, I nearly picked him up as well. . . .
[This note refers to a boy-messenger bringing a bunch
of flowers.]

*To S. S. Koteliansky*                        April 7, 1919

I wish you would come in now, this moment, and let
us have tea and talk.   There is no one here except my
cough.   It is like a big wild dog who followed me home one
day and has taken a most unpleasant fancy to me.   If only
he would be tame !   But he has been this last week
wilder than ever.   It is raining but it's not winter
rain.

This early Spring weather is almost too much to bear.
It wrings one's heart.   I should like to work all day and all
night.   Everything one sees is a *revelation* in the writing
sense.

Have you ever owned a cat who had kittens ?   Or have
you ever watched them from the first moments of their
life ?   On April 5th Charlie was delivered of two—He
was so terrified that he insisted on my being there and ever
since they have lived in my room.   Their eyes are open
already.   Already they smile and smack the spectator in

the face (the spectator being their mother). One is like a minute tigress, very beautiful, and the other is like a prehistoric lizard—in very little. Their tiny paws are pink and soft like unripe raspberries. I am keeping a journal of their first days. It is a pity that human beings live so remote from all animals. . . .

F. writes me that there is a ' rumpus ' between me and—them, I suppose. I see this ' rumpus '—don't you ? a very large prancing, imaginary animal being led by F.—as Una led the Lion. It is evidently bearing down upon me with F. for a Lady Godiva on its back. But I refuse to have anything to do with it. I have not the room now-a-days for rumpuses. My garden is too small and they eat up all one's plants—roots and all.

*To Mrs. Virginia Woolf*                         April 1919

I have burned to write to you ever since you were here last. The East Wind made my journey in the train an impossibility ; it set up ponds and pools in my left lung wherein the Germs and the Toxins—two families I detest—bathed and refreshed themselves and flourished and multiplied. But since then so many miracles have happened that I don't see how one will be able to bear real, full Spring. One is almost tired already—one wants to swoon, like Charles Lamb, before the curtain rises—Oh God ! to look up again and see the sun like a great silver spangle, big bright buds on the trees, and the little bushes caught in a net of green. But what I chiefly love, Virginia, is to watch the people. Will you laugh at me ? —it wrings my heart to see the people coming into the open again, timid, airing themselves ; they idle, their voices change and their gesture. A most unexpected old man passes with a paper of flowers (for whom ?), a soldier lies on the grass hiding his face, a young girl *flies* down a side street on the—positive—*wing* of a boy—

On April 5th our one daffodil came into flower and our cat, Charlie Chaplin, had a kitten.

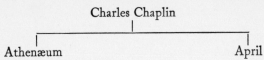

Athenæum                                            April

Athenæum is like a prehistoric lizard, in very little.  He emerged very strangely—as though hurtling through space—flung by the indignant Lord.  I attended the birth.  Charles implored me.  He behaved so strangely : he became a beautiful, tragic figure with blue-green eyes, terrified and wild.  He would only lie still when I stroked his belly and said, " It's all right, old chap.  It's bound to happen to a man sooner or later."  And, in the middle of his pangs, his betrayer, a wretch of a cat with a face like a penny bun and the cat-equivalent of a brown bowler hat, rather rakish over one ear, began to *howl* from outside.  " Fool that I have been ! " said Charles, grinding his claws against my sleeve.  The second kitten, April, was born during the night, a snug, compact little girl.  When she sucks she looks like a small infant saying its prayers and *knowing* that Jesus loves her.  They are both loves ; their paws inside are very soft, very pink, just like unripe raspberries. . . .

Virginia, I have read your article on Modern Novels.  You write so *damned* well, so *devilish* well.

But I positively must see you soon.  I want to talk over so much—Your room with the too deep windows—I should love to be there now.  Last time the rambler roses were nearly over and there was a sound of someone sawing wood.

April 26, 1919

That awful fair !  Never again.  The time has gone by when one was young and rude enough for such things.  It made me so utterly wretched.  I felt there was nothing to do but sit on the stairs and lift up one's voice and—weep for Babylon.  Were human beings in the mass always so shocking—or does one as one grows older shed a skin ?  I can't decide. . . .

I wonder what decision you are arrived at about the cottage with the tower.[1]  Perhaps the house itself is very imperfect in many ways but there is a . . . something . . . which makes one long for it.  Immediately you get there you are *free*, free as air.  You hang up your hat on a nail and the house is furnished.  It is a place where you sit on the stairs and watch the lovely light inhabiting the room below.  After nightfall the house has three voices.  If you are in the tower and someone comes from the far cottage— he comes from far away.  You go by the edge of the field to Katie Berryman's for the bread.  You walk home along the rim of the Atlantic with the big fresh loaf—and when you arrive the house is like a ship.  I mustn't talk about it. It bewitched me.

Saturday afternoon.  J. is downstairs discussing the theory of relativity with S.  I feel they are being a trifle portentous.  The kittens are trying to kill their mother with love in front of my fire ; the wind makes a pleasant sound but all my daffodils are fallen before it.  I feel awfully happy.  A husband, a home, a great many books and a passion for writing—are very nice things to possess all at once.

May 6, 1919

It is indeed thrilling to think that Higher Tregerthen is yours.  God forbid that you should find the rooms too small or some Dreadful Inconvenience that I have forgotten.  But when you sit at the tower window and look out upon that amazing hill I cannot but believe you'll feel its enchantment. . . .  Early this morning there was a white mist here and a smell of burning.  It made me think of Cornwall—of those enchanted misty days, when you go just outside the door and are spirited away.  It will be great happiness if I may come and stay with you in the summer—*great* joy to look forward to.  White and purple veronica would grow excellently well there.  But wait

[1] Higher Tregerthen, Zennor.  See letters of April 1916.

until you see the yellow irises and the foxgloves over six foot high—red indian encampments of foxgloves burning with passion and pride in the field next to yours.

The brilliant but cynical hero dined with us on Saturday. We ran over the eighteenth century in a very lively and high-spirited fashion—a kind of small tour with a basket of wine under the front seat—in the dog cart of the period ! A. H. came in later, lay upon the sofa buried his head in a purple pillow and *groaned* over the hor-rible qual-ity of Smollett's coarseness.

*May* 1919

I am very sorry you are not coming to the Party. I wanted everybody to be there and you to be there. I wanted the small private satisfaction of looking at the party *with* you. However, it can't be helped. If you do come to tea on Monday you will be very welcome. I am thankful people are buying a copy or two of *Prelude*. I hate to think of it loading up your ship. I don't see how your press can be other than a Prodigious success. It must be very nice, cruising about among the islands and deciding to put in—now here—now there—and seeing what the natives have to bring aboard. (Alas, my dear woman, I have no poem. I am not a poet.)

God be thanked for this divine weather ! The vicar called upon me yesterday and asked if he might come occasionally and administer a *little* Private Communion to me at any time . . . just a drain of wine, I suppose, and a crumb of bread. Why a little ? It puzzled me greatly. And I told him that while this weather continued I was nothing but a living Hymn of Praise, an incense, a harp responding. Which is more or less true. Addio.

Tchekhov has a very interesting letter published in next week's A. . . . What the writer does is not so much to *solve* the question but to *put* the question. There must be the question put. That seems to me a very nice dividing line between the true and the false writer.

*To Lady Ottoline Morrell*                     May 1919

I know I have not written for shamefully long, and my heart troubles me about it. It is always the same—if once I don't write—I fall into this dismal silence—and am nothing but a sorry wretch—the most graceless friend alive. Your exquisite letter made me feel the horror I am. And this weather, these first thrilling days of real spring always bring you before me so vividly. I know you love them as I do ; I know you have the same Horror of that endless winter—over at last. *Will* you come and see me when you are in town again ? There are so many things I long to talk over with you. So much seems to have happened and changed—I suppose it hasn't really. It is only the lifting of that appalling cold, dark wing that has hidden everything for what feels to me—an eternity—I really can hardly *remember* what happened before the winter. But I must not speak of it. The trees are trees again and one can face the light without shuddering. Garsington must be very lovely just now and your garden. It has been a miracle to watch the roots and bulbs *buried* by M. last October burst out of their little graves and put on beauty—rather meagre London beauty—but reinforced by nine immense dandelions, the garden, is, to a kind eye— quite gay—

M. and I seem to work like niggers at *The Athenæum*— I wonder if you really like it. *I* feel rather like the pink icing butterfly on the dark sumptuous tragic cake—Very unworthy. I thought the first numbers were too de- pressed but it is sitting up and taking more exciting nourishment now I think. It is great fun. We both enjoy it. It's such a funny company to be sitting at Athene's tea board—But I do wish the other guests would arrive—the gay, unexpected ones.

O this Spring—It makes me *long* for happiness. That is so vague. Each year I think—this year I shall not feel it so keenly—but I feel it more. Why are human beings the only ones who do not put forth fresh buds—exquisite

flowers and leaves ?   I cannot bear to go among them.   I
sit here or take small walks and there seems a blessing
fallen upon the world just as long as one does not see the
people or know of their ways.   We have all been wintry
far too long—Really, on some of these days one is tired
with *bliss*.   I long to tell someone—to feel it immediately
shared—felt without my asking " do you feel it ? "—Do
you know what I mean ?


*To J. M. Murry*                To Wate.
                                                Top Floor.
                        Ring 3.   (If Bell out of Order Please
                                        do not Nock.)
Sir,
    A highly Respecktable Party who as known the Best of
Everythink in er. Day and is oney come down in World
threw no Fault of Same but Illness loss by Death an
Marridge etc. would be greately obligded if Groun Floor
dark Gent would *lend* Same for Reading only Essays by
Wal. Pater.
    No chilren and is Agreed Book Shall not leave House.
                        I Am
                            Yours Faithfully
                                Geo. Mungrove.


*To the Hon. Dorothy Brett*                June 10, 1919

    About what you said—it depends so awfully what effect
company has on your work.   Perhaps it stimulates you ;
then I think you are ever so right to do it.   It does the
opposite to me.   I have to keep as solitary as I can, to
have nobody *depending* and to *depend* as little as I can.
Even if I had footballs for lungs I wouldn't go out often,
for instance—couldn't.   But then my particular Graces
are very jealous and very shy and I have to humble myself
and sit ready for their knock.   Well, it's no hardship—
There could never be a choice between them and the
present ' world.'   But I am no criterion—I want my

'flings' to-day to be oh! such delicate flings and if a
drunken C. blundered in I could not bear it. I can't help
it, I *do* feel so increasingly fastidious and frightened of
rudeness and roughness—Life to-day is such an affair that
I don't feel one can afford to rub shoulders with the world
that goes to Parties. You will think me a sad old frump—
but of course, like everybody else I don't think I am.
Gossip—tittle tattle—*spreading the news*—all that fills me
with horror—Were I perfectly sincere I'd have to confess
that I was always acting a part in my old palmy days.
And now I've thrown the palm away. . . .

*To Lady Ottoline Morrell*                                    June 1919

I have been working all the morning, trying to discover
why *Java Head* is not a good novel and trying to say it is
not a bad one. But one always seems to arrive at the same
conclusion—nothing goes deep enough—the *risk* has not
been taken. Whenever the crisis is reached they decide
to wait until the sea is calmer. How tired one becomes of
all these surfaces. Why do not more people live through
and through ? Must one spend one's life paying calls on
the emotions ? Why isn't the dreary fashion obsolete—
And if it is not this superficial nothingness, it is M. au
grand sérieux throwing himself bodily into the milk-jug
after the drowning fly !

But Oh, if we could have a few weeks Gaiety ! ! The
sun burns to-day and our mysterious plant, the anchusa, is
in bloom. But I should like to see whole vast plains
covered with it. But instead I must go down to the
Laundry office and ask why they have carried forward
10/8. Why—Oh why—and what a mission to take me
forth on a golden day ! And then B. R. says a woman is
incapable of real detachment—But only to think of the
things that do catch at our heels if we try to fly ! I can
imagine a whole rich Hell where the weekly books were
always late, always more than one expected and always
had unaccountable items.

How one grudges the life and energy and spirit that
money steals from one! I long to spend and I have a
horror of spending: money has corrupted me these last
years.

June 1919

The sound of the wind is very loud in this house. The
curtains fly—there are strange pointed shadows—full of
meaning—and a glittering light upon the mirrors. Now
it is dark—and one feels so pale—even one's hands feel
pale—and now a wandering broken light is over everything.
It is so exciting—so tiring, too—one is waiting for something to happen. One is not oneself at all in this weather
—one is a being possessed—caught in the whirl of it—
walking about very lightly—blowing about—and deeply,
deeply excited. . . . Do you feel that, too? I feel one
might say anything—do anything—wreck one's own life
wreck another's. What does it matter? Everything is
flying fast. Everything is on the wing.

On Bank Holiday, mingling with the crowd I saw a
magnificent sailor outside a public house. He was a
cripple; his legs were crushed, but his head was beautiful
—youthful and proud. On his bare chest two seagulls
fighting were tatooed in red and blue. And he seemed to
lift himself—above the crowd, above the tumbling wave of
people and he sang:

"Heart of mine, Summer is waning."

Oh! Heavens, I shall never forget how he looked and
how he sang. I knew at the time this is one of the things
one will always remember. It clutched my heart. It
flies on the wind to-day—one of those voices, you know,
crying above the talk and the laughter and the dust and
the toys to sell. Life is wonderful—wonderful—bitter-
sweet, an anguish and a joy—and Oh! I do not want to be
resigned—I want to drink deeply—deeply. Shall I ever
be able to express it?

Friday
June 28, 1919

This devilish cold persists.  I am still in my life jacket,
plastered underneath with unguents.  Oh, these nights—
sitting up in bed, waiting for the black trees to turn into
green trees.  And yet, when dawn does come, it is always
so beautiful and terrible—the coming of the light such a
miracle—that it's almost worth waiting for.  And then,
as the hours strike through the night, I wander through
cities—in fancy.  Slip along unfamiliar streets, invisible—
wonder who lives in these great houses with heavy doors,
or, down on some quay side, I watch the boats putting out
in the dark and smell the night scent of the open sea—until
lying awake becomes an ecstasy.

One's own life—one's own secret private life—what a
queer positive thing it is.  Nobody knows where you are—
nobody has the remotest idea *who* you are, even.

The Brontës—Last night in bed I was reading Emily's
poems.  There is one :

> I know not how it falls on me
> This summer evening, hushed and lone,
> Yet the faint wind comes soothingly
> With something of an olden tone.
>
> Forgive me if I've shunned so long
> Your gentle greeting, earth and air !
> Yet sorrow withers e'en the strong
> And who can fight against despair ?

The first line—why it is so moving ?  And then the
exquisite simplicity of " Forgive me " . . . I think the
Beauty of it is contained in one's certainty that it is not
Emily disguised—who writes—it is Emily.  Nowadays
one of the chief reasons for one's dissatisfaction with
modern poetry is one can't be sure that it really does
belong to the man who writes it.  It *is* so tiring, isn't it,
never to leave the Masked Ball—never—never.

The house is full of women, to-day.  The peevish old

234

lying cook in the kitchen who says it is *I* who make all the
work.   L. M. bringing my lunch with a ' Take, eat, this
is my body ' air, an old 'un sweeping the stairs away and
down in the studio a little dwarf sewing buttons and strings
on to M.'s clothes and making immense pale darns in his
Hebridean socks. . . .

M. has moved into his new offices and the burden is a
trifle lighter.   Tomlinson is in the same building and they
occasionally have a little gaiety on the stairs—heat pennies,
tie them on a string and slip them under Massingham's
door—or lean out of the window and angle for passing hats
with a bent pin. . . .   This cheers M. greatly.

I try and console myself with—half a lung is better than
no head—but at present I don't feel I've too much of the
latter.

July 1919

I, too, am sick and weary of the gossip-mongers.   Why
should one put up with them.   And what have they done
that they should dare puff themselves up so.   It's ridiculous.   I often feel you are far too tolerant of them.   The
absurdity, the utter absurdity.   What in God's name have
they ever given birth to ?

I confess that at heart I hate them because I feel they
are the enemies of Art—of real true Art.   The snigger is a
very awful thing when one is young and the sneer can
nearly kill.   They profess to live by feeling—but why
then do they never give a sign of it—and why do they do
their very best to ridicule feeling in others ?   It is all
poisonous.

Such a strange day,—a purplish sky—the rain falling,
falling—as one imagines the rain falls in China—and
through it the thrum-thrum-tinkle-tinkle of a little string
band.   For Mrs. D. is giving a Garding Party. . . .   I
have such a funny vision of the party—the vicar's straw
hat, so wet and sticky—Mr. D. blowing his nose in the
same charmingly intimate way *off* the stage as he does *on*—

and Mrs. flashing her teeth and her ten finger nails at Society. I saw these remarkable hands hovering over and positively shooting beams of light on to a box of plover's eggs at the fishmongers, the other day, while she cried for the pit, gallery, porter at the door and attendant in the Ladies Toilet to hear: "Are they *raipe*, Fishmonger? Are you sure they are *raipe*?"

What a world, what a world! The cook has given notice. How blessed! It is dreadful enough to be without servants but to be with them—is far more dreadful. I cannot forget the dishonest hateful old creature down in the kitchen. Now she will go and I shall throw her bits to the dustman and fumigate her room and start fair again.

I feel so much *more* sensitive to everything than I used to be—to people good or bad, to ugliness or beautiful things. Nowadays when I catch a glimpse of Beauty—I weep— yes, really weep. It is too much to be borne—and if I feel wickedness—it hurts so unbearably that I get really ill. It is dreadful to be so exposed—but what can one do?

Saturday afternoon
July 1919

It's raining and I feel lonely and cold and forsaken. Pray for me. How well I know that wraith-like, dis- embodied feeling; it has been mine all last, this week. One lay in bed and felt like a shell and wept and weeping made one cough and summer was over. I asked my doctor the very question, "What would one do if one had to cope with life," and he replied "Why, you'd be in an institution and paid for by the state." So there is one horror spared.

Why these young men should lean and lean over the decomposing vapours of poor Jules Laforgue is inexplic- able. . . . It only makes one feel how one adores English prose, how to be a writer—is *everything*. I *do* believe that the time has come for a ' new word ' but I imagine the new

236

word will not be spoken easily. People have never explored the lovely medium of prose. It is a hidden country still—I feel that so profoundly.

Monday. The weather has ' got me ' completely ; I am ill again. I have coughed so much that I feel like a living rattle. There's nothing to be done. Why won't the summer come back ? What has happened to it ? One must drug oneself deeply, deeply with work and try to forget.

Forgive me—I can't write—I feel *numb* with despair—and only want to creep away somewhere and weep and weep—

*To the Hon. Dorothy Brett*                            Friday
                                                    July 18, 1919

I have just been doing the flowers. They look so lovely—especially three in my room, which are small white roses with gay little leaves, fairy tale roses. Downstairs the Dwarf is making me what she calls a ' cotton body—a very useful possession, I should think. I wonder if she'd make me a fur body for the winter with a little hot piping round the waist. Further downstairs, in the tool-box Charlie has just been delivered of 6 kittens. She is in a dark cupboard, among the rakes and hoes and old bulbs, twisted with yellow twine and straw and red flower pots and bunches of twigs. I put my head in and feel I shall see a bright star in the back above Charlie and hear a chorus of angels. Athenæum *hates* them. When M. went to him and told him that God had sent him six little brothers and sisters he fell off the studio window ledge right through the glass house, breaking two large panes of glass. I love his sense of the dramatic necessity—but, all the same, next time he must *not* be told. C'est trop cher.

I am very horrified by your account of Mrs. B. Can't she be flung over the garden wall ? *Must* she cling ? Can't you harden your heart ? And if she threatens to kill herself why should she be stopped ? I don't know a

237

single enemy who wants to share a house and to whom I could fling a bramble. But be firm—don't have her in your room—that is the worst of brambles, there is never an end to them—they creep under the doors, they catch you whenever you want to fly, and they can be more than a nuisance—they can hurt. I think she ought to join something and become a ? or a ? or a ?. It's no use her staying Mrs. B. evidently. I am awfully hard-hearted about *clinging*—one must just use a knife as quickly as possible.

This house seems to be an R 34 to-day, rushing through the air. Everything is in flight. It's as much as one can do to catch anything. The windows all open—the curtains moving—a smell of cherry jam boiling from the kitchen. Gertie saying, " If you please, m'm, the nasturtiums in the front are out," as if they were walking up to the door—advancing upon us.

Oh Life—mysterious Life—What art thou ? Forster says : a game—I feel suddenly as though from all the books there came a clamour of voices—the books are speaking—especially the poets—How beautiful willows are—how beautiful—how the sun rains down upon them—the tiny leaves move like fishes. Oh Sun, shine for ever ! I feel a little bit drunk—rather like an insect that has fallen into the cup of a magnolia.

*To S. S. Koteliansky*                                    July 1919

I am going away the third week in September, I think—to the Italian Riviera—Then I shall have *unlimited time* to work. I do not want at present to start a new life in a new country, like Lawrence, but to be about and to work—really that is preferable to going to Heaven. . . .

My new kitten, Wing Lee,[1] is lying on his back on the sofa waving his legs and arms. He runs like a rabbit. I am longing to write a story where a kitten shall play an important rôle.

[1] The name of this kitten, who appears frequently henceforward, was shortened to Wingley and sometimes to Wing.

*To the Hon. Dorothy Brett*                          July 29, 1919

Are you drawing ?   Have you made flower drawings ?
I wish you would do a whole Flower Book—Quarto size—
with one page to each flower—its leaves, roots, buds,
petals—all its little exquisite life in colour—very delicate
with an insect or two creeping in or a blade of grass or a
tiny snail.   I see something wonderful.   Did you ever see
those books Karl Larsen made of his house and garden and
children ?   They didn't need any words at all—They
were *fascinating*.   I wish you would make such a book ;
you have just the vision for it—delicate—and light, light
as a flying feather.   But I daresay you will rap me over
the head for my imperence—But time is flying—soon or
late it will be closing time—let us be divinely drunk while
we may—

I wish you did not mind what they say—what anybody
says.   Why are you hurt by G.'s wooden airs ?   I think
like the man in *Mr. Polly*, he wants his head boiling—he
wants the MIGHTY to say to him, " Oh, *boil* your head ! "
Whenever I hear his absurd literary opinions I burn to
make that my cry.

Now, what is the news.   M.'s poems are out ! and he is
printing at lightning speed a long story of mine—We are
both *slaves* to the Athene but when we do escape we
are happy and talk and build sand castles.   Will the
treacherous tide have them—knock them flat ?   I don't
know.

The wind set up such a song in my bones that my dear
doctor is once more sticking longer, stronger needles into
my behind.   Although I walk like the only child of a
crab and an Indian colonel I feel it is going to do the trick.
Pray for me, Brett.   Burn a candle for me if there is a
Roman Catholic chapel in Oxford.

It is a very quiet day here, green and silver—the movement of the leaves is so secret, so silent, that I could watch
them all day—I try to find words for how they lift and
fall.

*To Anne Estelle Rice*                    August 13, 1919

I have been rather badly ill and am only up for the first time to-day. It was a thousand Joys to hear from you. I *searched* the wee photograph for all there possibly was to see of you and David. Ah, que vous avez de la chance! He looks a perfect lamb, distinctly as though he were thinking about that blackbird, taking it seriously, and making a thorough study of the bird. I hope I *shall* see him one day. My Pa arrives to-morrow and my plans are still rather en l'air until I have seen him. Why, I don't know. But he seems to me a kind of vast symbolic chapeau out of which I shall draw the little piece of paper that will decide my Fate. But that is absurd. For my plans are to go abroad in about three weeks' time and there to remain. We are on the track of several different places, and not decided yet, but c'est tout.

I shall be more thankful than I can say to be out of it all here. I hate the place and the people always more and more, and I am sure the whole of England is finie, finie. Perhaps it isn't if you have a baby to laugh things over with, but otherwise, and plus *life on a sofa*, it's just hell. What wouldn't I give for one of our *laughs*, ma chère? As it is, things aren't funny any more. They only make me feel desperate. " It's time for me to go," as the song says. The only thing I have got out of it all these months is pennies. I have earned quite a few. That gives me a good sense of freedom.

Forgive the dullest dog that ever lay beside a cottage door. I will write again, darling woman, when things are more lively. I'd give a world to hear your " Hil-lo! "

*To Mrs. Virginia Woolf*                    August 1919

This is the first day I am up again and able to write letters. I have been rather badly ill, and it has left me for the moment without an idea ... except that I must go abroad into a Sanatorium until next April. I can't take a villa or manage anything for the next six months. I must just lie in the air and try and turn into a decent creature. Do not think I am forgetful of you. You would not believe me if you knew how often you are in my *heart* and *mind*. I love thinking of you. I expect Asheham is a glory these days.

I will write again very soon. This is just really a wave. I would I were a crocodile. According to your Sir Thomas Browne it is the only creature who does not *cough* : " Although we read much of their Tears we find nothing of that motion." Thrice happy oviparous quadruped !

*To Lady Ottoline Morrell*                      August 17, 1919

Here's an absurd situation! My doctor strongly urges me *not* to put myself away, *not* to go into a sanatorium— he says I would be out of it in 24 hours and it would be a " highly dangerous experiment." " You see," he explained, " there is your work which I know is your life. If they kept it from you you'd die—then they *would* keep it from you. This would sound absurd to a German specialist but I have attended you for a year and I know." After this, I with great difficulty restrained my impulse to tell the doctor what his words did for me. They were breath, life—healing, *everything*. So it is the Italian Riviera after all, a maid to travel with me and a little villa —Being ill and bearing all the depression of those round me had, I think, almost made me insane. *I just gave up hope.* Now I am full of hope again, and I am off the third week in September. M. is going across the first week in September to find me a villa and then I go. It is a blessed relief. And to think there will be the sun and another summer and unlimited time to write—It is next door to Heaven.

Life is so strange—so full of extraordinary things. . . . To-day, this afternoon, waiting for my Father to come to tea—I felt I could have made—but only of that waiting—

a whole book. I began thinking of all the time one has
'waited' for so many and strange people and things—
the special quality it has—the *agony* of it and the strange
sense that there is a second you who is outside yourself and
does nothing—nothing but just listen—the other complicated you goes on—and then there is this keen, un-
sleeping creature—waiting to leap—It is like a dark beast
and he who comes is its prey—

Everybody has deserted me—I don't hear from a soul.


*To S. S. Koteliansky*                       August 21, 1919

I have re-read *The Steppe*. What can one say ? It is
simply one of *the* great stories of the world—a kind of
Iliad or Odyssey. I think I will learn this journey by
heart. One says of things : they are immortal. One
feels about this story not that it *becomes* immortal—it
always was. It has no beginning or end. Tchehov just
touched one point with his pen (.————.) and then
another point : *enclosed* something which had, as it were,
been there for ever.


                                    Poste Restante
                                    San Remo, Italy
                                    September 19, 1919

This is the first day I am able to answer your letter. We
were at the last moment forced to travel a day in advance.
This I telegraphed you on Tuesday but L. M. forgot to
send the wire, she says. I hate to think you came and
there was nobody there. We had a dreadful journey,
and this place is terribly hot and swarming with insects and
hotel profiteers. But I am better to-day and I have found
a small *solitary* little house away from everybody, hidden
by olive trees, overlooking the sea. In eight days I shall
be there. Please send me *as soon as possible* some more
Tchehov, as much as you can—I will work fast here—and
anything else. I will write again when I am stronger.

*To J. M. Murry.*                    Casetta Deerholm, Ospedaletti
                                          September 29, 1919

Your postcard from Paris has just come. Why it has
taken so long God only knows. I felt certain you'd have
sent me one from there, yet yesterday I gave up all hope of
getting one—indeed of hearing at all until you were back
in London. I feel quite different with this postcard.
When I die, just before the coffin is screwed up, pop a
letter in. I shall jump up and out. . . .

L. M. has broken my thermometer. *Good.* I got
another for 12 francs, which seems to play the same tune,
though the notes are not so plain. " I was pulling your
cupboard away from the nets and it just rolled on to the
floor." I suppose in Rhodesia you just have notches on a
bamboo or a tchetchetchetche branch.

I have been out since 9 o'clock. The sea is divine. It's
very hot. All last night I chased the midges Buzzing in
the nets afar Each one bearing, as it kindled, Message of
the open war. (Macaulay). It's perfect except for the
' afar.' They are a scourge here, now ; in hundreds.
On dit that they will go when the fruit goes, and that
flowers in the house are fatal for them. Well, what a
silly country !

I started a big story yesterday. I don't think it's very
good, but I am going straight on with it, whatever it is
like, just for the practice and for getting into my stride. . . .


*To S. S. Koteliansky.*                      October 1, 1919

I have taken this little villa for the winter, perhaps for
longer. It is nice, Koteliansky ; you would like it. It
is on a wild hill slope, covered with olive and fig trees and
long grasses and tall yellow flowers. Down below is the
sea—the entire ocean—a huge expanse. It thunders all
day against the rocks. At the back there are mountains.
The villa is not very small. It has a big verandah on one
side where one can work and an overgrown garden. No
hideous riviera palms (like Italian profiteers) ; everything

very simple and clean. Many lizards lie on the garden wall ; in the evening the cicada shakes his tiny tambourine. I have often pictured you here. We walk up and down, smoking. If only the mosquitoes were not like roaring lions—but they are. On the 14th is my birthday. Please send me a letter for that day if you are in the mood. I am working. I wish your eyes were better ; I wish you had good news. M. is back in London. Goodnight.

*To J. M. Murry*                                    Friday
October 3, 1919

I wish Wing could write letters. I should set him papers of questions and give him prizes for full answers. The weather is marvellous, like *silk*—very hot. and still. People are bathing below. It's so clear one can see their legs and arms, almost their toes. This house is rather like a fairy house. It is an adorable place to live in—and then the garden—and the view of Ospedaletti is exquisite. The view is for ever subtly changing. It's far more beautiful and remote than Pauline. The fact, too, that one is for ever conscious of this huge expanse of sea. . . . God knows I don't want to live here, but for a place to get well in, it could not be more ideal.

L. M. is off to San Remo to see if she can find a *litre* of fine muslin. Just as I thought, she loves that jaunt in, and " You don't mind, Katie, now you have your revolver, do you ? " No, I don't. . . .

? Monday
October 6, 1919

I am sitting outside in the bastick chair ; it is a mild, cloudy day. The morning was quite chilly—so was last night. Talk about the bounding horizon. . . . As I sit here I have to throw everything I write against it, and it seems to me the pink geranium beats me out of hand. It is a lesson in humility to write *or* think with that sea and sky there.

Where are you ?

How are you ?

When I know those things, and how you found everything I shall feel really settled, but while you are en voyage I'm restless. You understand that ? Augusta, the maid, has disappeared. She must have seen that furniture arriving.[1]

L. M. has broken :

      (1) The big fruit dish

      (2) Our plate

      (3) A saucer

all at one go from leaning on the sideboard. I shall buy crocks here but put them in your suit-case against the goldene Zeit. And the worst of it is I always feel she thinks it " so nice and homey " to occasionally smash a thing or two. You must keep me from getting over-stern, overstrict and overtidy. It's an obsession. I realised it this morning. Even out here I had to re-arrange the pick, the shovel, and the rake before I could do a thing—even though they were behind me. I hope I shan't say to our darling little boy " as long as your mud-pies have *form*, darling, you can make them. But there must be no slopping over the mould." He will like you best.

You know how, when we get hungry, we are at last even unable to play Demon for wanting the hash-hammer to sound. That is precisely my state of mind *re* a letter from you to say you are at home. Once I've got it, sat down to table with it, fed my soul on it, eaten every single scrap with all the appetite in the world, I fire ahead with other things. . . .

Tuesday

October 7, 1919

A workman has come who says they will have finished their part of the job to-day and after that it's only a

[1] The furniture was distinctly exiguous.

matter of quelques jours before the water is turned on here. Wonderful people! It's another summer day. As the waves break they are full of gold, like the waves we saw at Bandol. This early morning (6.30) the sea was *pink*, pale pink—I never saw it so before—and it scarcely breathed. . . . The washerwoman brought home your clothes last night (yes, the change of subject isn't a really absurd change. I'd think the pink sea all the lovelier if it had a boat in it with your blue shirt for a sail.) I have just put the clothes away among mine—and the carnation sachets. There are tiny false links in your cuffs which impressed me greatly. Here they are waiting for you.

The insect plague is *simply awful*. No nets or veils will keep them out. The tiny, almost invisible ones, who are so deadly, the laundress tells me are called ' păpĕtĕ-chĭkŏs.'

(Zuccinis are not cucumbers. They are a kind of elongated pale yellow marrows. L. M. bought one yesterday. I don't at all see why we should not grow them in Sussex.) I am longing to get out of the garden and make a small tour of Ospedaletti. Every day a new shop seems to arise; and the butcher is evidently a fascinating man. But I shall stick to the garden for the present and get my cough down. I feel wonderfully better, wonderfully stronger. I feel myself walking about like a normal person at times—quite lightly and quickly. Soon it will always be like that.

The olives are ripe and beginning to fall.

Wednesday
October 8, 1919

It is awfully hot here—as hot as when we came. The insects are *simply awful*. It's a good thing you left before they got really bad. My leg is so swollen I can only hop to-day. It is maddening because otherwise I feel so well and strong. Curse these confounded countries!! We have double nets, powder, bathe in verbena, oatmeal,

milk, salt water, fresh—but nothing cures them.   I think
they make the idea of a life in this country absolutely insup-
portable.   Enough of them.

I took the revolver into the garden to-day and practised
with it : how to load and unload and fire.   It terrifies me,
but I feel ' like a new being ' now that I can really handle
it and understand it.   I'll never give it back to V.[1]   They
are fascinating things ;  one is childishly fascinated.   I
almost understand old Brontë *père*.   No more coffee to be
had in San Remo.   The Government has taken it over as
it has the rice.   Dear knows when we shall get any more.
It doesn't matter really.

Thursday
October 9, 1919

I have just had an interview with a bonne who does not
speak 1 word of French—a pretty, nice, awfully nice girl
with pearly teeth.   What *she* said, what *I* said, I really
don't know.

*Me :*  La lettiere nonne arrivato attendre duo giorni
venuto Bordighera ?

*She :*  Si, si, cuisino.

*Me :*  Oh, dear, what a bother !

*She :*  Si, si, dimancho-sabbato.

I finally gave her a letter in French for the woman at the
dairy to translate, and off she went.   When (to make it
plain) I showed her the empty room with two coat-hooks
and a sheepskin in it, she seemed to think it superbly
furnished.   " Bono, bono, molto bono ! "   A sort of
Maori haka !   Wise old Feltie,[2] listening in the hall, is still
shaking with laughter.

I think she is just the person—young, strong, pretty,
with black, laughing eyes, a bit grubby, but only *de la terre*,
a kind of Italian Marie [3] of a lower class.   She gave a little

---

[1] The owner of the Casetta, who had lent the revolver to K. M.

[2] A large grey felt hat which we possessed in common.

[3] The bonne at the Villa Pauline.

half curtsey when we parted. What will come of it ?
She also wrote on a bit of paper, *Da muni vineri si*.
Whether that means she is coming or that she is fond of
wine I am still not certain. . . .

It's a lovely morning. I am working and very happy.
It's hot—grilling. I think I shall have a pet lizard here.
L. M. said a *sissida* (cicada) was buzzing round her electric
light all last night. What do you think of that ?

I had a letter from S. to-day which really boxed it.
I mean, he said it was only my " indomitable will " (!)
which kept me alive this last year, and he is sure I shall now
get absolutely well and " grow into your dream of achieve-
ment." This, of course, makes me feel *cicatrisé* all over and
also rouses my pride. I *will*.

Saturday
October 11, 1919

When I got up this morning, I put on my hat first and as
soon as the food had been arranged, went out for a small
walk. The day was so—what *can* one say ? there isn't a
word, perfect is not enough—that I had to go. First
thing I saw was a large daisy at the bottom of our steps, in a
pinafore—you know the kind, a Wingley flower. Then I
walked along the Boulevard which smelled of pines, gum
trees, heliotrope, geraniums and a dash of the sea, and
really had a look at Ospedaletti. But ! I hadn't the
faintest *idea* of what it was like. It's just a fairy tale ;
that's all. And the country above and beyond it—these
immense romantic glimpses ! I sauntered along, gripping
Mother's walking-stick. My heart was bursting with
happiness. The sun had his arm round my shoulder.
The sea made a sound you would have liked. There was
a breeze that filled one's mouth with pleasure like wine.
Hardly anybody about. A small scene from an opera
being enacted at the cabstand between two lovely girls
carrying baskets of fringed linen on their heads, a boy in a
blue undervest eating a loaf of bread, and the cab-driver
in white. That was all.

Then I kept coming to these glimpses of the old town, seen between the trees, and then to pine trees with rose-red geraniums climbing up to their topmost branch. The only work being done was gardening. One heard people gardening and felt them gardening, and that was all. By the time I got to the Poste I knew something very good was going to happen, and three letters were handed across. You know that row of darling little oleanders [a drawing of one]—little trees like that. I sat on a bench beneath them and read the letters and then walked off clasping them very hard and stopping occasionally and saying to a bush or a plant, " Darling ! " very quietly.

Really, when you come in May I dread to think of what we shall do. When it's spring here as well as everything else. You see, we shall trundle off with our *filet* in the morning, and then we'll come home ravenous as I did and see this little house as I did perched on the hill half in sun, half swept by the dancing shadow of the olive-trees. And there will be flowers everywhere.

I didn't feel in the least tired. I stopped at the drug store and bought four bottles of St. Galmier. It wasn't a luxury. I think one needs to drink here, especially while the skeeters are so skeeterish. Such a nice woman in there, extremely pretty, and awfully nice jujubes on the counter. Blow ! Everything was awfully nice. Beams came from the toothbrushes. She says it is like this all the winter except for an occasional day of wind or rain, just as hot, and people who come *pour se reposer* go away on wings. Cherry pie grows in trees in the jardin publique at Ospedaletti. Did you *see* that wonderful park-like place with all its flowers ? Lawrence was working in the garden with a handkerchief round his neck.

Well, *I* don't know. But really we seem to have found the most ideal place we could have found. I can *whistle* again. . . .

I wondered if you would ever publish a column from a Note Book. It is going to be called " From the Casetta " and it's a kind of day book about things like flies or a certain light or a fragment of talk over a table or workmen going home in the evening. . . . I want to write a whole book—ready in six months—of these . . . *observations*.

Oh, it is cruel to say how warm it is here. I never saw anything like the shadows in this house cast by the delicate trees outside. I have already noticed 5 different grasshoppers. They are great favourites of mine as insects : they are such *characters*. As for the cicada, every night he is here. I can't tell you how good the stove is. It is a gem, now that it is accustomed to go. Yesterday, when L. M. was out, I made my tea with about 2 leaves and a twig and the whole kitchen felt so warm and lived in. . . .

Sunday<br>October 12, 1919

I am sitting in the Bastick chair covered with the Jaeger rug, as although the sun is hot the air is chilly (it's about 4.45 p.m.). It has been a marvellous day here ; I've not moved except for meals. I've been reading and writing, and after lunch I fell asleep from the general *ship-board* atmosphere. Speaking of ships, such a small jewel of a sailing ship passed the house to-day, riding close enough in to see the men on board. She had two small sails at the bows, one big one at the stern, and a medium *very* movable one amidships. The sea is my favourite sea, bright, bright blue, but showing a glint of white as far as one can see. That lift of white seen far away, as far as the horizon, moves me terribly. In fact it is *the very thing* I would like to express in writing : it has *the very quality*. Here comes another most interesting little steamboat—a very small trader, she looks, painted black and red, with a most ridiculous amount of smoke coming out of the funnel. [A drawing of the steamer.] No, I can't draw her.

From where I sit, I cannot see any ground below the balustrade. That is threaded through with sea. One would think it was a sheer drop from there into deep water. What a place, eh ?

I had a nasty jar last night.  As there was no water last
week, the laundry was put ' out ' and it came home
exquisite, covered with a white net with a rose on top,
carried by the nicest old body on her head, who seemed to
take the greatest fancy to me, as I did to her.  Long
conversation.  " Comme vous êtes bien ici," etc., etc.,
etc., etc.  And under all this a bill for 37.85.  This, of
course, after the old 'un had gone and the rose had been
smelled and admired and Wig had thought how *much*
better, after all, they order these things in Italy.  L. M.
did not really " think it very heavy.  I don't think you
could have expected it to be less, Katie."  This with her
overall 4.50 and an immense white petticoat 3.85 !  As
to serviettes at 1 lira apiece, " Oh well, my dear, that's not
quite sixpence if the exchange is still at 41 for the £1.
It's about . . . let me see . . . hardly fivepence," and so on
and so on and so on.  How I should beat her if I were
married to her !  It's an awful thought.  She thinks I am
made of money.  That's the worst of it !  On her last
but one journey to San Remo she bought *one* hecto of
coffee for 4.50 from " *such* a funny little shop " and when
I protested she thought " the parcel was small for the
money, but the beans felt very tightly packed."  Could
you believe it ?  However,—let her go.  And I shall never
shoot her because the body would be so difficult to dispose
of after.  One couldn't make it into a neat parcel
or put it under a hearth stone, and she would *never*
burn.

Every day I love this house more for some new grace,
and every day I hold a minute review of the garden, and
there is always some thing fresh and wonderful.  Then
there is the wild hill, never the same, *satisfying* one's deep
love for what is living and ancient in literature.  I look at
the hill, and because I have not had a classical education,
it seems to me full of the spirit of those old boys—the wild
fig and olive, the low-growing berries and the tufts of
sweet roots. . . .

Monday
October 13, 1919

The weather has completely changed. It's chilly with
a thick, thick fog and heavy downpour of rain. The sky
is grey. It's like living inside a pearl to-day—very lovely,
for a change. . . .

Visitors last night. A *very* nice one. While I was
waiting for the beans, I saw two honey-ball eyes looking
at me from the hall. (The front door was open.) When
they saw me, they *flashed* away, but I immediately said as
much Wing language as I knew and went quietly to the
door with my soup plate. A perfectly lovely tiny cat
came in, *gold*, *white* and *black*, with a body rather like a
rabbit. It simply bolted the stray pasta : then I gave it
some milk, and it more than bolted that. Then it purred
more loudly than any cat I've ever heard. Its purring
machine must have been wound up until that moment.
It sat under a chair singing like this for a little, and then
fled into the night again. In my mind I called it "Gênet."

I have just looked up. The fog has rolled away. The
rain has stopped. The air smells of geraniums. To-
morrow the gardener comes for the day ; the ground will
be just right for sowing. There are carts going by.
*Yip-y-y-y-ip-yip*, say the drivers and the bells go *tring-
tring-tring*. The sea sounds as though it were somehow
exquisitely refreshed by that mist ; all the grass-blades
are bowed down by a diamond. Oh dear, I'm awfully
happy. It has been so lovely lying here in the rain. I
feel renewed, too, and bowed down with a diamond,
too . . . Look at the new leaves on the rose bushes—bright
red. Were they there yesterday ? There is one hidden
frog here ; he croaks every evening. He shall be invited
to the festa in May. . . .

Bites are still going strong. Does Tommy [1] know a
fly—just like an ordinary house-fly in the face, that
stings ? *It is here.*

[1] H. M. Tomlinson.

Wednesday
October 15, 1919

You should have seen after the rain was over yesterday,
little old men appeared from nowhere in peaked hats,
crawling over the wild hill looking for snails. They
carried coloured handkerchieves which *frothed*. Flowers
are coming up everywhere on the hill. I just went for a
glance to-day—not more than five steps high, and there
were 8 kinds there.

Caterina came yesterday (the pretty one from the
laundry). She brought me vivid pink carnations and two
eggs in cotton wool for a present. But I felt she could
afford to. All the same, she was fearfully nice—laughing,
gay, beautiful, *healthy* creature. She says May here is
magnifique beyond anything. The whole place is covered
with flowers, and all the little kinds *pour les distillations* are
out—tiny hyacinths, violets, small roses.

Well, now I'll tell you about myself. I feel marvellously
better. All that remains is my cough. It has bad
moments still, but that terrible boiling sensation when I
can't stop, I haven't had *once* since you left. Nor have I
*once* had a temperature. I get short of puff if I cough, but
my lungs don't hurt at all. Think of last October 14th.
S. B. came, and at night I had fever in that North Room
and thought I was going to die.

[Later.]

I am in the middle of a review of Brett-Young which I
will post to the office to-morrow unregistered . . I am
very glad that K. M. is liked a bit. She wishes she was
more worthy. That's *sincere* from my soul. But whenever I'm praised I always want to fall on my knees and ask
God to make me a better girl. It just takes me that way.

That Wing! What a fellow he is! I wish you could
bring him in May, but he would eat his way out of a suit-
case just as you were in the Customs Office. How I would
love to kiss him!

Yesterday ended in such a blazing glory of a sunset that

I was quite frightened. It really was the most superb day, and at night (all the windows open) the sea sounded like an immense orchestra; I could truly hear violins, especially, and great rushing passages for the wood-wind. The skeeters drank my blood last night, and I'm awfully bitten to-day—but to death—both hands, one face, and one leg.

I wish I was more of a stoic about under-linen, perfumes, little boxes for a toilet table, delicate ribbons and silk stockings. But the older I grow, the more exquisite I want to be, *fine* down to every minutest particular, as a writer, as a talker, in my home, in my life, and in all my ways—to carry it all through. Even now sometimes, when I write to you, a word shakes into the letter that I don't mean to be there, an old windfall, you know, from a tree in an orchard I've long forsaken. . . . Do you know what I mean ? It is my illness which has made me so bad-tempered at times. Alas ! one can't fight without getting battle-stained, and, alas ! there have been so many occasions when I've never had time to wash away the stains or renew myself.

A year ago I thought I was going to die, and I think I *was*. And now I know we are going to live. Don't let's forget how S. has helped. I really think I should just have died in that room upstairs if he had not taken me by the hand, like you take a little girl who is frightened of a dog, and led me up to my pain and showed it me and proved it wasn't going to eat me. That was what he did.

Oh dear, on the wild hill to-day I found thyme and rosemary—it reminded me of Bandol in the early morning. Very large astonished daisies are beginning to flower everywhere, even in the gravel. The cotton-pods are huge. Exquisite pale yellow butterflies flutter by. The Marygolds unclosèd are.

P.S.—A huge fawn-coloured rat just ran over the verandah. Tell Wing.

Thursday
October 16, 1919

It's bitterly cold, pouring with rain, a hard, heavy wind
blowing and the sky like an iron shutter. 4.30 and the
light is on. I went outside this morning but was blown in
again, and I've been writing at the dining room table.
My little table is too small. I am so thankful after all
that I brought really warm clothes. *On a besoin.*
To-day—thick jaegers, jersey and cardigan, and deux
pantalons.

That cat I made such a fuss about got in the larder last
night and stole our meat. It sprang in the window to-day
again and looked like a devil when I shooed it away. I
shall have *no* cats here. And *she* has broken our glass jug.
Well, well. First thing I saw was the fragments outside
the back door. It can't be helped. She said, " It was
very frail from the beginning." I suppose one would
make the same excuse if one dropped and broke a baby !
I hope my review is all right. I feel far away when I am
writing—as though I am being confusing, you can't *hear
me*. It makes me anxious.

Heavy thunder prowls round the sky. Now it is sunset,
and the shutter of the sky lifts to show one bright band of
gold. I am just a little bit tired ; it is the weather—the
thunder and sudden intense *heavy* cold like lead. Oh,
what a good idea ! I'll drink a glass of wine . . . Ge-
trunken. Really, England is never colder than this to-day.
Now it is hailing, enormous hail. I'd like to be in Sussex,
and very, very *snug*. But don't think I'm depressed. I'm
not—only *so* parky after such a long taste of heavenly fair
climate. And very angry because in spite of the cold the
mosquitos and gnats persist. Both my hands are bandaged
to-day. Why don't they die ? *She* caught one to-day
and put it out of window instead of killing it ! I expect
they've passed the word round that this house is an *asile*
for them.

Friday
October 17, 1919

I had just given your letter to L. M. to post, I had put
on my cape, and after walking through the rooms and
thinking how delicious apples and pot au feu smelt when
they were cooking ensemble, I went to the door to see the
sunset.   Up our steps came Caterina with a gardener in
tow.   (Caterina has established herself a kind of guardian
here.   She it was who brought me the eggs in cotton wool
and the pink flowers and who tells L. M. where to get
things.)   Alors, she has found me this gardener ; she
talked as though she had just picked him up somewhere on
the path.   He was very nice—a big grey kind old dog in a
cap.   Caterina was very cold.   She had her hands tucked
in the cuffs of a small grey woollen jacket ; her nose was
pink, charmingly pink, and her eyes sparkled.   " Do you
mind work on Sundays ?   He can come on Sundays ? "
Not at all.   " And he will bring you plants.   Would you
like quelques geraniums ? "   At that I held up my hands,
and I saw Caterina was having a joke, too.   So I asked for
violets, and he said he would bring them, both savage and
mild—little blue growling darlings and white meek as
milk ones.   He says they *poussent comme rien* here.

All roses flower in le mois de noël.   It is just time for
jonquils, narcissi, tulips,—rather late in fact.   He will
also bring roses.   But when he asked me if I wouldn't
like some little palms, and I said No, I loved plants with
flowers, I saw by his shrug and his ' moue ' that he rather
despised me.   " Ah, ces femmes avec ces fleurs ! " was
what I felt.   Then he asked if I'd like a lily that grew
about the size of the villa—*enormous*.   By the time you
came you would have had to hunt for me and the house
among the lily leaves and the big white flowers.   You
would have said, " There they are ! " and then " No, that's
a snail ! " because on such pasture the snails would grow
large too.

This rather frightened me.   I said if he had a smaller
one, I'd have it please, but not " those of the Lar-gest

size." Then in the late pale light with Caterina and the
gardener outlined against the olive, the deep blue sea and
the red sky, we had a little talk. The gardener meanwhile
spat very splendidly over the olive boughs. I was greatly
impressed by his performance.

(*Enter L. M. :* " Katie, do you mind if I put the pot au
feu through the sieve ? "

*Me :* " Terribly."

*She :* " Oh, I am so sorry. I was only thinking how
beautifully it would have gone through. It was just an
idea. Do you mind ? I won't interrupt again.")

Now it's dark. The big daisies in the vase on the table
have shut their pretty eyes. The shadows are wonderfully quiet. The sea sounds as though it were sweeping up
through hollow caves. A dog is barking, a bell tinkles on
the road. Through the window I see an olive tree growing
in a room just like this one and girl sits at a table under its
branches writing to her love.

Saturday
October 18, 1919

Please always tell me at once of the faults in my reviews.
Haul me over the hottest coals. It is only kind. I expect
you to do this. If anything is all right—let it be ; but
otherwise, do please beat me. Elizabeth Stanley is
sending two poems on Monday ; she wants to hold them
over till then. One longs to write poems here.

That Samuel Butler ! We knew it, didn't we ? The
ironing-board and the sewing-machine—they are in *all*
his books—he gave them to himself as well—was an expert
in the use of both really. What a surface he puts on
things ! What little crisp frills ! How neatly turned !
*How beautifully, enfin, he ' got up ' other people's washing.*
As to the sewing-machine, the 2nd half of *The Way of All
Flesh* is all machine-sewn. I wish I could see the woman's [1]
letters ; I'd *dearly* love to.

[1] Miss Savage, the original of Alethea Pontifex.

This afternoon I have been to San Remo. A great Ausflug—the first since you went away. We took the tram and went first class—velvet seats, very fine, but iron seats in velvet gloves alas! as the journey progressed. It was a beautifully light gay afternoon. I don't feel in the least tired, I feel *rested*; in fact, I went partly to rest my eyes. Oh dear, if I could tell you all I saw! But the very very thrilling thing was that I went to our china shop and bought another plate, (I am beginning our collection with ½ dozen soup plates : they are a late *dowry*) and the woman said at the end of this month she will have cups and saucers in this ware *all* sizes, from large café au lait downwards, also teapots and jugs. This is of international importance, isn't it? I *shuddered* with joy, seeing the large fluted cups, the sun on the breakfast table, honey in the comb to eat, you one end and me the other with three each side with their cups tilted up to their noses. But seriously, isn't it Great News?

The money flew out of my purse—but it was worth it. Then we caught the tram home. L. M. carried the parcels, and soon the kettle was boiling and we were having Tea. That is like the end of a 'composition,' *Describe an outing*. The villa trembling in the late sun and shadows was beautiful to return to. It *is* so beautiful. If only I did not get so bitten! Worse than ever—both my arms and hands.

San Remo is all in readiness for its visitors. Every second shop a cake shop : little cakes about the size of a cup for 3.50, and *Victory* with her car full of chocolates— you know the style—two sugar horses with silver wings, and little loves holding, staggering under, the bonbons, and then the stern, majestic, helmeted figure with her sword upraised, standing in a chariot of chées !

How strange human nature is! A clergyman and his waife in front of the postcar

" My dear, that view, I am share n from our window ! "

" Oh, do you think so, Arthur ? "

chill. The sea seems to be growing bigger and bigger,
pushing further and further out. . . . People shout as they
pass, against the wind. Two exquisite birds have been
walking in the garden. They had long, narrow, pale-
yellow bodies, little jackets in black and gold, very long
silver-grey tails. Happy tiny creatures, quite unafraid,
walking over the gravel and having a gay, gay little talk.

I have a feeling that my letter yesterday did not *ring*
properly. Please blame the insects. My hands feel as
though they were on fire, all swollen and inflamed. They
will be better in a day or two. It's so strange the insects
should persist, for it's really *very cold* at times, as cold as it
was in Marseilles. Yet in the evenings, even with the
windows shut and powder burnt, out they come. Bother
them !

I finished Stella Benson last night. I thought I might
do her with Hope Mirrlees—two women, both protesting
in the preface that their books are out of the ordinary.
But no bridge could be thrown from one to the other.
Miss Mirrlees lives in another world, and her world would
*shudder* at Stella Benson. I don't. On the contrary.
They are two interesting problems, *very* intriguing. I
hope I manage to say what I want to say. . . .

Please give Wing a foursquare kiss from me and Athenæum a *plain* (non-currant) kiss. Richard spoke of my four
brothers—you, he and the cats. We sound like a fairy
family, don't we ?

[Later.] If you write that novel you've got to have a
chapter called " The Birth of Wingley," don't you think ?
I have, as I always have, a sort of sweet scent in the air,
a sort of floating mirage of the novel. But I feel one
would be torn between tears and laughter all the while :
everything would be in rainbows. Already long before
the child is born I see the light above its head, a ring of
light—so lovely. Would it have cats and flowers in it, and
could B. wander there, wearing old Feltie, and Wing wave
at him from a high window ? There would be pain in it,
too, *agony*. Would there be a description of *the house*

after they were in bed—the fire dying in their room—the cat on the stairs—the moon coming through the window and shining on to the Shepherdess clock—on to her gay little dreaming figure sitting on the hill with her basket of fruit—and then his dark head on the pillow ? Do not be cross with me. I am only dreaming to myself of what the book might be. . . .

I'm in my room, lying down, the door and window open. The wind, thinking the house is empty, is taking a quiet *look through*, humming to herself. The shadow dances from the olive and there's no sound except the sea.

I dreamed last night that I had come home (a fever dream—horrible) and it was still October, dark, foggy, bitterly cold. And I was ill. I sent a note to S. who came. I was still in my travelling clothes : a black velvet cap and my peach-coloured shawl for a coat. He came and did not speak to me : you and he started talking about a new tobacco to be bought by the *sheet* : he had some to show you. Then you said, " Well, I'd better go," and left us alone. And S. wiped his glasses and said, very dryly : " Well, I'm afraid you've broken something more than your journey." I said : " Oh, but I'm leaving for Italy again next week.' He put his glasses on again. I said : " Doctor, I can see you'd rather not attend me any more." We shook hands and he walked out—and I saw the greenish fog in the window . . . and knew I was caught. To wake up and hear the sea and know I had not done the dreadful thing—that was joy.

I feel much better now—more normal. If it were anybody but you I could not say this, but really the gardener's wife had something to do with it. I felt her in my lung. Perhaps the truth was I was feeling weak, and she stabbed.

*To Richard Murry*                    Tuesday
                                October 21, 1919

I'm awfully interested in all you tell me about your job. I agree with you that the production of a book
262

should not assert itself but I think you're rather too hard on yourself when you say it shouldn't be noticeable. True, the writing is the important thing, but I think fine production, as it were, sets the seal upon its importance— and do you think it's too far-fetched to say it's an act of faith on the part of the producer in that he considers it worthy of a 'setting' and it's also his expression of delight in honouring it.   I suppose if a thing is really good and sound and honest there's no *need* to call attention to it, no *need* to praise it : but I like to think that people who are rich in life can afford to praise things—in fact, can't help praising them.   I don't think any of *us* will stop at what is necessary.   Take a domestic example.   I suppose a baby is the important thing and it's just as happy and content in a strong banana box.   But I can't help feeling that if I saw one flying in the direction of the Heron, or on the Heron's back (he looks a safe old bird according to Fergusson) I would make that banana box as marvellous as a banana box could be.   Of course, the whole difficulty about noticeable production is that if the idea gets into the minds of wrong workmen, vain workmen, there's no stopping them—and you can't see the great man for the wreaths and banners so to say.   But you can't afford to worry about that.   To be fantastical, I think a book should *look* like a herald, the author's herald, and as herald's *don't* carry trumpets it wouldn't be assertive but just very fine and on the proud side.   (I just then had a vision of Wing as a herald, but he would, in defiance of all the laws, have a most awful trumpet to blow in Athenæum's ear—)

I expect J. has told you about this little house—right in the sun's eye and the sea's eye.   It is built on the slope of a wild hill covered with figs, olives and tamarisk trees and a thick small shrubbery, and herbs like lavender and thyme and rosemary.   There are very small paths winding up it in all directions : I long to follow them, I shall by next spring.   We three could spend a wonderful time in this house.   It's a bit fäery—the light trembles on the wall from the water and dances in flecks from the olive

trees until you wonder if you're living in a bubble. . . .
Down below, *sheer* down there is the sea with a fine flat rock
for you to walk out on and dive off. Green sea with blue
streaks in it and violet shadows—so clear that from here I
can pretty nearly count the starfish star-gazing on the floor
of it. (That's nonsense. It's lunch time and I'm getting
what J. calls " shiny in the head.")

I wish though that the things that bite were not so
fierce. They are like the dragons my Papa used to draw.
Dragons with Seven Bellies—*i.e.*, never satisfied. They
must have had pints of me and you can't think I'd be
anything but rather inferior government ale, can you ?—
poor stuff compared to these rich fruity Italians.

*To J. M. Murry*                              Thursday
                                        October 23, 1919

I wish you could see this glass of flowers on the dining
room table—daisies and roses. Field daisies, but larger
than English ones, and very wide, with the petals dipped
in *bright* crimson and crimson roses from the wild garden
at the side of the steps. I have just gathered the third
rose and remarked that hundreds of buds will be blowing
in a week or two. The sea is very pale to-day ; small
boats go sailing by. I was out in the garden all the
morning : now I've come in to write. Don't you find
it very difficult to work without a large table and four
walls ? I try everything, I work on a tray—on a chair—on
a book—sit up high and arrange the ink and papers on
Table Mountain, on the verandah . . . but no, at the last
I have to come in. In our Sussex house we shall have a
real table and a real chair and a real ' abri.'

Except for my head to-day, I'm well again. I'm very
glad to have had the experience : it makes me feel so
secure. I should have had a doctor in London pour sûr,
but here I did without one, treated myself and cured
myself. This makes me feel so safe in case we should ever
find ourselves on a desert island—just in case. If there are

cannibals there our lives will be spared because of Wig the
Healer, and if there aren't, they'll be spared pour la même
raison. In view of the state of my *head* I am doing
Galsworthy this week. I know what I think about him :
I mean he has been in my mind for years and only wants
dusting, bringing to the light and *proving* by this new
book.

> (Oh why, why
> Did the Lord make the Fly ?
> And when we die
> Shall we find them spry
> In eternity ?)

To be *spry* in eternity seems to me particularly awful :
eternally spry ! I don't want eternity at any rate, so it
don't signify. Now it will be ideal for L. M.—time for
everything, time to get to know everybody and to wonder
about " this that and the other " to her heart's desire.
She is, indeed, made for eternity—one of God's own, as
you might say. But no—if the Lord will give me 30 years
starting on May 1st, 1920, he can do what he likes with
what's left of my bones and feathers after that.

I have 6 packets of cigarettes at 1 franc the packet,
black soldiers' cigarettes, I should think, made to be dis-
tributed to dying Zouaves in hospital and—held over.
But they are a great deal better than nothing.

Oh, is there *any* life of George Eliot so that I can write
an article for November 22—less than a month to do it in
—or if you could send me one or two of her novels—
*Romola*, *Adam Bede*, whichever are best ? I feel I'd love
to do something, but if there are other people on the spot
more competent and with more material, *c'est entendu*.

Friday
October 24, 1919

When you talk about Wing, I don't know what it is,
something in all you tell me goes to my heart. I see him
as he used to lie, in a kitten coma, while you kissed his nose.

Never shall we have such an adorable kitten again. When he slept on our bed, too, and wouldn't settle down (you remember), *would* dive off and swim about under the cupboard and up the screen-pier.

(*Oh*, the midges ! ! ! There are *three*.)

Your Sunday letter brought you and the house to me very, very clearly. It was wonderful how you conveyed the quality of the day—the one thing happening after another thing—in a silence.

I know what you mean about *people babbling*, even though je ne suis pas une silencieuse, moi. But the *years* one has spent, sitting with a strained smile trying to appear *of* the party, *in* the know . . . what foolishness, what waste of time !

But on those rare occasions when you and I talk, I do— I do feel the heavens opening and our thoughts like angels ascending and descending. Time, peace, freedom from anxiety—these things must be ours. Time to be silent in and to talk in. But especially that last. The *strain* we have lived under ! No one will know. Isn't it queer what a cold indifferent world this is really ? Think of the agony we've suffered. Who cares ? Who dreams ? If we were not ' set apart ' for ever before, this has been enough to do it. We could not, knowing what we know, belong to others who know not. If I can only *convey* this difference, this vision of the world as we see it ! Tchehov saw it, too, and so I think did Keats.

*To Richard Murry*                    Friday night
                                *S.S. Casetta* (Homeward bound)
                                    October 1919

I am at present being stared at by (1) very old winged beetle who is evidently looking to see if this is his club or not and whether there is an octogenarian or two to have a chat with ; (2) three white moths with their little moth's noses pressed as flat as flat can be ; (3) an Unknown, with six legs and the appearance of a diminutive lobster;

(4) one very large grey moth, apparently in a shawl who appears by her anxiety to be endeavouring to see if there really is a large barrel of butter hidden behind the counter for regular customers only or not. All these are on the outside of my windy pane, drawn to the light because I have not closed the shutters. It's a black night, calm, and with a great sweeping sound of sea.

I wish you could come into this room for a talk—sit before this wood fire with me and agree that the log has a head like a crocodile and one is like a poodle. The smell is good—of pines and blue gums—and I have one very large pine cone I would cheerfully sacrifice for a kind of illuminated address of welcome—my *dear, dear* old Boy.

Here comes dinner. I must sit up and prepare to attack it—We have funny food here—macaroni in all the most fantastical shapes and devices—in letters and rats' tails and imitation lace and imitation penny stamps and triangles and shavings. It must be fun to run wild in the Macaroni works. I wonder they don't have an Animal Series,— camels, frogs and Nelephants in one's soup would be particularly nice.

I am afraid that this letter is not, on the whole as serious as it ought to be. I trust, Sir, by the time it reaches you its demeanour will be composed, reverent, grave as befits one who is calling upon a young gentleman at a Publishing House in Thavies Inn.

Take care of yourself in these storms. Do not go up on deck without your big muffler ; do *not attempt* to stow the top-gallant sail but *be certain* to let go the fore top-gallant halyards while a squall rages.

But here's to Fair Weather for us all.

*To J. M. Murry*                              Sunday morning
                                              October 26, 1919

The Gardener is here ; he arrived at Aurora's heels, thumping his tail. I think he has done wonders, but Oh, I feel inclined to cry to the garden, as I do to you when

you've been to the barber : Why did you let him take off
*so much* ? When will it grow again ? My cotton plant has
lost its curls—a ruthless chopping of them : the roses that
had all started what I thought were the most exquisite
promising shoots are cut down to the bone and told to
try again. (I must plant sweet peas immediately.) And
he is so *delighted* with his work ; his good face beams ; he
shows me all stones he has taken out—it sounds like an
operation—and there on the path lie the pink geraniums.
*O Weh ! O Weh !* I feel there's an awful moral to be
drawn out of all this—Except ye can bear this to be done
unto ye, ye shall not bring forth. At any rate some old
Gardener or other has been doing it to us for years, and
God knows we've had our naked shivering moments. So
now I shall *fill* this garden with flowers. I shall make it to
blaze and shine and smell ravishing and look celestially
beautiful by the time you come, just to point the moral
further.

The wind with light, faint footfalls walks over the sea :
the water rings against the shore, like a bell, striking softly.
[Later.]

The gardener has gone ; there is a smell of blue gum :
that means the tea kettle is on. After tea I am going for a
walk up the road behind the hill. It's a marvellous day,
warm and yet *refreshing.*

Monday night
October 27, 1919

A picture. *Figurez-vous* your Wig on the verandah in
all the clothes she has, topped with the woolly lamb, and
with her cherry sunshade up, under a green fly-net ! It is
so perishingly cold to-day—a wind like ice. But for the
first time I seem to have weapons to fight it with, and I
am as snug as can be. As I walked into the garden wearing
the woolly lamb, I leaned on the green gate which is my
*confessional* and said to the daisy who remarked on it :
" Oui, c'est la jaquette militaire de mon mari qu'il a porté

pendant les trois hivers qu'il était au front. Le khaki était affreusement sale ; alors je l'ai . . . etc. . . ." If the daisy had been Catherina the same histoire would have been recounted : I am fascinated by these ideas sometimes. I saw you in this British-warm tucking your pocket-book away, pulling on immense gloves, and going off somewhere by motor-car. . . .

At break of day I went through all the paper and had a good read of it. The printers seems to get a bit scrimpy at times and will cut the noses off the words : it's very annoying. . . . Who wrote *What is Bolshevism* ? It's one of those reviews that begins with a bouquet and then gradually takes the flowers back again. And sentences like " It is of course impossible to estimate the number of people etc." are footle. Of course, it is. L. M. might try. At the end the reviewer decides to give him back a stalk or two—but . . . it's a bad style of reviewing, don't you think ?

Tuesday
October 28, 1919

I've just looked out of the window. L. M. is at San Remo. There is going to be an *enormous* storm ; terrible lead-coloured clouds are pulling over ; the sea is almost silent—just a deep beat—and the wind has arrived to clear the court, as it were, for the Elements. The cold is immense here, but I don't feel it at all as I did in the S. of France, thanks to all my warm woollies. But it's absurd to say this coast is warm *all the time*. Perhaps next month will be finer. Now I must work again and pray the house isn't struck by lightning. It's the moment to shut all the windows. You know that moment. Well, I've done it. I've also been into the garden, picked a rose, and brought in a bundle of kindling from under the verandah table, and I haven't coughed once or got out of breath. So I must be *furiously* better, really.

Wednesday
October 29, 1919

I have heard from F. at Mentone. Poor darling! he was robbed at Boulogne of his wallet—all his money, addresses, papers, £50 in banknotes, a letter of credit for £500. This really wrings my heart. I can't help it. If he does mind so terribly about money, it must have been so *ghastly* to be alone among foreigners, having to keep up and be a man of the world and look out of the railway windows as though it hadn't happened. I really literally nearly fainted when this swept over me and I ' saw ' him with a very high colour putting on a smile. I do hope to God people don't suffer quite as I think they do : it's not to be borne if they do.

I am writing this in a hurry. I seem to have such acres to plough and the horse is going so slow. I wish I could change the horse. He just sits on his hind legs and scratches his ear and looks round at me when we're half way through a furrow.

It's icy cold, thundering, blue-grey with a flash of steel. I should think it was going to snow.

Thursday
October 30, 1919

C. sent me a photograph of myself at three months old. It was *a dreadful shock*. I had always imagined it—a sweet little laughing thing, rather French, with wistful eyes under a fringe, firmly gripping a spade, showing even then a longing to dig for treasure with her own hands. But this little solemn monster with a wisp of hair looked as though she were just about to fall backwards head over heels. On her feet she wears, as far as I can make out, a pair of ordinary workman's boots which the photographer, from astonishment or malice, has photographed so close up that each tootsie is the size of her head. The only feature about her is her ears which are neatly buttonholed on to the sides of her head and not just safety-pinned on as most babies' are. Even the spade she clasps with the greatest reluctance. . . .

Friday
October 30, 1919

I sent a review yesterday. Before I forget—will you change the last sentence of all ? Substitute another word for the word "great." I can't remember just how it went, but I woke up in the night with the Lord crying "Samuel!" to me and saying, "Cut that bit out about a *great* novel!"

The sun came out this morning, took a cloud or two, did a little extremely high-class modelling on the grand scale —"The Banquet," "Greek Warriors Resting," "A Grecian Lady with a Bowl" and so on, all along the horizon for the benefit of a tiny little sailing ship and me. Then it went in again, and heaven knows how many doors are between us. It is bitterly cold and windy with great puffs of dust. I wonder if it will get warmer again ? I don't see why it should, and yet who would come for a saison d'hiver to get a blue nose and fingers ? A mystery to me.

I can't help feeling : Why didn't I go to Ventnor or some such place ? Why go so far ? It couldn't be colder in the Isle of Wight. Well, it only determines me never to do it again. . . .

Saturday
November 1, 1919

I had thought to have your Monday letter yesterday— but no, it wouldn't come. You must throw them more quickly down the letter boxes, *hurl* them, send them *flying*, tell them that if they come quickly there is nothing— nothing she won't give them. They can take whatever they please, pull off her rings and put them on their thumbs, peacock in her flowery shawl, eat all the honey jar at once. . . . Oh *no*, they are not children : I won't

have them children.  Little children must never travel.
How could I have written so !  It breaks my heart only
to think of them.  No, they are just—birds to whom the
journey is no labour.  Up they fly, out of sight, with one
beat of a delicate wing. . . .  But birds are so heartless,
alas !

It is a fearful day ;  long cold rain, a homeless wind
crying at the windows, the sea like ashes.  I am sitting in
my little room in a corner, wrapped up with a hot brick
at my feet.  I must work hard to-day.  Thank God for
definite work—work that must be done.

November 1st.  Six months to May.  After that don't
leave me alone.  I am not made to live alone.  I should
have gone to a place like Mentone where I could sometimes
go for a small walk without a climb and *lift the shutter* that
I live behind.  But work, work, work—simply to thy
cross I cling.  (Why must it be a cross ?  What a question
to ask at 31 !  But I *do* still ask it.)

Six months.  Only six months to cross.  A mountain a
month.  Six mountains and then a soft still quiet valley
where no wind blows—not even enough to fray the one
o'clock dandelion. . . .

Sunday
November 2, 1919

I am sitting in the dining-room.  The front door is
open, the cold salt air blows through.  I am wrapped up in
my purple dressing gown and jaeger rug with a hot
bottle and a hot brick.  On the round table is a dirty egg-
cup full of ink, my watch (an hour slow) and a wooden tray
holding a manuscript called " Eternity " which is all
spattered over with drops of rain and looks as though some
sad mortal had cried his pretty eyes out over it.  There is
also a pair of scissors—abhorrèd shears they look—and two
flies walking up and down are discussing the ratification of
the Peace Treaty and its meaning *re* our civil relations
with Flyland.

I am just sending L. M. to San Remo to ask the Hoch-wohlgeboren Doctor Bobone to come and see me. I *must* know from somebody how I am getting on, *i.e.*, I must be cheered up. Ten years passed this morning as I sat in my darkish little room. I am now 41 and can't lose a moment. I must know. If my depression continues, I shall try to get out of here in January, because if it does go on, we shouldn't have a May here, we'd be flinging our daisy chains round the tops of cedar trees. But on the other hand if Bobone consoles me and so on, I may feel better. . . .

Monday
November 3, 1919

No letter came to-day, but the paper did. We had the devil of a great storm last night, lasting for hours—thunder, lightning, rain, and I had appalling nightmares. I think it must be the noise of the sea which makes me dream so : it excites one's nerves at night. One longs for it to ' lie down ' . . . old age, I expect. After the thunder the day is very lovely, cool, but so *definite* and on *a big scale*. I began to write an article for the paper yesterday called " Eternity " ; I hope it will be finished to-day. If you don't care for it, please just keep it : it will go in some book some time or other. It's so nice to walk in this little garden. After yesterday I went up and down, up and down, thinking out things. It was then I hit on the subject for the article.

I've been out of doors all day, still am, in fact,—under a sunshade on the verandy. I feel quite all right, not a suspicion of anything is wrong with me, but I'm FLAT. It's the albatross round my neck. . . .

However, let us put a penny in the box, let us have a tune. Let us nod and grin while the others get up and do our dancing for us, as we sit over here in the corner, waiting, waiting—for the bead curtains to jingle, to be pushed aside, for La Santé to come laughing, laughing in, running over to our corner, putting her arms round our neck and saying, " My friend, my darling friend." The garçon hovers by, biting his nails and shooting me a glance or two. I've read all *the* illustrated papers—*all* the comics. Suddenly he swoops forward and piles two chairs on the table next to mine. Good Heavens ! it's really closing time ! Why doesn't she come ? Why doesn't she ! . . .

I don't know why I am writing this. Please forgive it. And forgive me for not being gay. Forgive me for that. Don't worry about me. I'll get out of this. See in your mind's eye Wig under an umbrella much too large, thinking it's still raining, and open the window and tell her how silly she looks and how that policeman with his scythe is laughing at her.

Tuesday
November 4, 1919

The storm at present is hanging over ; it has withdrawn to await reinforcements—a horrible lowering violet sky, a boiling sea like porridge, snow on the mountains. Fancy, with that, to get more air I had one side of the net up last night and I am bitten frightfully by mosquitoes. This is almost laughable. . . . Everything about this *côte d'azur* is lies. Why does one believe it ? One might as well believe that London is a rich, magnificent city, or that the Midland Hotel, Manchester, is the most comfortable place in the world. Why believe *liars* ? Everybody lies. I don't know : but there you are. Dostoevsky at least understood through and through. . . .

I feel a bit like the outside elements. At least I feel that they've had their way with me for the moment, and I'm now high and dry, on a rocky ledge looking up at the sky and simply vaguely wondering.

I hope to get work done to-day ; I long to—ah, so much ! ! If that were possible I'd get back my *spirit*. When that goes (the power to work) then I'm nothing, just a straw before the wind. And I feel *one must hurry* . . .

Believe that I try ALL I can, every single bit I can. Nothing less than La Faiblesse (who is really the toughest old hag of them all) keeps me from the performance of my promises.

Good God ! There's a little wavering gleam of sun on the wall—white, still. It makes everything look shabby and dirty. It's gone again.

Perhaps now I have encountered the whole troupe of fiends so early I shall get the better of them and be at peace. I suppose anyone who has lived my life of the last two years is bound to have these moments. That is what I hope. . . .

But to walk, kiss the earth, run, laugh, go in and out of houses and rooms—if I could do any of these things !

" You are always an invalid—hein ? " says Bobone, looking at me with absolutely inexpressive *red* eyes like an ox—no whites to them at all. " Vot is your age ? Dirty-five ? "

" No," I said. " Dirty-one."

" Zo."

Well, well, well. Why do I feel like this about Dostoevsky—*my* Dostoevsky—no one else's—a being who loved, in spite of everything adored LIFE even while he knew the dark, dark places ?


Wednesday
November 5, 1919

It's warmer to-day, with a huge wind blowing and working up for rain—all deep greys. The wind *tugs* at the trees, *tugs* at the waves. It's a vile wind. I wish the sun would shine, I wish it would—hot bright sun day after day.

But even Hampstead rests me to think of. It *is* my home. I *have* a home. I have every right to sit on the stairs and look at Wing come lopping up. I love 2 Portland Villas from here. I'd kiss the gate and the door. Often I go in and wander through and look out of the

windows, with love, with love.   My room was so beautiful
—the long glass reflecting the books—the Black Monk—
the exquisite clock, and the brass scuttle.   In my memory
I caress them—they are beloved darlings.   To turn that
unwilling key in the Black Monk [1]—oh, what joy !   To
curl up on the Stickleback and to have Wing climb up the
outer shell and then walk over unimportant me !   And my
chest of drawers—the special one !   Don't let us ever
give up our things—truly I *couldn't*.

I don't like foreign countries or foreign ways or foreign
houses.   It's only the sun that tricks them out.   When the
sun goes it is as though the flesh were gone, and there's
nothing to tell over but ugly bones.

This is an ancient wind.

Thursday
November 6, 1919

It has just stopped raining and is steamy, misty and cool.
I'm out on the verandah : the sea sounds heavy, so is the
air—one feels wonderfully *tired*.   The *Nation* came yesterday but no letter.

Not having heard from you I feel a bit dumb : I feel as
though I were standing at a door waiting for it to open—
or sitting up against it (more like that) just waiting.   I
wish I were a great deal more self-supporting.   It's a
thousand times harder for me to write reviews here where
I have no one to talk things over with.   I'm ' out of it '
and see so few papers and never hear *talk*.   I have to get
into full diver's clothes and rake the floor of the unpro-
fitable sea.   All the same *it is my life : it saves me*.

The woodman and his mate came yesterday.   I feel a
bit sentimental about him, because last time he was here
you were here.   He looked at the picture of Berne.
" C'est à Londres, ça ?   Londres est sur le lac de Londres,
n'est-ce pas ? "   And finding it was also a mirror, he

[1] A large black cupboard outlined in yellow which stood in
K. M.'s room.

twisted his moustaches in it.  How nice he is !  I thought,
etc., etc., until I had the bill.  Same amount of wood,
same size—115 francs, and it is to go up again this month.
He declared also it is défendu to take the wood from the
hillsides now.  Coal—does not exist for private houses,
only hotels.  This is all rather a blow considering the
climate, but we shall have to manage. . . .

Oh, God, let us try to make this our last separation.  At
any rate it will be.  I'd never bear another.  They are
too terrible.

Friday
November 7, 1919

It is all memories now—radiant, marvellous, faraway
memories of happiness.  Ah, how terrible life can be !
I sometimes see an immense wall of black rock, shining, in
a place—just after death perhaps—and *smiling*—the
*adamant of desire.*  Let us live on memories, then, and
when the time comes, let us live so fully that the memories
are no nearer than faraway mountains.

My " Eternity " seemed perfect rubbish.  I'll send it if
you like.  It seemed to go out as I wrote and I raked ashes.

Sunday
November 9, 1919

The papers have come ;  I've been reading them.  Then
I've read the ———.  The *disgraceful* dishonesty of it !
The review of Dostoevsky and the one of ———!  My
God !  what has happened to this age ?  It cannot have
been like this before.  Look here !  we must be bold and
beat these people.  We must be dead straight in our
reviews.  If they don't care for what we say, it doesn't
matter, but let us come bang out into the open while we
have the chance and say it.  I confess the world seems to
me really too hideous.  I felt after I had read the ———
that it was all like Mrs. F.'s party (you remember, when
we ran away).  My blood is up.  Let's up and at 'em this

winter. Send me as many books as you like. I'll do them. I have got my second wind from all this.

Blow me and my depression. What does my personal life matter! Let it go. It's hateful. But *we* matter: we have a chance to stand for something. Let's stand for it. Of course, I now see plainly that we shall never be successful writers—impossible. But let's be honest in the paper and give it them strong. There must be young people who see through this crabbed malice.

At the same time, I hate and loathe it all—these sets and dishonesties, don't you? I mean it is the stern daughter of the voice of God that makes one fight, not a joyful impulse. If it were not so tragic, it would be—no, it wouldn't.

As regards the———, there has been no War, all is as it was before. What a crew!

Monday morning<br>November 10, 1919

Here is another Monday. They do seem to come round so fast, like the horses we saw at the fair—no, the *roosters*—that was our one, wasn't it? Do you remember those little Princesses who went round for ever? They wore cotton frocks and tiny leather belts.

It's a chill, strange day. I breakfasted in Valhalla—cracks of lightning, thunder, tearing rain. Now I'm on the verandy and the clouds are immensely near and distinct like mountains.

Will you please say if my Dosty is all right? I sent it rather in fear and trembling, but I meant it. I am doing ——— for this week's novel. I don't like it. My private opinion is that it is a lie in the soul. The war never has been: that is what its message is. I don't want (God forbid!) mobilisation and the violation of Belgium, but the novel can't just leave the war out. There *must* have been a change of heart. It is really fearful to see the ' settling down ' of human beings. I

278

feel in the *profoundest* sense that nothing can ever be the same—that, as artists, we are traitors if we feel otherwise : we have to take it into account and find new expressions, new moulds for our new thoughts and feelings. Is this exaggeration ? What *has* been, stands. But Jane Austen could not write *Northanger Abbey* now—or if she did, I'd have none of her.

There is a trifling scene in ——'s book where a charming young creature in a light fantastic attitude plays the flute : it positively frightens me—to realise this *utter coldness* and indifference. But I will be very careful and do my best to be dignified and sober. Inwardly I despise them all for a set of *cowards*. We have to face our war. They won't. I believe our whole strength depends upon our facing things. I mean facing them without any reservation or restraints.

I fail because I don't face things. I feel almost that I have been ill so long for that reason : we *fear* for that reason : I mean fear can get through our defences for that reason. We've got to stand by our opinions and risk falling by them.

Do you want to know how I am ? Yesterday, upstairs in my room I suddenly wanted to give a small jump—I have not given a small jump for two years—you know the kind, a jump-for-joy. I was frightened. I went over to the window and held on to the sill to be safer. Then I went into the middle of the room and *did* jump. And this seemed such a miracle I felt I must tell somebody. There was nobody to tell. So I went over to the mirror— and when I saw my excited face, I had to laugh. It was a marvellous experience.

The sea is up to the brim of the world to-day.

Tuesday
November 11, 1919

I have just had the extraordinary comfort of seeing a really first-chop doctor—the man Ansaldi. L. M. was at

San Remo. It was getting dusky. There was a ring at the bell and I opened the door and nearly fell into the arms of a beaming, glistening Jewish gentleman mit a vite felt hat. I immediately decided he was a body-snatcher and said, most rudely, " Vous désirez ? " At which he replied " Ansaldi " and abashed me very much. He came in—dark bright skin, gleaming eyes, a slight stoop—and said, " Oh vot a nice little house you have here ! " The spit of the music halls. It made me feel terribly laughy. I don't know : L. M. away, this solitary spot, this queer stranger with his stethoscope in a *purse* (it would be a purse) and me in less time than it takes Wing to pounce, sitting draped in my flowery shawl, with my discarded woollen coats strewing the floor like victims. He examined me before he saw my chart.

My bad lung he says is drying : there's only a small spot left at the apex. (When I was in London there was a spot the size of a hand.) The other has also a small spot at the apex. I told him my history to date and he says that I have gained weight and can eat are excellent signs. There is no reason (bar accident) why I should not recover. " Never to be a lion or shoot the chamois or the hare "— *figurez-vous* ! I'd rather feed them with rose leaves—but to lead a normal life, not the life of an invalid. The chances are, he says, 99 to 100 that I can do this.

He was urgent about no mental worry, *very* urgent, but work—all you like and be in the air and walk, but never to tire yourself. Always stop everything before you are tired. I'll tell you the truth. He said I was not half warmly enough dressed. He was most emphatic on that, though I was wearing my jaeger and a jersey and a cardigan. He says this climate is admirable and especially here because the air is *balsamic* and positively healing, but one must take absolutely no risk as regards a chill. Never to go out uncovered and really never to know what it is to feel cold : he says that wastes one's energy—fighting the cold. This I am sure is sensible. But what was so good was his confidence in me : it made me feel so confident.

He told me I had so much *life* even in my skin and eyes
and voice that it was abnormal for me to be ill and that
was my great ' pull ' over other consumptives. He's
coming again in a fortnight. But after closely examining
my chart and reading *aloud* that writing we couldn't read,
he pronounced a definite improvement. Isn't that really
superb ? (I'll not always be such an egoist.) Of course,
he told me a chill or influenza might mean disaster, or
mental worry—but I must try to avoid those things. And
also he impressed on me that I shall never be a lion. That,
of course, is bad, one wants to be a lion, but after these
years to think I could lead a normal life is lion-like
enough.

But here's a brilliant, clever, sympathetic doctor on the
spot, see ? When I go to San Remo I must please to call
on him so that he may show me some little politenesses (as
though he had a collection of them. I saw them, darling
little tinies, sitting on his finger.) Then like the bee, the
lizard and the man in the poem ' he went away.' *I* went
upstairs, put on an extra pair of stockings and a scarf and
came down and had tea and ate four delicious fresh dried
figs with it. Terribly good !

Fancy calling my work " critical essays " ! I saw you
wink at Wing, and Wing, overcome, turning a catherine
wheel (with a K).

Wednesday<br>November 12, 1919

Strange, strange day ! My party has just gone—C., J.
(admirable person) and F. They arrived at about 10.30
(I expected them two hours later). But it didn't matter.
The Casetta seemed to turn into a doll's house. F.
couldn't even find room for his glasses. The cousins'
furs and coats and silk wraps and bags were scattered
everywhere.

F. suggested a run into San Remo, which we took. I
was just a little corrupted. That big soft purring motor,

the rugs and cushions, the warmth, the delicacy, all the uglies so far away. We 'ran' long past San Remo : it was *thrilling* for me. I didn't dare to speak hardly because it was so wonderful, and people laughing and silly F. talking Maori down the whistle to the chauffeur. Very silly— but very nice somehow. It carried me away. Then we got up and bought a cake and were as they say, the cyno- sure of all eyes, and that was nice, too. I was glad the chemist saw me (see what a snob you married !) and then while C. and J. were at Morandi's, F. and I talked and the sun streamed into the car and he said we were like a couple of hot-house plants ripening.

They have just gone. J. left me a pair of horn speggle- chiks of her grandfather's (the kind on a long black ribbon which suit me admirably). She took photos of the Casetta, too, and said, " They'll do to send your husband." I don't know what happened. F. at the last was wonder- fully dear to me. I mean, to be called my precious child was almost too much—to feel someone's arms round me and someone saying, " Get better, you little wonder. You're your mother over again." It's not being called a wonder, it's having *love* present, close, warm, to be felt and returned. And then both these women had been terribly homesick for their dogs, so they understood Wing. That was nice, too.

F. did not like this place, neither did they. They were horrified by the cold. F. said that at Mentone they have had none of this bitter wind, that it has never been cold like to-day. He seemed to think I had made a great mistake to be in such a thin house and so exposed. So, alas, did they. They said Mentone was warm, still, with really exquisite walks, sheltered. I said I'd consider going there in the spring. But I won't. When the bad weather is over, here will be warm too. And I don't want a town. I don't want to uproot. At the same time I was a bit sorry it was so much warmer. I *fed* them and F. left me five 3 Castles cigarettes ! ! ! He made the running, talking French, telling stories, producing spectacles. (He had four pairs of them. C. had three, and J. had three.) At one moment they were all trying each other's on—in this little room. [A drawing of many pairs of spectacles.] It was like a dream. . . . And here on the table are five daisies and an orchid that F. picked for me and tied with a bit of grass and handed me. If I had much to forgive him, I would forgive him much for this little bunch of flowers. What have they to do with it all ?

Thursday
November 13, 1919

This is the third day without a letter. I believe the Post Office does it on purpose. I have a box there which I bought for 14 lire where all my letters and so on are kept so as to avoid any mistake, but they don't care.

I went to the Post to-day down the road past the railway station through a small *place* and up some steps. Did you ever go that way ? I did not cough once all the way and came home past the shops and wasn't in the least tired. It is a brilliant day, bitter cold here, but on the level—gorgeous. There's no doubt about it, the Casetta is *not* a warm one. This morning, for instance, it was *icy* here, really perishing cold : even in my room the wind was so sharp. I went out dressed in furs and a shawl and woolly coat and after ten minutes on the level was much too hot. There was no wind there, either. But coming back, as soon as I began to climb the steps, the wind could be felt. The two front rooms are, of course, unlivable till after lunch, but that shelter is as bad—even worse : it's a wind trap. I shall always, when it's fine enough to go out, walk in the mornings now, and then (as usual) write here in the dining room in the afternoon. But the difference of temperature between here and in the village !

Did you ever explore the village ? It is so lovely— more beautiful than Bandol. All is seen against the huge background of the purple mountain. It was silent to-day except for an old woman crying fish and the boys flinging a ball among the trees of the *place* ; but it feels gay, rather fantastic. The air smelled of pines and of deep yellow roses which grow everywhere like weeds : they even climb up the aloe trees.

I can't describe (yes, I *could*) what real convalescence feels like. I decide to walk in the road, and instead of stopping, putting my stick off the pavement, then one foot, then the other, I take a little spring with all three legs and have to hold myself back from crying to an indifferent native : *Did* you see that superb feat ? (That is not intended for a F. joke).

I am reviewing ———— to send to-morrow. It's devilish hard. Talk about intellectual snobbery—her book *reeks* of it. (But I can't say so). You would dislike it. You'd never read it. It's so long and so tahsome. By the way, I gave C. the *Oxford Book of English Verse* to look at yesterday while she was testing somebody's specs and she said a moment after, "There are some quite pretty things here, dear. Who are they by ?" . . . What do you think of that ? I *should* have replied : Temple Thurston. Instead I pretended not to hear.

Friday
November 14, 1919

It's a bitter cold day, pouring rain, wind, fog, and air like acid. I am sitting in my room before the fire wrapped up snug with a hot bottle and Jaeger dressing gown over all. I am terrified of the cold and would go to any lengths to avoid it. Ansaldi's " chill will in your case be a fatal disaster " rings in my ears when the weather turns like this. At the same time, God ! what courage we have to remain apart, knowing that. It amazes me. But we could do nothing else, nothing else at all. It would be very wonderful to be rid of these melancholy thoughts, for them to withdraw into the forest and not come out again for, say, fifty years. The fog and ceaseless drip of rain makes them very *impish*.

How I hate furrin parts to-day ! I feel numbed when the sun goes in. That's a great mistake—to think it a good idea to live facing the sea. I've discovered it's a bad one. When the sun is not out the sea is like a mirror without light. It simply *asks* for the sun far more than the land does. " There's nothing to say, my heart is dead," says the sea and goes on saying it in a loud keening voice. . . . Another discovery is not to live alone and more or less tied to a house where the sea sounds so loud. If one broke up the noise with talk and kisses and walks it would be all right, but it has a frightfully depressing effect if one doesn't. Sometimes I lie awake literally all night, so excited that I play Demon, *sing* and talk out loud to try to work it off. If there were a second person I don't think one would notice it. L. M. says she never does. These things one just has to find out.

Saturday
November 15, 1919

I have just come downstairs and lighted my fire. Do you smell the blue gum wood and the pommes de pin ? It's a perishing coal-black day, wet, dripping wet, foggy, folded, drear. The fire is too lovely : it looks a stag's head with two horns of flame. I managed to get the review off yesterday, but *not* without a struggle. I wanted to be sincere : I felt I had a duty to perform. Oh dear, oh dear ! What's it all come to, I wonder ?

This morning J. sent me a box of Khedive cigarettes. That was very nice of her. I admire her terribly. F. sent me a letter. I feel that between them they are going to *move* me from here. It is I confess extremely cold and draughty here, but on the other hand—privacy, privacy, privacy. I won't go into a hotel or rooms where I'm not private. That's the *essential*. They (that is F. and his Co.) seem to think of Ospedaletti as a kind of rock that rears its awful form.

Oh, isn't it nice when I write so small ? I am taking

very tiny little stitches with my pen and making eyes of admiration at myself. I wish the Albatross would produce lunch : it's nearly *one* and lunch is at 12 and I'm shaking like a leaf and trembling with want of it.

Now a fly has walked bang into the fire—rushed in, committed suicide.

Lunch.

Lunch over. Pendant ce repas L. M. suggested I should take the tram into San Remo and get another back in ten minutes, just to enjoy the sun. I would not drive a *strong* pig to market to-day : it's such a weed-killer. So this suggestion for me made me angry. She then said : " Of course it is damp, the damp went right *through* me, but you do such funny things." Now, I *don't* do funny things : I haven't for ages and I hate to be reminded. I came back and smoked a cigarette and got over it. On the cigarette paper it declares :

Qu'à aucun moment de leur fabrication, ni par quelque procédé que ce soit, aucune substance aromatisante, opiacée ou chimique, *en un mot*, qu'aucun *corps étranger* n'est introduit dans le tabac. . . .

One feels there must be snippets of sheik brûlé in 'em after that.

Did I tell you ? When I was in San Remo in that motor I went to a bread shop, and there was a queer-shaped loaf which looked nice for tea. A kind of tea bread. So I said : Combien ? and he said : I must pèse it, Madame. Will you take it ? So I said Yes. And he pèsed it, did it up in a paper with a pink ficelle and said : Cinq-francs-Madame-juste ! ! ! Now, what do you do then ? I paid and took it and walked out—one living curse. But do the brave give it back ? Which is the lesser humiliation ? Have you ever decided that ? I was awfully ashamed of myself. Then I realised if it hadn't been for the motor, I wouldn't have paid. It was the price of corruption. . . .

All the same I read an article on small cars for tiny people (2 people, their luggage, a cat and its saucer and

bastick) for 3d. a mile all round the world from door to
door. Self-starter, electrical installation and a bag for
the money to roll into when you come to the place where
money rolls. That sounded to me the spit of us. I
thought Wing as cleaner would be so good—in overalls,
you know, wiping his little nose with a morceau of cotton
waste. The trouble with those cars is they ought to
cost 3d. to start with. It ought to be *all* 3d.—3d. all the
way through. " I'll have 3d. worth of petrol please, and
a thrippenny horse to pull us out of this hole."

I *wish* a letter would come. I'd like some good news to
put in this room—no, to wear in my bosom. I am very
well, with an old-fashioned face coming back, very bright
eyes and a pink colour like Bandol. I hardly know it when
I powder its nose.

Sunday, 8 a.m.
November 16, 1919

It was a fearful *blow* to get no letters yesterday again.
I shall never understand it. When L. M. came back after
the last chance, I *hid* for a moment or two upstairs, just
to delay the " No letters—nothing." Perhaps my luck
will turn to-day and the sea have a pearl.

Such a night! Immense wind and sea and cold. This
is certainly no ' pensive citadel.' This morning the
storm still rages. It's a blow. I long to go out and have
a walk, but I daren't face the wind.

What is this about the novel ? Tell me, thou little eye
among the blind. (It's easy to see who my bedfellow has
been.) But seriously, the more I read the more I feel all
these novels will not do. After them I'm a swollen sheep
looking up who is not fed. And yet I feel one can lay
down no rules. It's not in the least a question of material
or style or plot. I can only think in terms like " a change
of heart." I can't imagine how after the war these men
can pick up the old threads as though it had never been.
Speaking to *you* I'd say we have died and live again. How

can that be the same life ?   It doesn't mean that life is the
less precious or that ' the common things of light and day '
are gone.   They are not gone, they are intensified, they
are illumined.   Now we know ourselves for what we are.
In a way it's a tragic knowledge : it's as though, even
while we live again, we face death.   But *through Life* :
that's the point.   We see death in life as we see death in a
flower that is fresh unfolded.   Our hymn is to the flower's
beauty : we would make that beauty immortal because we
*know*.   Do you feel like this—or otherwise—or how ?

But, of course, you don't imagine I mean by this
knowledge   let-us-eat-and-drink-ism.   No,   I   mean
' deserts of vast eternity.'   But the difference is (perhaps
I'm wrong) I couldn't tell anybody *bang out* about those
deserts : they are my secret.   I might write about a boy
eating strawberries or a woman combing her hair on a
windy morning, and that is the only way I can ever mention them.   But they *must* be there.   Nothing less will
do.   They can advance and retreat, curtsey, caper to the
most delicate airs they like, but I am bored to Hell by it
all.

Here is the sun.   I'll get up.   My knees are cold, and
my feet swim between the sheets like fishes. . . .

Monday<br>November 17, 1919

It's a TERRIBLY cold day—really shocking.   I have
a big fire and a rug and bottle and am wrapped up.   The
air is like ice, the sea like a sheet of lacquer.   Truly this is
a cold spot.   Yet I don't want to leave it.   I *love* Ospedaletti.   I don't want Mentone and a band.   Here one
works, lives simply, is retired.   If I got there people
would call and so on, and it's no good :   I am not that
kind of person.   But I do wish it were not so cold.   Cold
frightens me : it is ominous.   I breathe it, and deep down
it's as though a knife softly, softly pressed in my bosom and
said ' Don't be too sure.'   That is the fearful part of
288

having been near death.   One knows how easy it is to die.   The barriers that are up for everybody else are down for you, and you've only to slip through.

Wednesday le midi
November 19, 1919

A most beautiful man has just been here to put the lock on the door—really a superb creature.   He could *not* put the lock on the door so he spent his time explaining (1) how easy it would be for a person to come in at night : (2) how unpleasant ; (3) how much wiser to trouver quelqu'un to sleep here seulement pour la bien garder.   Just give them a morceau de paille in the vestibule and the thing is done. Locking the horse in the stable *en pension*, so to say.

It has not been cold to-day—temperate air.   The result is I am a different child.   I've been out for a walk and I'm tingling with warmth and my bones don't ache half so much and my lungs open and shut.   The cold really *paralyses* me : I went to bed last evening and felt in despair about it.   First one couldn't work because of moustiques and moucherons.   Then because of L. M., then because of the cold—a sliding scale.   But when the day is fair one forgets.   I climbed about the hill at the back of the Casetta.   After you get up a certain height there's a perfect little promenade—quite flat, only used by the sauterelles, full of gay small flowers and insects. Below are pines and the sun shining through them makes them smell sweetly.   I was so happy there.   I thought how much more my kind these little boulevardiers were— the butterflies, the grasshoppers and the daisies—than the crowd at Mentone, par example.   How much lovelier to look at the wild thyme and the tiny honeysuckle than the shop fronts.   I stayed up there (like M. Séguin's goat, I felt) all the morning, and below ever so far as I came round a bend I saw the Casetta with its foreshortened geranium bushes, looking a jewel.   Just as I left I said out aloud : Thank you very much, it's been lovely—But to whom ? To the Lord who gave me consumption ?

Just then lunch was ready—curried pasta, fresh bread, marmelade de pommes and dried figs and coffee.   L. M. is off to San Remo to buy oatmeal and ' have a *little* look at the shops.'   So I shall write my review of Monkhouse and Stern and Stevenson.   The sun has gone, clouds have pulled over—soft grey ones with silver fringes—the wind is piping.   Of course, the locksmith man said they had never had such a year as this year.   The flowers are nearly spoiled with the gêlée, and snow on all the mountains. . . . Why do these things follow us ?   Wherever I go they never have known *such* a year.   I take back my Thank you. . . .

I have a suspicion that Eliot is finding himself as a poet in his analysis (not quite the word) of caricature.   I feel he is seeing why he fails, and how he can separate himself from Sweeney through Sweeney.   But this may be sadly far-fetched.

Friday morning, 8.30, after dejeuner
November 21, 1919

Here is your letter about the W.'s house.   They are lucky, aren't they ?   Shall we really have such a house ? It's not too late ?   We don't just make up dreams— precious dreams ?   It's not " all over " ?   I get over- whelmed at times that it *is* all over, that we've seen each other for the last time (imagine it !) (No, don't imagine it !) and that these letters will one day be published and people will read something in them, in their queer finality, that " ought to have told us."   This feeling runs exactly parallel with the other—the feeling of hope. They are two roads, I can't keep to either.   Now I find myself on one, now on the other.   Even when you tell me about the table I think How perfect ! but at the very same moment I think Will he sell it ?   Of course not. He must have a table after all.   It's all part of what I've said before, haven't I ?   I say it so many thousand times over in my mind that I forget whether I've written it. Once the defences are fallen between you and death they are not built up again. It needs such a little push, hardly that, just a false step, just not looking, and you are over. Mother, of course, lived in this state for years. Ah, but she lived *surrounded*. She had her husband, her children, her home, her friends, physical presences, darling treasures to be cherished—and I've not one of these things. I have only my work. That might be enough for you in like case. But God! God! I'm *rooted* in life. Even if I hate life, I can't deny it. I spring from it and feed on it. What an egoist the woman is!

And now, just supposing by a miracle the blissful thing should happen. . . . I don't remember where it was I stayed with the W.'s. It was near Marlboro' and the country was beautiful. There were forest glades—a beautiful forest. They took me for a walk that was miles too long: I remember that. I remember standing in a rank-smelling field and seeing them far ahead and waving very gaily when they looked round. . . .

But the country does not really matter a great deal, does it? As long as it *is* country and one can grow things (Oh, MAKE it happen!). But the money question is pretty dreadful. As to furniture, that we can always accumulate Eric-or-little-by-little. . . . I think we might do it by not paying down. We overdo the paying down, I believe. Other people never have their money in bags. But first we ought to find the house, take it and then consider. That is my idea. The house (like the Jew) first. (I never understood that text.)

Oh God! When you say we'll have to get a builder in, I suddenly dimly see a hall, a staircase with shavings, a man with a rule and a flat pencil measuring for cupboards. I hear a saw and the piece of sawn wood creaks and tumbles (such a *final* sound). I hear the squee-gee of a plane, and the back door of the house is open and the smell of the uncared garden—so different from the smell of the cared one—floats through, and I put my hand on your sleeve and rest a little against you, and you say Do you agree? and I nod Yes. . . .

But these dreams are so dear that they feel unearthly—they are dreams of heaven. How could they become reality ? *This* is reality—bed, medicine bottle, medicine glass marked with tea and table spoons, guiacol tablets. . . . Come, tell me, tell me *exactly* what I am to do to recover my faith. I was always the one who had a kind of over-plus of it ; you hated it in me ; it seemed to deny you so many of your more subtle emotions. You made me feel it was so crude a thing—my belief that wouldn't be shaken.

Take this all *coolly* : it's all—what ? Just add to my diseases a touch of melancholia, let us say.

Saturday morning
November 22, 1919

It is a brilliant bright day. The flowers against the sea flash and quiver with light. This house is full of roses : every jar, pot, spare glass has its share. Even the sauce-boat has a little cargo with their heads over the sides and their leaves trailing in the mer imaginaire. I am going off to San Remo this afternoon if it stays fine just to have a look at the gay world and to take the acid to the chemist. I ought to unwrap it and take just the bottle for I want the box. On the other hand I'd like him to see the seals just for him to know what an important person I am. . . . You're shocked ?

I sent off a review on Thursday night. Is it all right ? This copy of *Eve* is really too degraded. I wonder if *Vogue* is like it. It is written *by* imbeciles *for* degenerates. One gets so fastidious—oh, I don't just know what it is—living alone on a wild hillside. At any rate, what they call the ' semi-demi ' shocks me no end. I suppose there are a great many women who care for this sort of thing or it wouldn't be produced. It's positively *foul* and *filthy*. I do shrink from this world and its ways.

Yes, it's a beautiful day to-day, an opal. I am so looking forward to San Remo—to lose myself for a bit and

292

watch the people and perhaps the china will have come. I long to send you the superb fresh dried figs.  L. M. is making enquiries about them to-day. . . .

With my meals I am drinking *The Winter's Tale*.  It's again one of my favourites.  It's simply marvellous.

Saturday afternoon

As usual, I thought I was going to have it all my own way—get well, be happy, the horror of my disease (it *is* a horror) over, peace with L. M. and ease to work in.  What a fathead I am !  But of those . . . I'll get well ; and that's all and enough.  Let the others wait.  *Work*, of course. Work is second breath.  When you spoke of planting a tree of hope, I felt : Oh, it was *you* to speak so.  Plant it, plant it.  I will not shake it.  Let me sit under it and look up at it.  Spread it over me and meet me there often and let us hold each other close and look up into the boughs for buds and flowers.  No, there's no God.  That is queer.  This morning I wanted to say ' God keep you ' or ' Heaven guard us.'  Then I thought of *The Gods*, but they are marble statues with broken noses.  There is no God or Heaven or help of any kind but love.  Perhaps Love can do everything.  " Lo !  I have made of love all my religion."  Who said that ?  It's simply marvellous.

L. M. is ready to go.  I shall have the place to myself. It's nice.  Then I turn into a real mouse and make as tiny a noise as possible, so as not to disturb the life around me.

Sunday<br>November 23, 1919

I have just read your letter about the scarf.  I wish I'd seen that girl asking you if terra cotta suited me and you wondering if I was fair or dark or a hazel-nut.  I'm sure I shall love it.

The ACID is here : a bottle has been made up and it has a most superb effect.  Très potent—the best I have

come across. You did not see the bottle it was sent in,
did you ? A round glass-stoppered exquisite one, which
the chemist is not to be allowed to keep.

I didn't go to San Remo yesterday after all. Got all
ready and walked half-way down the steps, and the bells
rang Turn again Whittington. I had no puff, my back
ached. I felt it would only be going on my nerves. So I
sent L. M. and lay down with the window open to rest a
little. The bell rang. (The bell here when pressed rings
and goes on ringing till you open the door, unscrew the
top and stop it. This is a common habit. I never think
of a bell that stops by itself now. It makes all visitors
sound extremely urgent). *That* visitor was Catherina
with her minute Gus Bofa dog—Flock. She had just
given him a bath and was attired for the occasion in a
kind of white robe de chambre, très decolletée, with bare
arms, her hair just pinned up, her feet thrust into wooden
pattens. In her hand she had a large brush. Flock,
sitting in the garden, covered with what looked like
prickles of black and white fur all on end, shivered violently
and kept his eyes *pinned* on the brush ! He is an adorable
little animal—for sale—for 150 lire ! ! ! But he's worth
it really, he's such a personality.

Catherina had come to say three men were following
her bearing in their arms a porcelain stove. When she
and Madame Littardi had been discussing the coldness of
the Casetta, Mme Littardi had suddenly remembered she
had this put away dans la cave and *they* decided it would
chauffe toute la petite maison if it were installée in the
salle à manger. Would I like it ? It was un peu cassée, so
Catherina had brought three admirers to mend it for me.
Wasn't this very amiable ? There must be a rat somewhere, but I can neither see nor smell it up till now.[1]

Presently three good men and true hove in sight bearing
a small *terra cotta* crematorium. C. in her element,
ordered them about, made them put it in the garden,
sent them into the Casetta for a pail, a cloth, water for the

[1] There was, see letter of January 22, 1920.

cement, started them scrubbing, while she watched and
Flock sat with an air of intense pleasure watching the
sufferings of another while he still shivered and the blood
showed red in the muscles of his delicate little hind legs.
She came up to-day to have it put in the room. All my
thanks were over borne with : Je suis si contente, si
contente d'avoir trouvé quelque chose. And when I said
Wouldn't she at least have a bouquet of boutons de roses ?
she replied seriously *Demain*, avec grand plaisir. Mais
vous savez, Madame, I cannot walk carrying a bouquet
without my shoes on.

After she had gone I lay down again, and between my
book I heard the workmen whistling and talking, and then
there was a new voice, a child's voice, very happy. It
went on for about an hour. Vaguely curious, I got up to
see who it was. C'était le petit de la poste qui porte les
télégrammes, and he was beating up cement very firmly
with a little flat trowel—in *his* element, a workman, in
fact. When he saw me he paid no attention, and I just
chanced to ask if he had anything for me ? Si, Madame.
And off came his little cap with a telegram from F. inside
it ! I went in to sign the slip and he followed, leaned
against my table and suddenly, picking up the pig, pointed
to the old letters underneath and asked for the stamps for
his collection. Then he strolled over to the mantelpiece
and looked at your photograph while I humbly tore them
off for him.

I lay down again. The bell rang. A LADY to call. . . .
Elderly, typical, good family, dowdy gentlewoman with
exquisite greenish ermine scarf, diamond ear-rings and
white suède gloves. The combination suggested *arum
lilies* to me somehow. I liked her very much. She
knows a great deal about Italy : she was *gay*, *sociable*, full of
life and *pleasant talk*, and she was ' a perfect lady.' (I do
like fine delicate manners.) I made her tea as L. M. was
out. But you know, this form of social entertainment is
quite new to me. It is like playing ladies. Are they
playing, too ? They can't be serious surely, and yet. . . .

I see myself and hear myself and all the while I am laughing inside. I managed to inform her (I) we were not related to the John Murrays. We spell our name without the A. Yes, from Scotland. . . . The A was dropped generations ago. (Do you hear the A dropping? Hullo! There's the A dropped. We can't get it back. It's broken to bits.) My *private* idea is that the ship's carpenter dropped it over the side.[1] But never mind. Also—that F. *motored* from Mentone to see me : that my relatives there had managed to find *four* excellent maids : that my *cook* in London finds shopping so much easier : that (this is the invariable final and always comes in as natural as you please) Elizabeth in her German Garden is my cousin ! ! It is Butler's Montreal brother-in-law.

She was rather horrified at this Casetta : the coldness and the loneliness . . . the pity I was not at San Remo where ' we ' could have looked after you if you had let us and at least introduced you to our friends. *What* do you do when it rains, especially as you are not strong, etc., etc., etc. ? I am afraid I was a little brave-and-lonely at this. It's so nice to be cared for. . . . She is asking a few people to meet me at lunch on Wednesday, and I'm going. Do you wonder why ? I will tell you.

People steady and calm me. When I am not working, when I'm in pain, and conscious every moment of my body, and when my heart indulges in what S. calls disorderly action and my joints ache, I've no one to turn to. I can't forget my body for a moment. I think of death : the melancholy fit seizes me. Nature helps me when I'm well, but if the weather is cold and I am ill Nature mocks and terrifies me. Then healthy people help *beyond words*. I've noticed this many times. L. M. doesn't help : she always makes me feel she is waiting for me to be worse, but if I see people, the strain of her even goes. I feel I've cut away a few hundred octopus feelers and I feel refreshed. Do you understand ? Does it sound to you unworthy ?

[1] My great-grandfather and my grandfather were both ships' carpenters in the Royal Navy.

I swear when Catherina has been here sometimes, just to
be with her, to feel her health and gaiety, has been *bread*
and *wine* to me. . . .

I am looking at the little ring you gave me—the blue
stone with the pearls round it. I love it so. I feel you
made it of a flower for me when we were children, and it
has turned into pearls.

Glancing again at your letter I re-read the part where
you say you'd drive anywhere for a good table. Oh ! how
nice you are. *Too* nice. Terribly. I thought you meant
*food* first . . . ' to keep a good table '. . . then it dawned on
me. It's the spit of you to say such a thing. But be
careful, if somebody asks you to 'take the chair,' they won't
mean what you mean. I now see you answering an
invitation that you'll be very pleased indeed to take the
chair on Friday 20th, thanks awfully. How did they
know we were short of chairs ? And you will arrive at
8.30 as they suggest, with a small handbarrow. . . .

It has been the most perfect exquisite morning. I
went into the village. There were no letters. The whole
village is adorned with roses, trees of roses, fields, hedges,
they tumble over the steps in a shower, children wear
them, hideous middle-class women in chocolate-brown
' costumes ' with black button boots and hard velvet
toques pull and twist them from the stems. I walk about
wishing I knew the name of that white beauty with petals
stained as though with wine and long slender buds—those
pink ones, round and curled—those red ones with silver
shadows. Ospedaletti is an enchanting little village, and
the village people seem very nice. The visitors are
simply APPALLING. All the men are forked radishes,
but their strut, twirl, stare, ogle, grin is so bewildering,
and the women are all either chocolate brown or a colour
I always think of as Belgian grey—a second-class-on-the
boat grey. They have cold selfish faces, hard eyes, bad
manners, mean attitudes and ways. Serpents come out
of their eyes at sight of me—I don't know why—and they
draw the radishes' attention to me and then (*really*) burst

out into a loud affected laughing. I, of course, don't
notice, but I feel myself getting very English—but in
truth, one's heart is wrung. How *can* they be like that
with all these roses, with the air humming with bees, with
the great white bunches of sweet flowers on the promenade
—how *can* they? Divine weather—a crocus-coloured
sea—the sun embracing one's body, holding one like a
lover. . . . You know, people are *impossible* to understand. . . .

Monday
November 24, 1919

Master of the Cats! Hail!

I've gone and gained another 2 lbs. I weighed myself
and couldn't believe it and made the man weigh me as
though I were beurre frais at least and still there it was—
another kilo—that's a bit more than 2 lbs. Pretty good,
for a young 'un, don't you think? Please whisper the
news in Wing's ear. I now weigh 7 stone 4 and when I
left home I weighed 6.13. Having found out this fact I
phantasmagorically (see Miss R. Wilson) danced off to the
post and found hymn number 163—the one hundred and
sixty-third hymn (why do they always say that?) waiting
for me.[1] I read it in the public eye, but when I found
you had not given me the chuck absolute for my review I
lost my head and kissed it—looked up and saw an old
female leaning on a broom watching me and smiling very
broadly. This was awkward because I blushed and had to
climb up a flight of steps so as not to pass her. Her broom
by the way, was made of those great reddish stems that
grow in the centre of palms with tiny dates on them—a
very nice broom indeed.

Don't ever flatter me. Beat me *always* before you
would beat anyone else. But God! to think that review
was all right. I've been on the point of wiring my regret

[1] Our letters were numbered. No. 163 meant that there were 163
days to K. M.'s return.

that I had failed you. That's enough to make a person
gain 20 more. . . .

I am so glad that the precious cats have won S.'s heart.
I sent them each a card yesterday. I *see* little Wing
rabbiting on the stairs. They are blessed creatures and
must have perhaps a whole tiny cottage of their own in
Sussex. I see Wing leaning out of the window pouring a
jug of water on to Athy in the garden below. Athy will
get very ' pa ' in his old age, don't you think ?

The furniture makes my mouth water. A *chest*, a
*cupboard*, a *couch*, a delicious cabinet. I should like to have
a cabinet—tall—you know the legs. Oh dear ! Why
aren't we rich ? We want £800 a year *without* working,
please, and just a few lump sums, that's all. It's not much
to ask. If I ever went to Mentone I might meet an old
dying American there who for sufferings-nobly-borne
might well leave me twice the sum. But I don't want to
go to Mentone. Terra Cotta, the new stove, has been
installed to-day. It's a regular German stove with a flat
top [a drawing of the stove]. It looks awful there. But
that round thing is where the red shows and below is a
sort of baby oving. I should think it would box it [1]—the
cold, I mean.

You see I can't afford to go to Mentone and live there.
It would cost quite double this place, I am sure. No, if
I see tumpany here and go into San Remo and see people,
I think I can manage, and this place must be terribly
healthy for me to have gained 4 lbs., stopped all my fever
and planted in me a roaring appetite. And then—
MAY ! ! I feel so well to-day that only to write that
makes me almost unbearably excited.

I have to do the books for *Art and Letters* this week.
It's a dreadful sweat having to *re*-read two, and *The Mask*,
which I imagine I am supposed to admire. I dislike it
intensely. It's a very vulgar ill-bred book with *two*
climaxes where the little Jew is forced to expose himself

[1] To ' box ' something, in K. M.'s private language, was to settle
it satisfactorily.

—— would think it a masterpiece : that's the exact measure of it, but I can't quite say that, though I'd like to.

I had 8 pages from F. at Toulon, written just before he left. You know how in the old days you used to *wring* my heart in letters—*all* the ghastly things that happened just to you. F. does it. If he manages to secure one egg on a journey, it's a bad egg. He loses things, people cheat him, he goes to a hotel where they won't give him a fire—he " feeling very shaky "—, he peels the bad egg, letting the shells fall into the crown of his hat so as not to make a litter, and the ' juice ' spirts out all over the lining that he showed me with such pride the other day when he was here,—and so on. Of course, he *has money*, but it makes no difference to him. He falls into absolute *pits* of depression and loneliness.

Tuesday,<br>November 25, 1919

The paper has come. May I talk it over a little ? And please remember I am nobbut a cabinboy and you are the skipper.

I don't think S. W. brought it off with George Eliot. He never gets under way. The cart wheels want oiling. I think, too, he is ungenerous. She was a deal more than that. Her English warm ruddy quality is hardly mentioned. She *was* big, even though she was ' heavy ' too. But think of some of her pictures of country life—the breadth, the sense of sun lying on warm barns, great warm kitchens at twilight when the men came home from the fields, the feeling of *beasts*, horses and cows, the peculiar passion she has for horses. (When Maggie Tulliver's lover walks with her up and down the lane and asks her to marry, he leads his great red horse, and the beast is foaming—it has been hard ridden and there are dark streaks of sweat on its flanks—the *beast is the man*, one feels *she* feels in some queer inarticulate way.) Oh, I think he ought really to have been more generous. And why drag Hardy in ?

300

Saintsbury I like *awfully*. I wish we could lay down a little piece of excellent vintage. But ours will be dandelion, elderberry, cowslip and blackberry. (Oh, won't it be heaven !) I say : Who did Fisher ? Do you altogether approve ? I read bits of the book in *The Times*. He's a presumptuous, self-conscious, high-stomached old roarer. No doubt the Admiralty was at fault, no doubt everybody was a fool—but Fisher could have put nought right. And as for saying he was a great man. . . . Or are our sea-legs being pulled ? ? I was a bit sorry to read that.

I like the way Tommy keeps hitching up his trousers as he writes and just not yarning. He's always full of life somehow.

Lewis is extremely interesting, I think. He hurls lumps of sentences at you, but that doesn't matter.

—— frankly disgusts me. Oh, I wish that first paragraph had not appeared in the paper. " Gave herself ' in commas! Oh, the unspeakable journalist! Shoo him off ! He simply revolts me. Apart from his vulgarity, he's got nothing but a very old newspaper in his head.

The Duhamel is, of course, another eye-opener. The idea that they should surrender something of their personality . . . that started a terrific excitement bubbling in me. It's true of all artists, isn't it ? It gives me another *critical point of view* about an artist, and quite a new one. I mean—to find out what the man is subduing, to mark that side of him being gradually absorbed (even as it were without his knowing it) into the side of him he has chosen to explore, strengthening it, reinforcing it, even while *he thinks* it is subdued away. Oh, that's frightfully vague. . . .

It's raining, a heavy, misty rain—most beautiful. I went out to the post in it and after so long, it was thrilling to hear the fine rain sting the stretched silk of my umbrella, the sudden heavy drops drum on it from the gum trees. All the coast is soft, soft colour : the roses hang heavy : the spiders webs are hung with family jewels. Aged men in pale blue trousers are sweeping up the dead leaves, and there is a succession of bonfires—puffs of white, fine smoke,

with the old figures moving in it, sweeping and bending.
The sea is still very full—faint to see with dreamy lines
upon it, and my two little royal birds are back in the
garden.

Wednesday
November 26, 1919

What's the day like ?   I am thinking of you.   I have
got our house on the brain as well as the heart.   I feel
such a frenzy of impatience, but that must not be.   We
must be wise children and hard to please, for this time it
really is more important than ever before.   This time we
decide to live in the land with our flocks and our herds, our
man-servant and our maidservant and our two sacred cats.

All the same, I keep seeing *chimneys* in the landscape of
my mind, so to say—chimneys that are going to be ours.
Think of the first time we visit together, sitting on a step
with our hats on our knees smoking a cigarette (man with a
vehicle waiting for us somewhere round a corner) looking
over the garden, feeling the house behind us, saying : We
must have peonies under these windows.   And then we
get into the station cab and the man drives away and we
hold each other's hands and think how familiar this road
will become. . . .

It's a wild, glittering day.   I can't go to those people
for lunch.   The wind is like a great bird tumbling over
the sea with bright flashing wings.   I am upstairs in my
bedroom sitting in the sun.   The windows are open.   It
is very pleasant.   One could make a charming room of
this.

At three o'clock I woke up into the middle of a terrific
thunderstorm.   The thunder seemed to set one's bones
vibrating.   One heard the sea, not breaking regularly, but
*struggling* and only now and again with a great harsh sigh
the waves spent themselves.   It is strange to be alone in
such a storm.   I kept feeling I must write this, I must
write this ; but it must be a man who feels it, rather an

302

elderly man away from home, and something must happen to him—something, you know, which could not happen to such a man—and then the morning must follow, still, clear, 'poised,' like it is after such a storm, and he. . . .

It's afternoon. I've just had another caller. A woman who lives here in Ospedaletti with her Italian maid, her English maid, her mother, and I should think a few Spanish menservants. She asked me to tea on Monday. Her villa has a flat roof. She was swathed in fur, violet perfume, and I thought she was M. The spit of M. M.'s eyes, teeth, extravagance. *Chicken*, 18 *lire*, *butter*, 20 *lire ! !* Did you ever ! 'You must go to Algiers next year. Algiers is *perfect*.' She is, I should think, very rich and what they call 'fast'—plays golf, bridge, *our car*. No 'swank.' She has a house in the South of England. I had no time in this *race* (so familiar !) to ask where, but it was that which interested me. But I must have cards. Here are 5 people I ought to leave cards on. What an absurd predicament. Oh, how nice our name is ! My husband bulks very large in these conversations. What a dark, romantic, brilliant creature he is, and as he need never see the people he is quite safe.

My God ! the wind. It's blowing great huge guns.

I send J.'s letter just to give you an idea of her. She is a nice woman, streets above these *callers*. This woman has left rather a faded taste of white suède gloves in my mouth after all. She is unhappy, dissatisfied like M. was. I don't know : one's work sets one *finally apart* from the idle world, doesn't it ?

> Wednesday night
> November 26, 1919

About the 10 stories. They won't all bear reprinting, Boge. I can't afford to publish my early works yet. If you don't mind I'd rather let them lie and deliver you the new goods in May.

The wind has been joined by the robber cold. Both are in highest spirits. There is a perfect uproar going on outside.  It makes my room feel like a lighthouse.  I seem to see you in another light house. . . .

*Thursday*.  Hail, rain, wind, dark.  The terra cotta in full blast, smelling dreadful as the plaster bakes dry.  No, the point about this climate is its extreme variability of temperature.  It's never a whole day the same.  That's what puts such a terrific strain on one, I think, and that's what makes it truly preposterous for people who are not as well-covered and as solid as L. M.  They may win through.  But why have to fight so hard ?  Why have to use up one's energies in keeping warm ?  It's so wasteful.  The sea sounds like a big old rake.  I was awake more then half the night.  At one o'clock I called L. M. and she went down and made some tea.  In my *home* I shall always have the things for tea in my room, so that in the middle of the night I can brew a cup.  Mr. Salteena's thrill for tea in bed I feel for tea in the middle of the night.  Ten years ago I used to have tea and brown bread and butter every morning at half past two.  I don't know why it should be such a gay little feast then.  I long for somebody to *laugh* with.  I think of such funny little jokes—minute little jokes.  Wing would perhaps be the perfect companion of such revels.  I see him stuffing his paw into his mouth or the end of his tail so as not to laugh out loud and wake you.

Oh, I hope I get a letter to-day or something.  It's the *vilest* old day.  However, I've just *got* to stick it.  There's nothing else to do.  God ! how lonely I am !  You know, I sometimes feel a violent hate of S., E., T., all of them, because they have never suffered what I have had to suffer, and expecially not THIS.  It's just one of the many poisons, I suppose.  But to have been *alone* here—that even you will *never* know.

Saturday
November 29, 1919

We had a severe earthquake last night at 11 o'clock. The little Casetta gave a creak and then silently shook.

And to-day it is dead calm, airless, real earthquake weather. . . .

I couldn't get to sleep last night. When I shut my eyes *gardens* drifted by—the most incredible sort of tropical gardens with glimpses of palaces through the rich green. Trees I've never seen or imagined—trees like feathers and silver trees and others quite white with huge transparent leaves passed and passed. My heart just fluttered. I scarcely had to breathe at all. It was like a vision brought about by drugs. I couldn't stop it and yet it frightened me ; but it was too beautiful to stop. One is almost in a state of coma—very strange. I've often got *near* this condition before, but never like last night. Perhaps if one gives way to it and gives way to it one may even be able to get there. . . . Oh, I don't know, but it *was* a vision, not a memory. I am going to San Remo to-day to try to get some tea plates for you. Those two items don't hang together.

No sign of the scarf yet. Did I tell you I'd paid 8 francs for a box for my letters so as to have them secure. Now L. M. tells me it's 8 *francs par mois* ! ! ! I thought it was for the season, for after all they won't deliver here : they refuse. Another robbery, alors, and I dare not quarrel with les gens de la poste. On the contrary L. M. takes the little box-faced girl bouquets of roses from Madame. If she'd like me to burn candles I'm only too willing. But, they do make one pay.

Sunday morning, 8 a.m.
November 30, 1919

It's a real Sunday, calm, quiet, with the sea practising over a voluntary while the verger tiptoes laying out the hymn and prayer books in the strangers' pews. There's a lovely piece of bright sun in my room—but, bother, it is moving towards great banks of unruffled cloud.

I went to San Remo yesterday afternoon. It was *very* exciting. The shops are all prepared for the Great Fleece.

A great many antique shops are open. I suppose they are all frauds. At any rate the prices would be appalling, but, by Jove! they have got some lovely things! There was a chair yesterday that can't be a fraud, covered in the most exquisite needlework on old ivory brocade. Figs and their leaves, pomegranates, apricots, pears, a spotted snake or two, all in most gay delicate colours, and then there was another great piece of embroidery, all flowers, with a little running border of wild strawberry fruits, leaves and blossoms. The shops are rather darkish. One looks in and one sees a flash of silver, a mass of copper, dark polished furniture, lace, a glass case or two of miniatures and jewels, and the old spider with a silk handkerchief over her head sitting quiet, on the watch. I'd be the first fly to go in if my purse were full.

I went to the market. It was gay there. You remember where they used to sell fried cakes? Yesterday there was a stall covered with them and to the side on a charcoal stove women were cooking pancakes. A queer feeling markets give me. I feel that—once every hundred years or so—I walk about among the stalls, price the fruit, note that the new raisins have come, smell the fried cakes, and see the woman's gesture as she rattles for change in the money-bag at her side.

Waiting for the tram R. came up. Well! He'll commit murder one of these days. If ever man looked like a murderer.... He's a fascinating character, a *real* villain. Not a fool, not merely vague (*far* from it). He'll end by having a small hotel at a place like Boulogne or Calais or Dieppe, and he'll meet the trains wearing a straw hat and sand shoes.

It's autumn here now: the vines are red and yellow: the dark women carry pale chrysanthemums, and oranges and lemons are ripe. I came home, lit my fire, began to take my shoes off and fell asleep. When I woke up it was dark—the fire just burning, not a sound. I didn't know how long I'd been asleep. Everything was still. I sat there for about half an hour, then I heard steps outside, and

L. M. came in, back from the village. It was nearly seven
o'clock. I ate dinner, came up, got into bed, fell asleep
again and woke at eleven, bitten to death by three *huge*
mosquitos in the net. Murdered them, went to sleep
again and slept till seven ! What a pa woman ! Oh, find
the house ! I am *longing* for it. Christmas is near.
*Shall* we next year really keep Christmas ? *Shall* we have
a tree and put it in a room with the door locked—only you
and I allowed to go in and decorate it—and then have a
small party on Christmas Eve ? ? We shall go out all
wrapped up to the noses, with a pruning hook to cut holly
and we'll burn a Christmas log. (PERHAPS !)

You know it's madness to love and live apart. That's
what we do. Last time when I came back to France do
you remember how we *swore* never again ? Then I went
to Looe—and after that we *swore* : never again. Then I
came here. Shall we go on doing this ? It isn't a married
life at all—not what I mean by a married life. How I
envy —— ; no wonder she can write. There is always in
her writing a calm freedom of expression as though she
were at peace—her roof over her, her possessions round her,
and her man somewhere within call. What have I done
that I should have *all* the handicaps—plus a disease and an
enemy—and *why* should we believe this won't happen
again ? We've said as sincerely as we can ever possibly
say : " It will not. This is to be the *last* time. We'll
*never* let each other go again. We *could* not." But the
time comes and there's nothing else to be done, and before
you say Jack Knife, we're apart again, going through it all
again. Shall I be in Malaga next winter, or Algiers ?
Odious, odious thought. But really, I'd better get used
to it. We are the sport of circumstances. It's obviously
impossible for us to do anything. But how tired the dice
get of being rattled and thrown !

Sunday evening
November 30, 1919

Weather report: Dead calm. Warm. Some sun.
Earthquaky.

Yes, the Fakeists quite overcome me. That *Observer*
had, par exemple, a review of *L——*. *If* you read *L——*!
Humbug—deplorable humbug—rant—rubbish—tinpot
provincial hysterics. But they couldn't have said more if
C. D. had written *The Tempest*. It makes me feel quite
queer sometimes when I read that *Saint's Progress* is one
of the great masterpieces of all time, and yet I never feel
for an instant I'm not right. There can't be any doubt
about such rot as *L——* and the *Times* raved! Perhaps
when 1,200,000 people a year buy *Georgian Poetry* we
shall be burned together.

It's getting dusky. The house is full of small shadows.
I can hear the kettle having its lid taken off and then it's
filled and now it's on the fire again—all this very distinct.
It's sunset. The windows are shut, the sea is pale. Oh,
how dare I lean on you as I do? Do you feel I'm a weight?
I want to lean so light, so light, and then suddenly I get
heavy and ask to be carried. You ought not to have
chosen me to travel with. Ah, I don't agree with that.
We made the right choice, the marvellously right *choice* at
any rate. *We've* done all we could. It's only the . . .
Boss Omnipotent who's been so horrid.

Monday
November 31, 1919

I'm rather dashed to-day. I've got fever and that
makes me frightfully depressed. Ansaldi came yesterday.
Don't *count* on him. He's a charlatan. He owned
yesterday that the reports he gave me were because " I
saw dis lady wants vot you call sheering up. Like de
Irishman I told you you can trot and I hope you may be
able to walk." You observe the polite smile with which I
listened. The whole interview seems to have been more

or less of a fake.   He said yesterday, for instance, *emphat*
ically that I could not winter in England next year or the
year after :  that I must have sun and warmth.   In fact,
he behaved precisely as all other doctors in the world but
S. do behave.   S. is the only man one can trust at all.
This one wasn't like D. in the face for nothing.   He *did*
give me a good beating.   And when I told him of my
melancholia, he said it was part toxin poisoning and part
because you are alone wiz nobody near you to love and
sherish you.   I tell my patients dat is better than medicine.
*Mrs.* Murry, and so on and so on and so on and so on.
And then he went away and I sat in my dressing gown and
watched it grow dusk and then dark here, and *realised* how
I had been taken in again.

Doesn't matter.   What must be, must be.   I am writing
to J. to-day to ask her if I may come to Mentone for a few
days.   But what's the good ?   I couldn't go to-day.   My
temperature's 102.   So one goes round and round and
round like the squirrel in the cage.   It's a cold, grey day.

Wednesday
December 3, 1919

Last night under the inspiration of a fever attack I
wrote these verses.   Keep them for me, will you ?   I feel
a longing to write poetry.   Don't forget you were going
to send me Hardy :  I feel passionately eager to read his
poems.   Did we mention the review in *The Times* ?   It
was superficial, " silly," and the snail under the nasturtium
leaf again.   That don't fit Hardy.   Talking of snails, the
*Nation* and the *Guardian* came to-day.   Did you see the
one in the eye Wayfarer gave me ?   He *had* his quarrel I
own, but he was unfair all the same

R.'s old gardener is outside—bless him !—sowing sweet
peas.   He's a dear old root of a man.   He peers at me
through the window and when I open it to speak makes
the gesture of pulling his coat round him so that I'll keep
covered up and mutters " d'vent, d'vent " as though it

309

were spelled *devant*. It's all right. I shall be better
still to-morrow. It's always a comfort not to feel worse.
But don't rush a house. Who knows that I'm not turned
out of England by the Lord—that I'm not a wandering
tribe, complete with lamentations. It looks jolly like it
to me.

Thursday, 5 p.m.
December 4, 1919

It's sunset with a wide, wide pale yellow sky and a blue
sea gilded over. I feel horribly weak after this fever
attack, but calmer—just now—thank the Lord. My
heart is so hateful. If you had such a heart. It *bangs*,
*throbs*, *beats* out "Tramp, tramp, tramp, the boys are
marching," double quick time, with very fine double rolls
for the kettle-drum. How it keeps it up I don't know. I
always feel it's going to give out. I think every day I
shall die of heart failure. I expect it's an inherited feeling
from Mother. Oh lucky, lucky Mother, so surrounded,
so held, so secure ! Can't I hear her " Child, you mustn't
be left here *one instant*," and then she'd make miracles
happen and by to-morrow she'd have me wrapped up and
defied everybody.

But we are firmly held in the web of circumstance.
We've got to risk it, to see it through. No, once I'm
better I go to Mentone and I'll return here later in the
spring when I'm stronger.

L. M. is out to tea with some people in Ospedaletti—
gone off with a big bunch of roses for them. The wind
sighs in the house and the fire goes *chik-chik*—very small.
My fever makes everything 100 times more vivid, like a
nightmare is vivid. But it will be over in a day or two, I
expect. A bad business.

I am sure Mentone will do wonders for my old depression. I've great hopes of it. Forgive me, all you tell me
about the house—I can't help feeling it's all part of a
hideous vile joke that's being played on us for les autres to
read about in days to come. I *can't* see it except like this.

Friday
December 5, 1919

Oh, your new book has just come. It looks superb.
I'll read it to-night. It looks terrific. And then I
looked at the title-page and decided, No, he's forgotten,
and then saw that TO MY WIFE, I had a moment of
such *ancient bliss* you cannot conceive. No, that TO MY
WIFE, TO MY WIFE is written on every wave of the
sea at the moment. It's to me just as though I'd been
going home from school and the Monaghans had called
after me and you—about the size of a sixpence—had
defended me and p'raps helped me to pick up my pencils
and put them back in the pencil box. (I'd have given you
the red one.)

I had by the same post an awfully nice sympathetic
letter from Grant Richards asking me for a book. He can
have *White Roses* when ready. I feel better to-day. The
brandy was a great point. "Very Old Pale Cognac"—
one can't help pitying it. Yet that it should have such
fire!! My temperature was only just on 100 last night.
Now I've got to climb back again, curse it.

The sea comes rolling in—rolling in. There's not a
sound but my pen. L. M. is somewhere out in the village.
Catherina came to see me yesterday guarding against the
infection de la fièvre with a shawl, but an *immense* shawl!
which she kept held up to her lips till I made her smile and
then forgot all about it. I was asking her if she was going
to help with the tea-room that Mme. Littardi is opening.
"Ah non, Madame, ce n'est pas mon métier, vous savez"
—and here she flushed lightly and put her hands in her
pockets—"je suis *née* pour le repassage . . .e—t puis . . .
c'est ma passion!"

There's the secret of her charm.

Sunday
December 7, 1919

I wonder what you are doing with your Sunday? And
if it's fine or dreadful? It's very fine here—a little

windy, that's all.   My day has been like my last few days.
I rise at 12, lunch, lie on the sofa till 6, and then say, " Are
the hot water-bottles upstairs ? " and go to bed.   It's a
small beat, but there is a large Policeman on it who
frightens me a bit.   My fever returned last night, I don't
know why.   It decided me to take a step.   Your " clock "
complex is surpassed by my doctor complex, but my
collection, unlike yours, never is reliable, never tells the
real truth, or strikes the real hour—except the beautiful
clock S.   But I am going to call in another.   I don't want
to see Ansaldi again.   What *is* the good ?   Who wants
" sheering up " only ?   And besides he repels me.   But
yesterday that Miss S. came here and though she was *far*
too kind and concerned, she did implore me to see F., the
Englishman.   In fact, she asked me if she could go back
and telephone him, and I said Yes, perhaps it's just as
well.   He comes to-morrow.

But I must get Richard to print off a decent little
pamphlet entitled " The Physical History of K. M.
1917-19— ? "   It's so wearisome, so—I don't know—like
ashes, to hear myself recite my *one* recitation—a bird with
one song, " How the Fowler Trapped me."   Perhaps
that's what all birds in cages sing.   Next time you pass
me, listen and hear it :

> I was flying through a wood
> A *green* wood,
> A spring wood,
> It was early, early morning. . . .

The fire is all right, but it's become a burning bridge
with no heart—just an arc de triomphe.   I can't get up
and put it together, I am so wound round in my Jaeger
rug.   There *was* a purchase.   It's dusk here.   My pen
seems to make such a loud noise.   The wind swings in the
shadowy air.   The sea cries.

Thursday
December 11, 1919

About Constables. If they will give £40 in advance
and Richards won't, it must be Constables of course. A
book including *Prelude*, *Je ne parle pas* and so on would be
interesting. But I must make very sure of what they
collect from *Rhythm*. The story " The Wind Blows "
from *The Signature* is in the collection. It's the only one
worth reprinting. The book had certainly better include
*Prelude*. It makes a longer book. S. says even if an
arrangement is come to, nothing can be published for
several months. In that case the final decision as to
*which* stories could perhaps be left for my return in the
first week of May.

Saturday, 7 a.m.
December 13, 1919

I've been lying here while my dream ebbed away. I
never have had such vivid dreams as I do here. Campbell
in this came to warn me (we were at ' some strange hotel ')
" Mansfield, I'd lock your door to-night. There are two
Chinamen downstairs, and they're very *predatory*." He
repeated this word while he made some small tentative
golf-club-swinging motions, immensely familiar. Campbell belongs to another life, doesn't he ? But so does
everybody, every single person. I feel they're all quite
gone. Even Hampstead and the tapestry in the studio
and the sommier. They are not in this world—not for
me. What is in this world ? Nothing. Just a blank.
It's fine this morning, sun and blue sea,—and I don't even
care to look out of window. How long was Dostoevsky in
prison ? Four years, wasn't he ? And he came out and
did his finest work after. If only one could rid oneself of
this *feeling of finality*, if there were a *continuity*. That's
what is so intolerable. The feeling that one goes on, just
as the sea does for hours and days after a storm, presenting
an appearance of agitation and activity, but *it's really all*

*over*.  Could it be possible that I am wrong ?   I think I'd
better not write stories but only my confessions here, and
keep them out of letters.

G. B. S. on Butler is very fine indeed.[1]   He has such a
grip of his subject.   I admire his tenacity as a reviewer
and the way in which his mind follows Butler with a steady
light—does not waver over him, find him, lose him, travel
over him.   At the same time it's queer he should be
(G. B. S.) so uninspired.   There is not the faintest hint
of inspiration in that man.   This chills me.   You know
the feeling that a great writer gives you : " My spirit has
been fed and refreshed : it has partaken of something
new."   One could not possibly feel that about Shaw.   It's
the clang of the gate that remains with you when all's
over.   What it amounts to is that Shaw is anything you
like, but he's not an artist.   Don't you get when you read
his plays a sense of extraordinary *flatness* ?   They may be
extremely amusing at moments, but you are always
laughing *at* and never *with*.   Just the same in his prose :
You may agree as much as you like, but he is writing *at*
not *with*.   There's no getting over it : he's a kind of
concierge in the house of literature—sits in a glass case,
sees everything, knows everything, examines the letters,
*cleans the stairs*, but has no part, no part in the life that is
going on.   But as I wrote that, I thought : Yes, but who
*is* living there, living there as we mean life ?   Dostoevsky,
Tchehov and Tolstoy and Hardy.   I can't think of *anybody else*.

Oh God ! What wouldn't I give for a TALK.   Well, it
can't happen.

Don't move my shepherdess if you can help.   I *see* her
there so plainly : I'd hate to think it was another dream :
she wasn't there at all, only a little carriage clock.   She is
the gentle little spirit of the room to me.   I always,
always until I die shall remember how we listened to the
tiny bell striking—from a world of faery.   Please don't put

[1] A review of Mr. Festing Jones's *Life of Samuel Butler*, by Mr.
Bernard Shaw, which appeared in *The Manchester Guardian*.

her away.   Think what she has meant.   Put the carriage clock on the writing table, can't you ?   But she is everything to the room, the poet to the landscape.   Have you moved her ?   Tell me.


*To S. S. Koteliansky*                         Saturday night
                                              December 14, 1919

   Your letter has made me very happy.   Thank you for it. You know, it is still here, in my room, sounding, like music that has been played.   " Be well."   And I am ashamed that I broke down in my last letter.   That night I went to bed with pneumonia.   That was why I was so depressed. Of course I am still in bed but it does not matter.   *All is well.*

   We are quite alone here to-night.   It is so far away and still.   Everything is full of silent life—complete with its shadow.   From the sea there comes a soft *ruffled* sound and its beat is regular and soft like the beat of mowers cutting through a deep meadow.

   Yes, one day when we have enough money we shall meet somewhere and talk quietly for as long as we wish—It will happen, I think.

   Your loneliness is precious to you, I know.   Does it disturb it to know you are dear to me ?   Do not let it.   It is such a quiet feeling.   It is like the light coming into a room—moonlight—where you are sitting.

   I shall try and get well here.   If I *do* die perhaps there will be a small private heaven for consumptives only.   In that case I shall see Tchehov.   He will be walking down his garden paths with fruit trees on either side and tulips in flower in the garden beds.   His dog will be sitting on the path, panting and slightly smiling as dogs do who have been running about a great deal.

   Only to think of this makes my heart feel as though it were *dissolving*—a strange feeling.

   Lawrence wrote from Florence.   He said Florence was lovely and full of " extremely nice people."   He is able to

315

bear people so easily. Often I long to be more *in life*—
to know people—even now the desire comes. But immediately the opportunity comes I think of nothing but
how to escape. And people have come to see me here—
*What* are they ? They are not human beings ; they are
never children—they are *absolutely unreal* Mechanisms.

And those people in England—When one goes away the
memory of them is like the memory of clothes hanging in a
cupboard. And yet the beauty of life—Koteliansky—
the haunting beauty of " the question "—Sometimes when
I am awake here, very early in the morning, I hear, far
down on the road below, the market carts going by. And
at the sound I live through this getting up before dawn,
the blue light in the window—the cold solemn look of the
people—the woman opening the door and going for sticks
—the smell of smoke—the feather of smoke rising from
their chimney. I hear the man as he slaps the little horse
and leads it into the clattering yard. And the fowls are still
asleep—big balls of feather. But the early morning air and
hush. And after the man and wife have driven away some
little children skurry out of bed across the floor and find
a piece of bread and get back into the warm bed and divide
it. But this is all *the surface*. Hundreds of things happen
down to minute, minute details. But it is all so full of
beauty—and you know the voices of people before sunrise
—how different they are ? I lie here, thinking of these
things and hearing those little carts. . . . It is too much.
One must weep.

Forgive a long letter.

I do not know if M. is coming. I have sent him several
wires asking him not to come. It is not at all a good idea.

*To Miss Fullerton*                                    Tuesday
                                             December 18, 1919

The doctor came yesterday and put his British foot down
on all the lovely plans. I am not to get up yet and when I
do only to lie on a couch or on the verandah for a few

hours a day at present. My heart which evidently feels its turn has come for a little attention has been playing me tricks and I'll have to give way to the jealous creature for the present. So bang goes the lovely Christmas ! We're more than sorry and it was lovely to have been asked to the party and I hate to be such an unsatisfactory creature. Will you and Cousin Connie forgive me ? But what can one do when ones heart gives the most marvellous imitations of the big drum in a brass band—first, heard very far away in the distance, then coming nearer and nearer, then thumping so loud that you think it must break the windows and then wonderful faint, far away ' distant ' effects—and all for an audience of *one* ! But it's not really ' serious '— only a temporary thing. I'll have to learn to play the fife to keep it company—

A comfortable old Scottish party from San Remo came to call the other day and seeing the chaste nudity of the Casetta she has since sent us a great roll of carpets and rugs that she had in store so we are a great deal snugger and warmer here. The doctor is definitely opposed to my moving at present. Ida takes little jaunts into San Remo and she has made several friends and I've plenty of work to keep me going. So that's my programme for the present, quite a satisfactory one except that it prevents me from spreading my wings.

*To the Hon. Dorothy Brett*         December 20, 1919

I've been ill with pneumonia, and too wretched to write. Forgive me. I have thought of you so often. And I want to thank you for the photographs, to talk about them. I will, at length, now I am ' better.' Now M. has brought over his exquisite little coals of fire for Xmas from you— So lovely. Such gay greetings. Thank you ever so much for them. This is an exquisite little place—and the weather—like June. The whole village is under roses as other villages are under snow. I hope you have a happy Christmas and Joy in the New Year, real, real Joy.

# Index

## VOL. I.

PRINTED IN GREAT BRITAIN
BY ROBERT MACLEHOSE AND CO. LTD.
THE UNIVERSITY PRESS, GLASGOW